The Exact
Location of
the Soul

ALSO BY RICHARD SELZER

SHORT-STORY AND ESSAY COLLECTIONS
The Doctor Stories
Imagine a Woman
Taking the World in for Repairs
Letters to a Young Doctor
Confessions of a Knife
Mortal Lessons
Rituals of Surgery

NONFICTION
Raising the Dead

AUTOBIOGRAPHY
Down from Troy

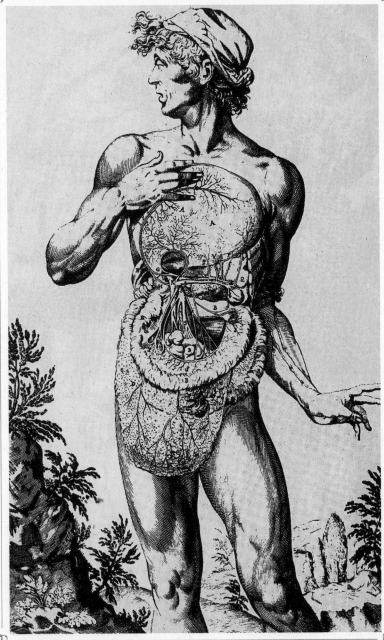

The Exact Location of the Soul

~NEW AND
SELECTED ESSAYS~

Richard Selzer

Picador USA
New York

www.picadorusa.com

Picador® is a U.S. registered trademark and is used by St. Martin's Press under license from Pan Books Limited.

Acknowledgments for previously published material can be found on page 337.

Anatomical drawings by Casserius (late sixteenth century), courtesy of Richard Selzer.

Designed by Lorelle Graffeo

For information on Picador USA Reading Group Guides, as well as ordering, please contact the Trade Marketing department at St. Martin's Press.
Phone: 1-800-221-7945 extension 763
Fax: 212-677-7456
E-mail: trademarketing@stmartins.com

Library of Congress Cataloging-in-Publication Data

Selzer, Richard.
    The exact location of the soul : new and selected essays / Richard Selzer.
        p. cm.
    ISBN 0-312-26146-2 (hc)
    ISBN 0-312-26313-9 (pbk)
    I. Title.

 PS3569.E585 E93 2001
 814'.54—dc21   00-047834

First Picador USA Paperback Edition: March 2002

10 9 8 7 6 5 4 3 2 1

To the Boys Friendly

Maynard Mack

Eugene Waith

Louis Martz

George Hunter

Fred Robinson

Murray Biggs

Claude Rawson

Contents

Acknowledgments

I would like to express my thanks to Katherine Rodgers for an early reading of the manuscript followed by her advice and encouragement, and also to Wally Needham. My thanks also to Alicia Brooks for her intelligent, careful, and warmhearted editing. I am grateful to Georges Borchardt and Lourdes Lopez for shepherding this book to its destination.

~R.S.

The Exact
Location of
the Soul

Introduction:
The Making of
a Doctor/Writer

—⁀⁀—

The making of a surgeon/writer would seem to demand an explanation. It is that odd a marriage of professions. And so I shall try.

Throughout the 1930s and 1940s, our family lived on the second floor of an old brownstone whose first floor was Father's medical office. It was only half a block from Troy Music Hall, where Mother, Troy's only diva, gave occasional song recitals. At any hour of the day, she would be practicing her scales. Billy was a year older than I. Now and then, I have a vision of two small boys, dressed in identical cotton suits—short pants, and with cross-stitching on the collar and sleeves. They are sitting on the landing of the darkened staircase, hoping not to be noticed. (Once, Father had had to shave their heads for lice. Then they resembled ferrets.) Now the slim older boy has flung one arm about the shoulders of the pudgy younger boy, the one wearing glasses. They have the inconsolable look of the Princes in the Tower. What are they doing there? They are listening to the cries and moans of pain coming from the downstairs office. They hear their father's voice, commanding.

"All right now, you're going to feel a sharp stick and then a burning. Ready?" The two boys on the landing tense to receive what they know is coming. A scream splits the air and races up the staircase like lightning to strike them where they are sitting. "No, no! You mustn't holler like that. Try to be brave." The bigger boy withdraws his arm from around his brother's shoulders and covers his ears with his hands. He screws up his face and shuts his eyes. The younger boy's face is serious, grave. You cannot read any reaction on it at all. Only, perhaps, a glistening of the eyes. The scream cascades down the chromatic scale—do, ti, la, sol, fa, mi, re, do. Then, by some alchemy of sound, it is transmitted into Mother's voice ascending the scale again—do, re, mi, fa, sol, la, ti, do. Thus is pain changed into song. It is more than sixty years later. Billy and I are two old men.

In Father's office, there was no such thing as a nurse or receptionist. The door was always unlocked; you just walked in and took a seat in the Waiting Room. To my knowledge, he never sent a bill. If the patient had the two dollars for the visit, fine. If not, or if he needed change for a ten-dollar bill, there wasn't any, so payment was postponed, or more likely forgotten.

At the age of seven, I was promoted to keeping Father company on house calls. I remember him walking up to a bed, observing its contents for a minute or two, then, without a word, scooping up a young girl quickly as if she were melting and he didn't want to lose a drop of her. Into the backseat of the car she was deposited, now whimpering like a dog dying to be petted, and we drove up to the Samaritan Hospital. An hour later, when he came out to the car, I asked.

"She died," he said, under his breath. Then added, because I had to know, "Sugar diabetes."

"Sugar?"

"Too sweet," he said. I didn't know that anything could be too sweet. He glanced sidewise and saw whatever he saw in my face. "It's all in the cards, Dickie. We do what we can, but Fate has her own way with everybody."

"What's Fate?" He gave a small laugh, the kind I knew was make-believe, and started humming to himself, the humming that was a cocoon about him that meant no more questions.

On another visit, the patient was a man with an injured hand that had become infected. Two fingers had turned black with gangrene. There was the smell of putrefaction. Father advanced into the stench, parting it with his hands as he stepped into the bedroom.

"Let me have your hand," said Father. The man held it up to him as though he had no hope of ever getting it back.

"I don't know, Pat," said Father in a voice saturated with regret. The man's Adam's apple ran up and down his neck like an elevator. My legs were so heavy you'd think I was being hanged by the neck. Long after we had left that house, my eyes retained the sight of that hand. A buzzing followed me from room to room. I went out into the backyard to escape, but it was there too. That night, in my bed, with my head under the covers, I smelled it. After a while, I opened my eyes to see Father standing by my bed. I raised my hand to touch him. I met his hand coming down to me.

Already my eyes were in wanton pursuit of everything that Father did, watching the way the lips of a wound would open wider as if to welcome his penetration. It seemed to me that he could snuff wounds as if they were the flames of candles. A person who could do that would waste his time doing anything else. After each house call, Father would give a brief explanation of the clinical condition, why he had done what he had done, as though I were a colleague instead of a small boy.

"Why did you place your hand on his forehead?" It had hovered for a moment above the man's face before drifting away. "That's for me—to give me courage and for him as well—to break down the natural mistrust a man feels when his body is to be confided to another man."

"Why do you need courage?"

"Wait till you're a doctor, then you'll find out why."

I didn't understand much of what he said, but I knew that he was proud, and glowing. Sometimes, when leaving a house we'd visited, I had to touch the ground carefully to make sure it was still there waiting for my feet. Mother's eyes were large and made of milk and sapphires.

"The child is trembling. You are making him sick," she said, *sotto voce*. She put some milk on the stove to boil, then set it down in front of me, stood there to make sure I'd eat the "skin," which made me gag every time.

"Birth pangs," said Father.

"You are taking away his childhood."

"He wouldn't have had one anyway. Not that boy." He had a habit of rolling a pencil between the fingers of his two hands, looking down at it, instead of at her. His hands always had to be holding an instrument. If not, they looked blank and dumb.

"Show me your hands," he said one day. I held them out palms down in case they were dirty. He flipped them over, bent to study them intently, ran his finger over the creases. "Just as I thought," he said at last. "You're going to be a surgeon." I didn't know it then, but those were moments of great happiness. We rarely recognize happiness when we are living it. Only later, when we are no longer happy, do we find it again in memory.

I am no more than my father's child. The great discovery of 1937 was his novel *Goldie*. It had been written at night after supper, when Billy and I had been dismissed to our homework. No sooner had quiet descended upon the household than Father would go back downstairs to his Consultation Room. Any little sneak could peek through a crack in the door and watch him take off his collar and cuffs, put on a green eyeshade, and secure his sleeves with rubber bands. At last, he would fill his fountain pen from the bottle labeled Higgins' Eternal Ink. An ear pressed to the door would receive the groans of creation, the hissing of his hand as it drove the pen across the paper in small bursts from left to right, then a longer hiss as his hand flew back to start a new line. Now and then there was the crackle of gashed paper as the pen burst into flames. Billy and I died to know what he was writing.

"None of your business," he said, and that was to be that. After a while, we stopped asking, and came to accept his lucubrations as a fact of family life. It came to pass that, having finished the novel at last, Father typed it onto looseleaf pages that he placed in a brand-new three-ring folder. One night he showed it to Mother, said she could read it if she wished. A week later, she delivered her verdict.

"Keep it away from the children." But keeping anything away

from children is a theory. It wasn't a day later that Billy found the manuscript in a cabinet in an unused closet at the back of downstairs. She had stashed it there under some old blankets. For the next two weeks, Billy and I spent the hour from eight to nine at night in that back closet reading what seemed to us the most heartrending story ever told. By candlelight, we took turns reading it aloud, our voices breaking, tears streaming.

It was all about a beautiful young girl driven into prostitution in order to feed her two younger brothers. (They were exactly our ages!) There came the day when Goldie was accosted on the street by a man she thought just another customer for her charms, but who turned out to be a brilliant atheistic doctor who had observed that she was desperately ill. He brought her home where he lived alone (!) above his medical office. There he endeavored to nurse her back to health, and in doing so, fell in love with her. And she, it goes without saying, with him. But happiness was not to be theirs. When Goldie died in the doctor's arms, Billy and I sobbed without shame or restraint. (It was the death of Little Nell, all over again.) For weeks, we moped and mourned, now and then screwing up the nerve to return to that back closet and read again some part of the story.

Then one day, rummage under those blankets how we might, the novel was nowhere to be found. One of them had taken it away. Nor was it ever seen again. But for me, *Goldie* by Julius Louis Selzer is the emblematic work of American literature. How often through the years I have longed to hold it in my hand, letting my tears fall again upon the pages where his prose was strewn. But I had read it. And so had Billy. We thank God for that.

A portion of this book is a return to the past. Lucky the writer whose first childhood runs right into his second. The rest of us who would recapitulate our beginnings must rummage and reinvent. The memoirist seizes time by the forelock, forcing it to stand still. But there is danger in the backward glance. Lot's wife knew she was not to look back, but she couldn't resist. Here's the poet Anna Akhmatova urging her to do so:

It's not too late, you can still look back
At red-towered Sodom, where you were born,
At the square where you sang, where you sat to spin,
At the windows of the high house, forlorn,
Where you bore your beloved husband children.

For that human act, she was punished by a cruel God. Such a rendering casts quite a different light on the woman, who has been vilified and ridiculed for her disobedience. Orpheus too looked back, to make sure that Eurydice was following him out of Hades. He had been forbidden to do so, but could not resist. There is no more mournful sound in all literature than that of Eurydice's footsteps receding.

To write about the distant past, it is not enough to sift the ashes of memory. A good part of the process is reinvention. While the past looms larger and larger right up to the moment of death, it is impossible to recall it precisely. If anyone could, it would be just such a hateful child as I was, one who sits and watches and listens while fantasy furnishes every corner of his mind. Such a child doesn't smile, doesn't speak. He observes, his pupils dilating and constricting, his breath gone shallow and quick, or stopping, even, in the receptacular act. He is always in the shadow, or gives that effect. You glance over your shoulder to see if anyone is there; no need to wonder, he is. And you lower your voice so as not to be overheard. No use to tell this child to go outdoors and play ball. He clings to the indoors as he clings to his privacy. Attic and cellar know him. It is indoors that he finds his calling. He is a daemon.

Most of my writing is done at Yale's Sterling Library, a great gray stone beast that squats in its wisdom on High Street, flashing its windowpanes at you in the morning. Most weeks, I go there every day. Sometimes I have the feeling that I was there first, that in the beginning there was me, and that over the years I have secreted the library around me, the way animalcules of the sea secrete a coral reef. Trouble is, I've become the Resident Physician at the library. No one hesitates to come to where I'm sitting to present a list of symptoms and ask for a diagnosis. "Feel this, will you, Doc? What do you think it is?" is a not uncommon beginning. Last Christmas, the security guards presented me with a sphygmomanometer, so now I have to take everyone's blood pressure. Come to the same place at the same time every day, and willy-nilly the world will come unto you. Such is my predicament when I unlock my carrel in the morning. No sooner have I sharpened a pencil and opened a notebook then they start showing up, patients and pilgrims alike. Would I write a letter of recommendation to medical school? Would I sign these eight books? "One is for my doctor in Albany. And this one's for my nephew Jake, who wants to be a doctor—he's ten years old." Do I by any chance know a doctor named Clancy? Would I read this manuscript? "I know it's a long one, but I'd appreciate your opinion. And give it to me straight, Doc. I can take it." Then too there are the penitents who come to wipe off their sorrows on my sleeve. Honestly, I should have a lattice to sit behind. So many interruptions that I hardly get anything done. Then it is that I long for my cell in the Abbey of San Giorgio Maggiore in Venice, with its narrow bed, tiny table, single chair, and just enough room for my flagellations. Even my postprandial fifteen-minute nap is observed with impatience by several supplicants who stand about like cows needing to be milked. When is he going to wake up? Why does he need so much sleep? One day, I shall not wake up. Never mind; to meet death while at your work is a blessing. It should be welcomed the way a sweaty brow welcomes a dry bandanna.

I have learned more from studying the human body than I have from all the reading of my life. For me, the body is the source of truth. I continue to gaze and gaze at it until what gazes back at me is what, by some, might be called the soul. There are differences between science and art that can never be dismissed. Science is almost always fatal to sentiment. The personality of the scientist is absent from his work, as it should be. It is quite otherwise with the artist, whose own taste and temperament are always visible in the work. The scientist does no more than find in Nature what is already there, and to manipulate, or recombine it into new configurations. The artist invents a unity, creates something new that will fire the imagination of others.

Lest it be supposed that, having left Medicine, for writing, I have lost fascination for Science, it is not so. Not long ago, I learned, for example, that in Surinam there lives a four-eyed fish named, with utter disregard for euphony, *Anableps tetrophthalmus*. In the muddy waters of the creeks of that country, an armada of these small submarines will swarm over the tidal flats. The surface of the water is cleft by triangular wakes, at the forward apex of each of which a pair of tiny periscopes glides. *Anableps* is unique among animals in that its eyes are divided horizontally into two halves. The upper half is so refracted as to see clearly in the air. The lower half is focused for seeing underwater. As it glides along in search of food, or to watch out for danger, *Anableps tetrophthalmus* sticks the upper half of its eyes out into the air. With the lower half, it performs these functions below the surface of the water.

I have learned too that there is a plant called *Tribulus,* with pale yellow flowers each with five petals and a fruit that is beset with sharp bristles. It is a pernicious vine that flourishes in the presence of evil, and wilts at the least whiff of goodness. *Tribulus* likes to grow on the old stained walls of dungeons, palaces, harems, and morgues. Always, it takes the shape of the stain by which it is nourished. You see *Tribulus* growing on a wall, and right away, you know that unspeakable acts of depravity go on just behind it. There is a stain of damp on the ceiling of my study. Six months ago, it was the size and shape of New Hampshire. It has since grown to annex Massachusetts and a portion of lower Maine. I shouldn't be a bit surprised to look up one day and find a *Tribulus* over my desk right here in Connecticut! Hurry past, traveler. Or knock on my door, if you dare. There is a Chinese poem entitled "The Things Done in the Inner Room of the Palace of Wei Were Shameful." It was written in 700 B.C. and translated by Helen Waddell.

The tribulus grows on the wall,
upon the stain.
The things done in that room
Man cannot name.

The tribulus grows on the wall.
The stain is old.
The evil of that inner room
May not be told.

Thus are science and literature wedded in the pages of a diary.

The one science for which I have the wrong-shaped head is Physics. All through school, it was my nemesis. This mental block can be traced back to Christmas 1935. The entrance to 2145 Fifth Avenue consisted of two sets of glass-paneled doors separated by a shallow foyer big enough for the patients to remove wet boots and stack umbrellas. In the all but unanimous Christianity of Troy at the time, life and Christmas were synonymous in December. No house but was festooned and trimmed. No house but ours. Kindhearted as they both were, neither Mother nor Father gave the least nod in the direction of the holiday season, Christmas or Hanukkah. It was less a matter of unbelief than of distraction, and . . . well . . . yes . . . carelessness. It simply did not occur to them that Billy and I might suffer the deprivation keenly. But then, we had already learned the arts of renunciation and forgiveness. We'd had to. Still, the feeling of exclusion from felicity hung heavily over us.

One evening, I came home to find (Be still, my heart!) a beautiful Christmas tree in the front hall just inside the glass doors. It couldn't be! But it was! A miracle. I hollered for Billy, who, infected by my wild surmise, came running. I saw his eyes widen as he too accepted what had doubtless come from on high. Flinging open first the outer doors, then the inner, we gazed in expectation of joy. Where a moment ago the Christmas tree had been there was only the old wooden hat rack. Bereft, we stepped back outside, closing the doors behind us. No sooner had we done so, than presto! There again was the lovely tree—tinsel, angels, golden horns, candy canes, Star of Bethlehem, and all. With mounting anguish we turned to look across the street, where in the bay window of Kinnicut's, on the second floor, stood the identical tree. It was indeed from on high that the tree had come—one flight up. By some demonic optical conjunction, the image of that tree was thrown down into our front hall, giving the appearance of a tree, but the appearance only.

It was the cruelest deception of our lives. Even now, more than sixty years later, the memory is bitter as the apples of Sodom. It was the first of a lifetime of mortal lessons that it isn't the truth that sets you free; it's the imagination. The disappointment has long since vanished, though not the sympathy for those two small boys. But now I see that reflection on the glass door less as a manifestation of the science of Optics than as a beautiful ghostly tree that was no less ours than the solid one was Kinnicut's, and all the more to be relished for its mystery. If only I had thought of that then.

Be all that as it may, I have never enjoyed Christmas presents more than I did the ones imagined prior to the rude jostling-awake. Anticipation is always better than the event would be. Why undeceive yourself until it is absolutely necessary? Besides, those presents, whatever they might have been—toys, books, candy—could not be broken, or swiped by anyone of woman born, or eaten up by greedy cousins. They were beyond the reach of Fate, as was the magical tree beneath which they were strewn. It is also why I have nothing to do with the science of Physics, of which Optics is the meanest branch, the one most apt to "unweave the rainbow."

When I was a surgeon, I thought how lucky writers are not having to look at things better left unseen. Now that I'm a writer, I think it is the surgeon who is lucky for the same reason. I used to worry about discomfiting the squeamish reader with an explicit rendering of the unlovely aspects of disease. I don't any longer. It occurred to me that even the most refined and delicate woman, on Thanksgiving morning, will thrust her hand up to the wrist into the belly of a dead turkey.

So much of this book has for its subject the events that take place in a hospital. I am the conduit through which flows onto the page the building with its cargo of patients, wounds, lesions, cadavers, doctors, nurses, next of kin. Try as I may to efface myself, I cannot entirely disappear from the rendering. As it passes through my imagination, it becomes indelibly marked with my fingerprints. Authentic merit must be splashed with vivid personal experiences. Take the essay entitled "Textbook." Let us say that the act of writing this piece took a certain amount of energy, both mental and physical. From the moment it was finished, that same energy was there to be passed on to each of its readers, in turn. And each new reader, by his intellectual and emotional response to the writing, stakes a claim on the work, making it his own. It becomes as much the reader's as it once was mine.

Were I to try to characterize the writing in "Textbook," I would use the word "passionate" in both of its meanings—suffering and intensity of feeling. The patients presented here are sufferers. My attempt was to match their suffering with a prose that had the same rich texture as their wounded bodies. It is the opposite of the dry clinical language whose purpose it is to inform, to teach. Rather, the language of "Textbook" is allusive and full of imagery and color. No gray, good-natured words for me. It may be said that this language is the scalpel with which I am trying to open the reader's heart. As their author, I can admit that what I felt immediately upon writing these sentences was a pure and perfect joy. By the act of writing, that which had lain asleep in the dark burst forth into the light. Then too, there was the pleasure of finding an adjective, surprising, eccentric perhaps, but splendidly precise, which satisfies the request of the noun it is intended to modify.

By just such acts of willful play, carried out in solitude, this solitude that is little more than loneliness domesticated, "Textbook" has become an instrument of pedagogy. Without intending to, I have assumed the role of a teacher, directing his remarks to students and to eager listeners-in, eavesdroppers who are no less welcome to me. This is why I must bend every effort to make clear my meaning, to avoid the elliptical, the obscure. Which is altogether different from the ambiguity and mystery which shade our daily lives. It is a paradox that while the subject of "Textbook" is the vulnerability and sad fate of the human body, the mood of the piece is decidedly cheerful. There is a palpable relish in my descriptions of the photographs. What at first might be thought a preoccupation with the morbid, under the influence of a meticulous language is revealed as beauty. The horror has fallen away.

It is a quarter of a century since some of these essays, memoirs, and meditations were first published. In choosing the contents of this book, I have included those pieces that have evoked the strongest response from readers as well as those that I believe have withstood the test of that much time. Such are the excerpts from *Mortal Lessons* and *Letters to a Young Doctor*. In reading these works to make the selection, I was inclined to use an editorial pencil in order to spare myself a number of embarrassments this time around. For some reason, I did not. Perhaps it is because I have the uncanny feeling that these chapters were first written in a foreign language and that I was but their translator rather than their author. Still, I am surprised that the author (perhaps it is better to consider that he and I are not the same person) came so close to expressing precisely what I think now. In a way, that writer of twenty-five years ago is the older of the two, as I don't seem to think of myself as anything but a mere pickle of a boy. Even in my dreams, I am a youngster making love for the first time. It is both ridiculous and exhausting. And whenever my opinion about anything is asked, I have to try not to smile. Let this volume be my attempt, then, to introduce myself to a new generation.

There is no one way to write. The minimalists have shown that plain, unadorned prose in words of one syllable can reach the heights of beauty and power. "There, but for the grace of God, go I" for example. Or this:

Drink to me only with thine eyes
And I will pledge with mine.
Leave but a kiss within the cup,
And I'll not ask for wine.
—Ben Jonson

I'd rather have written that than the whole of the *Encyclopaedia Britannica*. But such was not given to me. Style is something that rides in on a writer's DNA. Like fingerprints, it cannot be changed. The contents of this book reveal a writer intoxicated by words, one who grabbed up great armfuls and ran across the page letting fall what may, and only then stopping to select, sort, rearrange. In surgery, the scalpel must be restrained rather than given its head. Holding back is the primary mode of surgery. After so many years of reining in, a surgeon-turned-writer must be forgiven the exhilaration of the newly liberated. As a sapling long bent down by the weight of winter's snow springs up in April, so did I spur my new instrument, the pen, and ride it with relishment. The pen and the scalpel are about the same size. In using either of them, something is shed—blood or ink. But there the similarities end. In writing, the risk is all the author's; in surgery it is taken by the one lying on the operating table.

The essay entitled "The Corpse" was not meant to shock but rather to invite the reader into the mausoleum of the newly dead and hold up the lamp of language. In this, as in many other essays, I have used the grotesque and humor as instruments of illumination. In writing "Bald!" I had meant only to entertain. Now, twenty-five years later, bald is beautiful. Many is the partially bald man who, unwilling to suffer the slow and steady loss of his glory, has seized Destiny by the lapels and shaved his own head. Just so does a martyr seize the everlasting kingdom of heaven. About baldness, I now feel differently. It has to do with chemotherapy. A young boy suffering from cancer was receiving chemotherapy, and had become totally bald. What was his surprise, upon returning to school, to find that all of the boys in the fifth grade were also bald, as was their male teacher. To spare their classmate embarrassment, they had all chosen to have their heads shaved. Such an act of communal grace gives reason to hope for the future of mankind.

The excerpts from *Letters to a Young Doctor* were an effort to tell what it is like to be a doctor, to tend the sick, and to be sick. Rilke, from whom the title was borrowed, was right when he wrote that the events of the body lie outside the precincts of language. Pain cannot be rendered, nor can orgasm, despite that countless novelists have perspired to do so. In order to approach these bodily happenings, I have roamed the imagination, gathering metaphor, myth, and memory. In "Textbook" and "Rounds" I strove to photograph the patient and to nail that picture to the page. "A Mask on the Face of Death" is the diary of a visit to Haiti, ravaged by AIDS. "Brain Death: A Hesitation" asks an impertinent question of those who harvest the brain-dead.

Not a single thought of social or ethical purpose brought about any of these essays. But it happens that some of them do have relevance for society in that they confront such subjects as abortion, physician-assisted suicide, organ transplantation, AIDS, and the doctor/patient relationship. Looking back, I see that so many of my characters seem to be knocking at the door of this world in an attempt to get into the next.

I'm told that art is best achieved in misery, toil, and disappointment. I don't know about that. I know only that writing has made me happy, just as happy as doctoring once did. Happiness has taken a great part in the making of these small creations of mine. I love the self-imposed exile of the writer, the giving up of everything else and the pledging of oneself as a bridegroom or a monk does. To enter my small brown nutshell of a study, close the door, and wait. That is all.

Throughout these writings, there is a strong note of spirituality. It would be hard to find a page without it. This is only natural for a writer who sees the flesh as the spirit thickened. Again and again, in patients ravaged by disease, or deformed, we are stunned by a sudden radiance. This is not always comforting; there is terror in lifting the veil from the ordinary world. In my study, over the desk there is a message written by John Donne: ". . . our blood labors to beget spirits." I believe I know what he meant.

It is thirteen years since I walked away from my beloved workshop in the Operating Room. It was a departure not done with a cheery wave of the hand. The Operating Room was my native land. A writer leaves his native land only at great risk. There was a feeling of dislocation, as though I were standing on the bank of a river, and it was the bank that was flowing while the stream stood still. Would I be punished? Suffer impotence of the pen? After all, my subject as a writer was my work as a doctor; the two cross-fertilized each other. I need not have worried. There is always the sharp and aching tooth of memory. Even now my dreams are filled with surgery. I am convinced that my best writing was done in the hospital charts of my patients. It had none of the vanity of an author or the pomp of language. It was truly a matter of life and death. And say what you will about writing, there is no more thrilling an achievement than the successful completion of a difficult surgical dissection.

The Exact Location of the Soul

—◊—

Someone asked me why a surgeon would write. Why, when the shelves are already too full? They sag under the dead weight of books. To add a single adverb is to risk exceeding the strength of the boards. A surgeon should abstain. A surgeon, whose fingers are more at home in the steamy gullies of the body than they are tapping the dry keys of a typewriter. A surgeon, who feels the slow slide of intestines against the back of his hand and is no more alarmed than would be a family of snakes taking their comfort from such an indolent rubbing. A surgeon, who palms the human heart as though it were some captured bird.

Why should he write? Is it vanity that urges him? There is glory enough in the knife. Is it for money? One can make too much money. No. It is to search for some meaning in the ritual of surgery, which is at once murderous, painful, healing, and full of love. It is a devilish hard thing to transmit—to find, even. Perhaps if one were to cut out a heart, a lobe of the liver, a single convolution of the brain, and paste it to a page, it would speak with more eloquence than all the words of Balzac. Such a piece would need no literary style, no mass of erudition or history, but in its very shape and feel would tell all the frailty and strength, the despair and nobility of man. What? Publish a heart? A little piece of bone? Preposterous. Still I fear that is what it may require to reveal the truth that lies hidden in the body. Not all the undressings of Rabelais, Chekhov, or even William Carlos

Williams have wrested it free, although God knows each one of those doctors made a heroic assault upon it.

I have come to believe that it is the flesh alone that counts. The rest is that with which we distract ourselves when we are not hungry or cold, in pain or ecstasy. In the recesses of the body I search for the philosopher's stone. I know it is there, hidden in the deepest, dampest cul-de-sac. It awaits discovery. To find it would be like the harnessing of fire. It would illuminate the world. Such a quest is not without pain. Who can gaze on so much misery and feel no hurt? Emerson has written that the poet is the only true doctor. I believe him, for the poet, lacking the impediment of speech with which the rest of us are afflicted, gazes, records, diagnoses, and prophesies.

I invited a young diabetic woman to the Operating Room to amputate her leg. She could not see the great shaggy black ulcer upon her foot and ankle that threatened to encroach upon the rest of her body, for she was blind as well. There upon her foot was a Mississippi Delta brimming with corruption, sending its raw tributaries down between her toes. Gone were all the little web spaces that when fresh and whole are such a delight to loving men. She could not see her wound, but she could feel it. There is no pain like that of the bloodless limb turned rotten and festering. There is neither unguent nor anodyne to kill such a pain yet leave intact the body.

For over a year I trimmed away the putrid flesh, cleansed, anointed, and dressed the foot, staving off, delaying. Three times each week, in her darkness, she sat upon my table, rocking back and forth, holding her extended leg by the thigh, gripping it as though it were a rocket that must be steadied lest it explode and scatter her toes about the room. And I would cut away a bit here, a bit there, of the swollen blue leather that was her tissue.

At last we gave up, she and I. We could no longer run ahead of the gangrene. We had not the legs for it. There must be an amputation in order that she might live—and I as well. It was to heal us both that I must take up knife and saw, and cut the leg off. And

when I could feel it drop from her body to the table, see the blessed
space appear between her and that leg, I too would be well.

Now it is the day of the operation. I stand by while the anesthetist administers the drugs, watch as the tense familiar body relaxes
into narcosis. I turn then to uncover the leg. There, upon her knee-
cap, she has drawn, blindly, upside down for me to see, a face; just
a circle with two ears, two eyes, a nose, and a smiling upturned
mouth. Under it she has printed SMILE, DOCTOR. Minutes later I
listen to the sound of the saw, until a little crack at the end tells me
it is done.

So, I have learned that man is not ugly, but that he is Beauty itself.
There is no other his equal. Are we not all dying, none faster or more
slowly than any other? I have become receptive to the possibilities
of love (for it is love, this thing that happens in the Operating Room),
and each day I wait, trembling in the busy air. Perhaps today it will
come. Perhaps today I will find it, take part in it, this love that blooms
in the stoniest desert.

All through literature the doctor is portrayed as a figure of fun.
Shaw was splenetic about him; Molière delighted in pricking his
pompous medicine men, and well they deserved it. The doctor is
ripe for caricature. But I believe that the truly great writing about
doctors has not yet been done. I think it must be done *by* a doctor,
one who is through with the love affair with his technique, who
recognizes that he has played Narcissus, raining kisses on a mirror,
and who now, out of the impacted masses of his guilt, has expanded
into self-doubt, and finally into the high state of wonderment.
Perhaps he will be a nonbeliever who, after a lifetime of grand gestures and mighty deeds, comes upon the knowledge that he has
done no more than meddle in the lives of his fellows, and that he
has done at least as much harm as good. Yet he may continue to
pretend, at least, that there is nothing to fear, that death will not
come, so long as people depend on his authority. Later, after his
patients have left, he may closet himself in his darkened office, sweating and afraid.

There is a story by Unamuno in which a priest, living in a small Spanish village, is adored by all the people for his piety, his kindness, and the majesty with which he celebrates the Mass each Sunday. To them he is already a saint. It is a foregone conclusion, and they speak of him as Saint Immanuel. He helps them with their plowing and planting, tends them when they are sick, confesses them, comforts them in death, and every Sunday, in his rich, thrilling voice, transports them to paradise with his chanting. The fact is that Don Immanuel is not so much a saint as a martyr. Long ago his own faith left him. He is an atheist, a good man doomed to suffer the life of a hypocrite, pretending to a faith he does not have. As he raises the chalice of wine, his hands tremble, and a cold sweat pours from him. He cannot stop, for he knows that the people need this of him, that their need is greater than his sacrifice. Still . . . still . . . could it be that Don Immanuel's whole life is a kind of prayer, a paean to God?

A writing doctor would treat men and women with equal reverence, for what is the "liberation" of either sex to him who knows the diagrams, the inner geographies of each? I love the solid heft of men as much as I adore the heated capaciousness of women—women in whose penetralia is found the repository of existence. I would have them glory in that. Women are physics and chemistry. They are matter. It is their bodies that tell of the frailty of men. Men have not their cellular, enzymatic wisdom. Man is albuminoid, proteinaceous, laked pearl; woman is yolky, ovoid, rich. Both are exuberant bloody growths. I would use the defects and deformities of each for my sacred purpose of writing, for I know that it is the marred and scarred and faulty that are subject to grace. I would seek the soul in the facts of animal economy and profligacy. Yes, it is the exact location of the soul that I am after. The smell of it is in my nostrils. I have caught glimpses of it in the body diseased. If only I could tell it. Is there no mathematical equation that can guide me? So much pain and pus equals so much truth? It is elusive as the whippoorwill that one hears calling incessantly from out the night window, but which, nesting as it does low in the brush, no one sees. No one but the poet, for he sees what no one else can. He was born with the eye for it.

Once I thought I had it: ten o'clock one night, the end room off a long corridor in a college infirmary, my last patient of the day, degree of exhaustion suitable for the appearance of a vision, some manifestation. The patient is a young man recently returned from Guatemala, from the excavation of Mayan ruins. His left upper arm wears a gauze dressing which, when removed, reveals a clean punched-out hole the size of a dime. The tissues about the opening are swollen and tense. A thin brownish fluid lips the edge, and now and then a lazy drop of the overflow spills down the arm. An abscess, inadequately drained. I will enlarge the opening to allow better egress of the pus. Nurse, will you get me a scalpel and some . . . ?

What happens next is enough to lay Francis Drake avomit in his cabin. No explorer ever stared in wilder surmise than I into that crater from which there now emerges a narrow gray head whose sole distinguishing feature is a pair of black pincers. The head sits atop a longish flexible neck arching now this way, now that, testing the air. Alternately it folds back upon itself, then advances in new boldness. And all the while, with dreadful rhythmicity, the unspeakable pincers open and close. Abscess? Pus? Never. Here is the lair of a beast at whose malignant purpose I could but guess. A Mayan devil, I think, that would soon burst free to fly about the room, with horrid blanket-wings and iridescent scales, raking, pinching, injecting God knows what acid juice. And even now the irony does not escape me, the irony of my patient as excavator excavated.

With all the ritual deliberation of a high priest I advance a surgical clamp toward the hole. The surgeon's heart is become a bat hanging upside down from his rib cage. The rim achieved—now thrust—and the ratchets of the clamp close upon the empty air. The devil has retracted. Evil mocking laughter bangs back and forth in the brain. More stealth. Lying in wait. One must skulk. Minutes pass, perhaps an hour. . . . A faint disturbance in the lake, and once again the thing upraises, farther and farther, hovering. Acrouch, strung, the surgeon is one with his instrument; there is no longer any boundary between its metal and his flesh. They are joined in a single perfect tool of extirpation. It is just for this that he was born. Now—thrust—and clamp—and *yes*. Got him!

Transmitted to the fingers comes the wild thrashing of the creature. Pinned and wriggling, he is mine. I hear the dry brittle scream of the dragon, and a hatred seizes me, but such a detestation as would make of Iago a drooling sucktit. It is the demented hatred of the victor for the vanquished, the warden for his prisoner. It is the hatred of fear. Within the jaws of my hemostat is the whole of the evil of the world, the dark concentrate itself, and I shall kill it. For mankind. And, in so doing, will open the way into a thousand years of perfect peace. Here is Surgeon as Savior indeed.

Tight grip now . . . steady, relentless pull. How it scrabbles to keep its tentacle-hold. With an abrupt moist plop the extraction is complete. There, writhing in the teeth of the clamp, is a dirty gray body, the size and shape of an English walnut. He is hung everywhere with tiny black hooklets. Quickly . . . into the specimen jar of line . . . the lid screwed tight. Crazily he swims round and round, wiping his slimy head against the glass, then slowly sinks to the bottom, the mass of hooks in frantic agonal wave.

"You are going to be all right," I say to my patient. "We are *all* going to be all right from now on."

The next day I take the jar to the medical school. "That's the larva of the botfly," says a pathologist. "The fly usually bites a cow and deposits its eggs beneath the skin. There the egg develops into the larval form, which, when ready, burrows its way to the outside through the hide and falls to the ground. In time it matures into a full-grown botfly. This one happened to bite a man. It was about to come out on its own, and, of course, it would have died."

The words *impostor, sorehead, servant of Satan* spring to my lips. But now he has been joined by other scientists. They nod in agreement. I gaze from one gray eminence to another, and know the mallet-blow of glory pulverized. I tried to save the world, but it didn't work out.

No, it is not the surgeon who is God's darling. He is the victim of vanity. It is the poet who heals with his words, stanches the flow of blood, stills the rattling breath, applies poultice to the scalded flesh.

Did you ask me why a surgeon writes? I think it is because I wish to be a doctor.

Down from Troy, Part I

—⌘—

From early on, I loved going with Father to St. Mary's Hospital. Actually that was its nickname, short for St. Mary, Consoler of the Afflicted. Or as Father liked to say, and made me say it too, Maria Consolatrix Afflictorum; he was of the conservative branch of atheism and insisted on the Latin. The hospital was a three-story red-brick building built in 1914, a long rectangle with two pavilions, or wings, extending from either side. Since it was operated and staffed by the Sisters of Charity, the building was winged in more ways than one. St. Mary's was situated halfway up the slope of a steep hill, from which you could look down over the town. Ever since, I have always thought that halfway up a hillside is just where a hospital belongs, midway between a cathedral on the top and a jailhouse at the foot, in touch with both the sacred and the profane. Whether it was prophetic or simply a matter of logistics, the cemetery was right up the street. From the hospital's solarium on the second floor you could watch the smoke from the crematorium chimney rise and diffuse over the city as the dead insisted upon mixing with the living. In summer, with the windows open, you could even catch a whiff of it, a compelling early lesson in death, resurrection, and ecology. I can still close my eyes and smell that blend of starch, candle wax, ashes, and roses that permeated St. Mary's Hospital. It is an odor that I have not smelled since in any of a lifetime of hospitals; it is the odor of sanctity, I think.

The nuns ran the place as though it were the flagship of a fleet on the eve of a naval battle. Here, if nowhere else, cleanliness *was* next to godliness. The polished floors wore a perpetual fanatic gleam, dirt was rooted out as though it were sin. It would take more than mere senility to make me forget Sister Michael's evening inspection of the long marble corridor. Behind her limped a wretched porter, who had spent the entire day washing and waxing the floor. I remember the stiff white wings of her cornet slicing the gloom, the crusader's curve of her nostrils, her eyes that reconnoitered every corner, then turned upon the miscreant with the glare of black olives as she pointed to a bit of smudge that was invisible to me. I remember how the Nun of Wrath aimed one bony finger at the spot for the poor devil to see, how he stood there with the good-for-nothing look of a dog that has just made a mess on the carpet. With the student nurses, she was equally exacting. Like that precise princess in the fairy tale, the one who was put out of sorts by a rose leaf out of place in the garden, just so did Sister Michael appear in the doorway of a ward, sniff once or twice, and go directly to the very bed where one corner of a sheet had not been tucked to ferocity.

The habit of the Sisters of Charity was black and full and fell to within an inch and a half of the floor. From a cord about the waist, a black rosary hung. The wimple was topped by a starched white cornet with a broad lateral flap on either side of the head. One alone was a sailboat, two side by side a regatta, three a whole armada. These sisters did not walk; they skimmed, they hovered. Free of the drag of gravity by which the rest of us are rooted to the earth, they floated quickly and noiselessly, save for the soft click of wooden beads tossing among the folds of their habits. With each step, the black nose of a shoe would peek from beneath the hem, then dart back inside the flaring recesses as though each of them were sheltering a family of mice.

More than once in the springtime I sat in the many-windowed solarium that was filled with vases of lilac and peony and gazed down the long hall in full expectation that the very next thing I would see coming toward me would be Maria Consolatrix Afflictorum Herself, to whom I would, oh yes I would, hold out my wounded heart. One evening Father came to collect me there.

"What were you doing?" I asked him.

"I was bringing a baby boy into the world," he replied. That's the way they used to talk in those days.

"Where did you bring it from?"

"A sealed garden."

"How did you get in if it was sealed?"

"The gate was opened just long enough for me to reach in and take him out. *Next subject.*"

I opened a new line of questioning. "What is the Holy Trinity?"

"It's just an expression."

"No, what is it really?"

"It means the three who are one."

"I don't get it," I told him.

Father thought for a long moment. "Well, look," he said. "Here we are walking this corridor. Do you see those three wall lamps along the way? Let the first one be the Father, the next one the Son, and the third the Holy Ghost. Each lamp gives out its own light but as we walk down the hall passing from one light to the next we still get some of the light from each one no matter where we are standing. Now do you get it?"

"You made that up."

"Then shut up," he explained. It is fifty years later, and as for the Holy Trinity, I still don't quite get it, but of all the explanations I have been given over the years, Father's makes the most sense.

At St. Mary's, the beds were lined up along the walls of large ward-rooms. In time of need, a movable curtain screen could be placed so as to conceal the newly dead or to afford, if not privacy, at least the implication of it. To this day I am of the opinion that private rooms are a wrongheaded idea. Once encaged in a private room, the patient is out of sight as well as alone. This cannot be as safe or as functional as a great ward with fifteen beds lined up on either side, over which one sharp-eyed nurse can keep constant surveillance. To say nothing of the lovely commiseration that prevails in a ward and the hustle-bustle that is the antidote to the boredom of the bedridden. What architects and doctors have lost sight of is the pleasure the sick take in just plain gossiping. It is on a ward, not in a private room, where the craving for gossip is more likely to be satisfied. Besides, unless the gift of prophecy has deserted *me,* a ward is not one inch farther away from Heaven than a private room. When the time comes for me to be put to bed in a hospital, let it be in a ward, where my sighs and groans can mingle with the sighs and groans of my fellow human beings in the consolation of fraternity, and where it might be given to each of us in turn to utter the most beautiful sentence in the English language: There but for the grace of God go I.

As severe as Sister Michael was with the porter and the students, just so kindly did she move among the sick. Mercy, just before leaving the world of medicine forever, lingered awhile among those nuns. How different those sisters were from the doctors, who stepped importantly among the puddles of patients, especially the surgeons, each of whom was quite convinced that once he had left the ward his disembodied radiance lingered on. Father was the sisters' favorite. Their affection was based on his good-humored teasing, to which they responded with a commotion of cornets and a rolling up of the eyes. With what wit and gallantry he returned to those laborious virgins a glimmer of their long-forsworn sexuality. Temperamentally unable to surrender to faith myself, I have remained in a condition of awe at the faith of others. It is what constitutes for me a belief in God, only once removed, like a cousin. When I was twelve, Father lay dying in St. Mary's Hospital. Long before my eyes had had their fill of him. I remember the vigilant nuns grouped like lamps in the darkened room, his face graying away, theirs glowing with an imperturbable golden light.

Years later, during summer vacations from college, I worked as a night orderly at St. Mary's. It was on my first night of duty that I was told to wheel a stretcher from the emergency room to the operating room and to go as quickly as I could, for the cargo in my charge was a young woman who, I was told, was hemorrhaging briskly. With one hand holding aloft a bottle of saline solution and the other pushing, I set off at a speed just short of reckless endangerment, only to find that the single working elevator was in use. When minutes went by, or hours (what does it matter how long?), and still the elevator didn't come, I began to despair for the life of my patient. From the head of the stretcher rose moan after moan to break the heart of Caligula. Was the red stain on the sheet spreading? A sister arrived also to wait for the elevator. At last, from the upper regions of the shaft, I heard the door slide shut, the gears engage, and the car set in motion. Like a sentry on the alert, I prepared to storm and capture that elevator and rescue my first patient from certain death—only to watch as the empty car passed sluggishly by without stopping. Its slow disappearance from view remains one of the most sickening events of my life. Again and again I kicked the door and pounded it with my fist and I cursed it much as Jesus cursed the fig tree that bore no fruit. Goddamn elevator! I cried aloud. May your cables rust, your gears be stripped, your door go unhinged so that never again shall you know the bliss of ascension or descent. To all of which the sister responded with one of those sad little smiles those people keep in their repertoire. Then she reached for her beads and began to *offer it up*. That nun hadn't got past bead one when the elevator appeared out of nowhere, and we all rose to a happy ending. That was the trouble with working at St. Mary's. You were always at risk of having Her called in on consultation, which kept a permanent sheepish expression on the faces of the heathen.

From St. Mary's on, like the gaucho who spends half his life on horseback, I have spent half of mine inside a hospital. That is bound to affect the way one perceives such a place. Lacking the least knowledge of architecture and unable to read blueprints, I have now and then built a hospital in my mind.

I have a son, Jon, who makes metal sculptures in the garage. What with his worktable, tanks of acetylene gas, the hoses from which spurt jets of bluish flame, and the piles of derelict iron, steel, copper, and brass, I have to leave my car out on the street. Believe me, I am glad to do that. For no mere automobile, were it a Rolls-Royce done in gold leaf or my Chevrolet at the height of its decrepitude, can match the solidified dreams that issue from Vulcan's cave: little dancing frogs made from coat hangers, a giant bumblebee from a bag of tenpenny nails, and even a red-tailed hawk out of what, in a former life, had been horseshoes. Just so does a garage become a temple of reincarnation. Again and again, the tongs and metal are thrust into the flame, then hammered or bent to suit. From time to time, a shower of sparks flies up in celebration. Only last spring, he made a set of wind chimes out of some old copper pipe and plaques of tin weighted with lead. If my years be Methuselan, I shall never forget how, goggled and aproned, he emerged from his forge holding aloft those wind chimes. When, at precisely that moment, a breeze took the chimes and I heard for the first time that sweet confusion of notes, it was as though a lamp had been turned on somewhere deep inside my ear.

Surely, there is no more beautiful object made by man than wind chimes, a thing born of metal, of fire, ravishing equally to the eye and ear, whose spatial configuration is no mere geometry, but geometry that at any moment may be galvanized into life. Unlike the ticking of a clock, the voice of wind chimes is not Swiss, that is to say, automatic and regulated, but pagan, in that it is dependent upon the surprise of streams and currents of air. The soft concussion of its parts cools the heated mind, inviting it to reverie. Ever since Jon made them, the wind chimes hang outside the back porch, near the kitchen, animating the paralytic old house, offering it the dream of movement; at any moment, the house with all of us in it might rise into the air as though it had been painted by Chagall. Thus has space been mastered and inertia overcome by the artist using nothing but fire, wind, and earth. At night, lying in my bed, I wait to hear its soft palaver like a blind man who cocks his ear to hear the stars come out. There! It begins! And I am filled with a sense of harmony with the natural world. I am once again a pagan, for whom every tree, waterfall, rock, and cliff is inhabited by spirits.

Just as I would never again live in a house without wind chimes,
I would not call a building *hospital* that did not have a fountain on
the premises. Were I to design a hospital, I would cause it to be built
around a large reflecting pool, from the center of which would rise
a fountain. Let it be a tall fountain with a powerful upward thrust
and, at descending intervals, lateral leaves or petals to catch the fall,
breaking it into a thousand secondary and tertiary *cascatelli*. There
can be nothing so consolatory to the sick as a fountain. To such a
waterfall, the sufferer will attribute all the antidotes to his symptoms.
The mere contemplation of such a sympathetic element—water—
leads naturally toward the ideal of recovery. Each night, with the
fountain stilled, the sick and those who tend them might watch from
their windows as Cassiopeia and Orion are enticed into the pool,
glittering evidence of the celestial connection with earth. For those
who cannot get well, a fall of water, by offering its destiny in full
view, teaches the incurable how to die. Falling water knows how to
comply with death by surrendering its voice, place, shape, and identity to peaceful horizontality. It is the same complicity that wood has
with the flames that devour it.

My hospital would face west. Before drawing the first line of my
blueprint, I would imagine the building at sunset, those few minutes
when it shows its true color—red, as though the building itself were
hemorrhaging. Moments later, with every window ablaze, it becomes
a crucible in which a core of radium is glowing. Hemorrhage, irra-
diation—these are events not unheard of within the precincts of a
hospital. At noon, the building would resemble a great supine human
body, its corridors a labyrinth of arteries circulating corpuscles of
light to every corner. At such times—sunset, noon—a hospital is
transformed and exalted by the elements. And so water and sunlight
must not be underestimated any more than the architect would
ignore the lessons of brick, wood, or glass. What is brick, after all,
but the earth taken up, molded, and burned in the fire? Each brick
is a fragment of the planet, wrested free, purified, then placed in
precise juxtaposition to its fellows. What is wood but a creature that
was once no less alive than the architect who will use it? Years after

wood has become what some call dead, it is capable of vitality. Perhaps not in the same way as was Aaron's rod when it burst into leaf, but with no less striking implications. Take down an old table from the attic, where it has stood for decades gathering dust. Dribble on its surface a few drops of lemon oil. It has a familiar odor that serves to awaken the buried past of childhood. Now, using a soft cloth, preferably a fragment of shirt that someone has once worn to work, begin to polish. Make broad circular strokes, leaning into your labor, delivering all the force of your shoulder and arm to the tabletop. Within minutes you will see the old wood begin to glow under the animating force of your body, lighting up, until what you see rekindled is the life that has lain dormant in the long-dead tree. Each material that goes into the making of something has a characteristic and unique emanation of which the artist must remain cognizant. And each thing, be it wind chimes, fountain, or hospital, must take part in the mysterious correspondence between man and the elements. To create, it is necessary to dream; the artist who cannot imagine cannot prophesy.

Just as a writer surrenders to language, permitting the words to lead his hand across the page, so will stone, brick, wood, glass and marble suggest to the architect the manner in which to use them. To denounce these correspondences between artists and material as mere animism would be to misunderstand. The architect who denies these connections does so at his own risk. The soul of his building will not be visible. He will have become a barbarian.

Say what you will, there are some aspects of life that do not have an artistic solution. Perhaps architecture, as it is applied to a hospital, is not an art at all. Visit a few dozen medical centers around the country, as I have, and you will come away with an impression of sameness, monotony, derivation, rather than of inspiration or originality. Lacking entirely in majesty or the least intimation of the sacred, not one of these hospitals would fulfill the criteria of a future ruin. Perhaps the solution lies not in architecture at all, but in language. That which eludes the architect presents itself to the writer. After all, a hospital is just a building until you listen and hear the slate hooves of dreams galloping across its roof. Perhaps what an architect cannot give a hospital a writer can.

Not so long ago admission to a hospital was tantamount to a sentence of death. Even the jailhouse, that one at the bottom of the hill, was preferable, for it did not necessarily imply physical suffering and there was always the possibility that you would one day be let out. The fact was that there wasn't too much that could be done for you in a hospital. Mostly it was the therapy of subtraction: Something was taken away from you. After you'd had an amputation, a series of enemas and cathartics, and as much bleeding as necessary to placate the resident vampire, you'd had everything the hospital had to offer but the chaplain. And then there *he* was with an ecclesiastical smile etched on his face, exhorting you to make peace with your Maker. The best that could be said of it all was that your suffering would not be prolonged. Those were the good old days, when a single martyrdom was enough. Under present conditions, the hospitalized sinner, rescued from crisis to crisis, is apt to endure enough punishment to *die out of debt* no matter how unrepentant.

Nor did it reassure that the premises were called Mercy Hospital or Memorial Hospital or Misericordia or even Martyr's Hospital, which at least has a certain unvarnished candor. Were I placed in charge of naming hospitals, I would call a moratorium on the letter M, a dirge-y sort of letter if ever there was one. Who would not rather go into the Strong Comeback Clinic than into the Strong Memorial? Or the Florida Hall of Bodily Restoration?

Imagine yourself being led into a hospital by firm and loving relatives. To the pain and bleeding by which you have already been separated from the rest of your kind, now add terror. "Don't be silly," says your next of kin. "Of course you're going to get out of here, and before you know it." But you know better. Just look at the place! Not the least sign of a gate leading into a garden with, above, a bay window looking down; no chimney wearing a feather of smoke; no attic with dormers; no dark, cool cellar for exploring. Soon you have been "signed in" and braceleted like a child in danger of being lost, conducted to your room. How pathetic your little suitcase with its

shamefaced cargo of pajamas, slippers, your toothbrush. You hold
on to it as a refugee would clutch his possessions at a port of em-
barkation. A nurse enters and asks your name. "What brought you
to the hospital?" she wants to know. "I took a taxi," you say in a
feeble attempt at graveyard humor. "Roll up your sleeve," she replies.
Now you surrender all the measurements that you have always taken
for granted: your blood pressure, pulse, temperature, and you satisfy
her with your blood and your urine. More to the point, you think,
would be to snip a lock of your hair to be given to your family when
the time comes. The nurse leaves, but not before ordering you to
strip and don the special raiment of the place. You do, then look
around the room, your heart full of longing for the lares and penates
of home, for the familiar roof beams, whose every notch and nick
you have committed to memory; for the flames in the grate, rising
and falling like voices in a choir; for your afghan, hand-knitted by a
prophetic grandmother, who knew from the very first pass of her
needles that one day you would take relish in lying beneath it. The
doctor enters, and with that first step, he makes the room his own.
The bed trembles; the walls worship. For is he not the omnipotent
one, who has come to take you into his wise hands? His voice is
courteous but with an underskin of granite. *Behave yourself*, it seems
to say. Exit the doctor. Once again you are alone. Your eyes engage
the mirror; your chin quivers with restrained tears.

But. And upon that conjunction, I will hang my hat. *But* there is
the indomitable human spirit that cannot be entirely snuffed. In
Auschwitz as in the Soviet gulag, in the dungeons of Piranesi as in a
room at the hospital, it flickers on. Before long, you have tested the
bed for softness, then flicked the bed lamp on and off. Next thing
you know, you will have assessed the view from the window. Perhaps
you can see your beloved house from up here? Within hours you
will have befriended, if nothing else, a pattern of sunlight on the
window ledge, a water stain on the ceiling that has the exact shape
of Yugoslavia. Even in the sound of the wind tricking along the outside of the building, you will hear snatches of a familiar song. With
all the force of memory and nostalgia, you will search here for scraps

of intimacy. It is the same impulse that causes a prisoner confined to a dungeon to fall rapt at the play of a sunbeam on the wall or a child sent to his room for an infraction to take comfort in a spiderweb in the corner where ceiling and wall meet. The process of nesting has begun. It must be one of the most ancient urges of mankind. In so doing, you will people this room with the whole of your remembered past.

Now you have been in the hospital for a week. You have undergone every one of the tests devised by a diabolical science bent upon stripping your body of its carnal mysteries. Surgery has been performed. Your world has shrunk from the room to a single bed. It is a narrow house, hardly larger than your body. Only the strong, capable arms of the nurse can enter this narrowness to bathe or nourish you or dress your wounds. Unable to tend yourself, you are once again a child in its cradle. Still later, if Fate decrees, you will be a small creature in its cocoon. Either you will emerge to life, or you will not. Narcotized, you are only dimly aware of the tiny place, this bed, which nonetheless embraces tenderly its small parcel of humanity. Take heart, little patient, there is reason to feel at home.

Unlike other buildings constructed for public use, a bank, say, which, once erected, holds to its shape through whatever transaction passes hand to hand, a hospital, the moment a patient is bedded in it, becomes an extension of that person. No, a hospital has not the solidity of a bank or a courthouse. A hospital has a heart and lungs. It has a bloodstream; the tide of it flows back and forth along the corridors. Each room expands and contracts in accordance with the breathing of its occupant. The walls palpitate to the rhythm of his heart, while in and out the window fly daydreams and nightmares. It is a dynamism that is transmitted to the hospital by the despair and the yearning of the sick. Who has not experienced the strange, surreal resonance of a hospital room in which a loved one is lying? I have often felt, while fighting in the middle of the night to keep drowning lungs afloat or to stanch a flow of blood, that the room about me was participating in the struggle, how more than once the walls gasped, then stood still at the instant of death. Can this be said of any other structure made of bricks and mortar and prestressed concrete? And how often I have watched a nurse scrub and polish an old beshrivelment until its ribs smiled and the room smiled back in shared pleasure. Little patient, take heart. More than human hands helped make this place.

Time was when every great building owed its existence to some life destroyed. A living person was buried in the wall or foundation. It was done to provide a spirit for the building that would occupy and give it a life of its own, to make a beginning. In the Middle Ages, gargoyles and other ornamentations took on the function of warding off evil spirits that might threaten inhabitants. Long after the practice of immurement was abandoned, it still happens that, during the labor of construction, blood will be shed, a life lost. The hospital differs from those ancient buildings in which living people were immured in that its house spirit enters the premises *after* it has been built and put into use. This spirit is born out of the suffering and death of those who occupy it. Year after year the building becomes re-created in the form of spirit as the suffering of the sick is set free within its walls.

But what, you ask, has all this to do with the architecture of a hospital? All these fountains and wind chimes, the sacredness of brick, the vitality of wood, the house spirits—these are the fantasies of a mere scribbler who cannot even read blueprints. And I, in turn, ask: Where is the architect who, without sacrificing function and practicality, will think of the hospital as a pregnant woman who suffers the occupancy of a human being who enters, dwells for a time, and ultimately passes forth? Where is the architect who, from the very moment he begins his design, will be aware that in each room of his finished hospital, someone will die? Who, while seated at his drawing board, will pause to feel upon his naked forearms the chill wind of his mortality? One day, he too will enter this building, not as its architect but as a supplicant in direst need. If I am wrong, and such human emotions cannot be expressed in architecture, why then it is time to surrender the hospital to writers, who will build it out of words and dreams.

—m—

It was a five-block walk south on Fifth Avenue to Public School No. 5. Every morning at precisely eight-fifteen I was picked up by the twins, Alice and Lucy, big chubby girls who lived around the corner on Jacob Street. "Dickeeee! Dickeeee!" they would bawl, filling the street with their brays and giggles until, mortified, I ran downstairs to shut them up. For some reason Mother found this daily summons exceedingly funny. At the first "Dickeeee!" she would cover her mouth and gasp. Had she known what we talked about on the way to school and what we might or might not have done in the backyard of their house, she would have been less amused. It was Alice who first suggested that we show each other what we had "down below," although, years later, she insisted it had been Lucy. Suffice it to say, there were any number of occasions in their backyard when I lowered my knickers and they their bloomers while we examined each other with immense clinical curiosity.

The children of Public School No. 5 were for the most part blond, blue-eyed, and pale, which was impractical in a town enveloped in soot. Pale children show the dirt so. In the lower grades the first half hour of each day was spent taking attendance. Roll call was a feast of beautiful names: Fully half the girls were tailed with an 'een. There was Maureen, Colleen, Mavoureen, Kathleen, and Evaleen, along with a number of Bridies, Sybils, and Bridgets. The boys were Liam, Conal, Conor, and Patrick. And Patrick. And Patrick. And Patrick. Next to them, Richard sounded like the strewing of ashes on pavement. As each name was called, we were required to leap to our feet and recite a proverb.

"Kathleen McGuire!"

"A rolling stone gathers no moss."

"Patrick Logan!"

"Empty barrels make the most noise."

"Richard Selzer!"

"A stitch in time saves nine."

A mindless exercise in rote and obedience? Never mind—it was an incantatory ritual, nothing short of a system of belief by which we could live. In the sixth grade, a new girl appeared. She had the unfortunate name of Cleopatra Reilly. While the rest of us whose tissues were not "subtly spun" could hide our imperfections behind quite ordinary names, poor, pigeon-toed, frizzy Egypt stood naked in the gale and had to suffer daily the pain of odious comparison.

Public School No. 5 was a cheerless two-story gray-stone building with a concrete play yard in front. By some eccentricity in the pipes, the great corridor was frigid while the classrooms were stuffy and overheated. At the vicious bell whose clang marked the end of one period and the beginning of another, the children rose as one and filed into the corridor to stand in silence like the newly dead being shunted from one mansion to another until we should arrive at Heaven or Hell.

The classrooms smelled of chalk, ink, and urine. The teachers were Irish spinsters who had obtained their certificates at normal school, large bosomy women given to wearing flamboyant silk dresses with tiny lace handkerchiefs tucked into a sleeve. Given also to wearing toilet water. Each teacher wore the particular scent that was her trademark: lily-of-the-valley, gardenia, carnation. Ever since, I have agreed with Cicero that the woman smells good who smells of nothing. Miss Feerick was famous for her ability to look out the window while you were reciting, then say, "Thank you," in a way to let you know that you had performed abominably. Miss Vaughan, long after she had gone stone deaf, continued to call out "Silence!" from force of habit. Miss McTammany taught by the ruler and wore the perpetual glower of the archangel on the day of Expulsion. Mademoiselle Bouton, a Québécoise, taught anatomical French, acting out the phrases. *Je m'hausse les épaules* was followed by a shrugging of shoulders. *Je me fronce les sourcils*, and she wrinkled her forehead. Miss Foyle taught manners by requiring each boy to stand and bow to her, each girl to drop a curtsy while she sat at her desk as upon a throne accepting the obeisance of her subjects.

"No, no, Colleen. That was clumsy. And don't twitch so." Then, rising from her chair, she would take a bit of her skirt in either hand, cross one fat ankle over the other, incline her head just so, and, slowly, with infinite grace, sink precisely three inches. "There, now you must do it again."

Each desk had an inkwell at the upper right corner. It was considered honorific to be chosen to fill these inkwells from the large nozzled can labeled Higgins' Eternal Ink. The pens were of tapered wood with detachable steel nibs. I never mastered the knack of controlling the flow of ink to the tip of the nib. The paper upon which I practiced the Palmer method of penmanship was always soiled with great blobs. It was an early lesson that ink has a mind of its own. It goeth where it listeth. So many years later, in the throes of writer's block or, like Flaubert, rolling on the floor in search of *le mot juste*, I long for an inkwell full of Higgins' Eternal in which to dip my pen and come up with just the right word. As for those recalcitrant pens, they put me in mind of Sir Walter Scott. How one day, while out hunting, he suddenly thought of the sentence he had been trying to write all morning. He quickly shot a crow, whittled a pen from one of its feathers, and wrote it down in crow's blood. Once or twice I tried making my own ink from a formula in *The Old Farmer's Almanac*, but it came out like weak tea, and such was the prose it produced.

In those days the handicapped children were not isolated but kept together with the rest of us until the seventh grade, when the logistics of transporting them to and fro became too difficult. While this was occasionally disruptive—the unpredictability of their outbursts and all—it was never less than entertaining, and surely it promoted tolerance. It was expected that some people would "take fits" or be "deaf and dumb" or "feebleminded." For the most part, these afflicted children were models of patience, sitting quietly while the rest of us recited the particularities of the French and Indian wars, rejoicing when we performed well, sharing our disgrace when we did not. I remember one Spanish girl who could neither hear nor speak, but whose gaze was more eloquent than any speech. All her ethnic ebullience shone forth from her dark eyes, which overflowed with the zest of expression. And I remember a boy with the vague helpless smile of someone who had misplaced himself.

As unrefined as were their pupils, just so exquisite were the teachers. They were, to a woman, hypersensitive to drafts, and only when the rancid odor of the unwashed reached the level of toxicity would the biggest boy in class be asked to lower one window an inch with a long hooked pole. It was another unsought privilege to be sent to the teacher's kitchen for her lunch tray while the rest of the class played in the schoolyard. More than once, for my sins, it was I who carried a tray of asparagus on toast or chicken croquettes and Jell-O with a nipple of whipped cream.

There was one black boy in the school. Clifford was handsome and had a beautiful baritone voice, with which he rendered "Old Man River" and Negro spirituals at assembly. He was also the victim of prejudice. Once, driven to wild rebellion, he dipped his pen and shook it at Miss Rogers. Higgins' Eternal Ink flew in gobs over her silks.

"You goddamned nigger!" she shrieked and slapped him back and forth, back and forth, across the face.

From time to time, the school was swept by impetigo, lice, or pinkeye. Of the three, lice was the worst, for it involved mortification of both flesh and spirit, itching and shame in equal portion. No classroom but had its quantity of freshly shaved scalps, each with a bloody nick or two from the paternal straight razor. It was in the fifth grade that pediculosis struck home. O dire was the twang of Apollo's silver bow when he shot his crab-tipped arrows down upon my head! To have one's head shaved for lice was humiliating. One wished for death. When Father had finished, I looked in the mirror and was shocked to see how small my head really was, scarcely more than a doorknob. And cold! The sight reduced me to tears.

"You look like a penis," said Billy in a burst of generosity. When, two days later, his own depilation took place, I had the ignoble pleasure of returning the compliment.

During the polio epidemic everyone wore a green cloth amulet called a scapular tucked inside shirt or blouse. These were rectangles of green felt bearing a white cross from the center of which blazed the sacred heart of Jesus. Unbeknownst to Father and Grandpa, Mother had gotten hold of two of these scapulars from the McGucken sisters. When Father discovered them pinned to our undershirts, he gave her a look.

"It is just to please the McGuckens," she said. "And anyway it can't hurt."

Perhaps out of some notion that clothes make the artist-to-be, Mother dressed me in baggy knickers, thigh-length tan cotton stockings held up by garters, a beret, and a loose black bow beneath my collar. Any departure from the uniform of poverty worn by the boys at Public School No. 5 was greeted with derision in the schoolyard, and mine would have drawn comment from the clowns at the circus. Even Billy joined in.

"You look like the sack of Troy," he said.

When I related the story of my martyrdom, Mother, herself given to wearing costumes—veils, sashes, and feathers—was impervious. "I'm surprised at you," she said. "It is a mark of character to rise above the taunts of the rabble."

I took to feigning illness so as to be allowed to stay home. I had already mastered the knack of looking dangerously gaunt. Now I managed spells of labored breathing; I coughed hideously. Mother, fearing that I might be developing "a chest," began to knit furiously. I lay in my bed reading and listened to the clicking of her knitting needles.

"What are you making?" I asked.

"You'll see. It's a surprise." Two weeks later, she held up the surprise. It was a helmet made of heavy gray wool with holes for the eyes and mouth and a broad "skirt" that covered neck, shoulders, and upper chest both front and back.

"What's that?" I demanded.

"It's a balaclava. They wear them in the Crimea."

"I won't."

"Yes you will. Not another word!" She pulled the thing over my head and twitched it into place.

"There. Now you can go back to school." The smell of the wool was suffocating, and my head itched. Furthermore, it didn't fit; the eyeholes were not always over my eyes. In the mirror I looked like the Man in the Iron Mask. I hated it as I have hated nothing else since. The next morning Alice and Lucy took one look and screamed, first in terror, then in hysterical laughter. Dying of shame, I could not hold back the tears. The girls insisted on trying it on, each splitting her sides at the sight of the other. It is to the everlasting credit of those hefty, spirited girls that, in the ensuing weeks, no one dared poke fun at me in their presence. To show my gratitude, I taught them to say 555 in French.

"Cinq cent cinquante cinq," I repeated over and over.

"Sank sonk sank-on sank," they chanted in unison, and to that cadence we marched to school prepared to face the Cossacks.

It was Father who rescued me. One evening, I knocked on the door of his consultation room during office hours, an action forbidden under all but the most urgent circumstances. Once inside, I burst into tears and announced that I would rather die than wear that crown of thorns.

"It's just a kind of hat," said Father.

"This is not the Crimea," I sobbed.

There followed a long, pondering silence. All at once, he brightened. "It must be done delicately," he said in a conspiratorial tone. "Your mother has placed a good deal of faith in that hat. It has become her religion. We'll do it with her weapon—poetry." He then instructed me to learn by heart Tennyson's "Charge of the Light Brigade." Did I think I could learn it by tomorrow? Did I!

"Right after supper, I'll give you the signal. Put on the balaclava. For atmosphere," he added slyly. "You won't want to be crying either." I shrugged and raised my hands to show I couldn't help it. "Just you imagine you're right there galloping between the cannons to right and left. You might be scared but you won't cry."

By midafternoon of the next day, I had all six stanzas down pat. At the table, rigid with anxiety, I waited for the high sign from Father. It came. I rose to my feet, pulled the hated garment over my head, and spurred my horse. I got as far as

> Boldly they rode and well,
> Into the jaws of Death
> Into the mouth of Hell . . .

when all at once she said: "Take that silly thing off and give it here." And that was that. I never saw the balaclava again, but months later there was a newly knitted afghan on the couch, some of whose colors made me think of the Crimea. To this day I give thanks to Tennyson for the repetitious meter and the predictable rhymes that made his poem easy to memorize.

In contrast to Billy, who made every room his own by merely setting foot inside it, I was shy and shrimpish. Upon entering a room, I would sidle for a corner rather than risk the exposure of the open middle. Part of this had to do with my wardrobe, whose wormy circumstances made me look like John the Baptist. It is to these years of unwelcome attention to my attire that I attribute my lifelong lack of interest in dressing up. No matter what I put on in the morning, by noon it has taken on the patina of burlap and begun to ravel. But the role of a surgeon in our society demands otherwise, and my desultory efforts to look presentable were a pitiful attempt to suggest decorum without ever living up to it. A long white doctor's coat covers a good many lapses of haberdashery. For this reason alone, I had chosen the right profession.

Down from
Troy, Part II

—⁓—

Every once in a while, when my eccentricities threaten to get out
of hand, I send myself back to Troy, where they're not so apt to be
noticed among the general oddity. Even when I'm not able to make
the physical journey, I will dispatch my astral body there to nose
among the old alleyways and corners, revisit the pergola in Frear
Park, the site of that first confirmatory kiss, swim naked in the Hudson River, and go a-haunting with all the gusto of which a disembodied spirit is capable. In returning to Troy in these pages, I have
chosen Enthusiasm and Nostalgia for my companions. They are as
endearing as they are contagious. If theirs is a colored slant, never
mind. In my Troy, all the women were pretty, the men handsome.
In my Troy, all the dogs were of the same melancholy breed in which
something had gone wrong with an ear, the tail, whatever. In my
Troy, each street had its own personality. That block of Second Street
where I lived for the first seven years of my life was a scene out of
an Edith Wharton novel. It came as no surprise that when *The Age
of Innocence* was made into a movie, it was filmed right there. In my
Troy, if nowhere else, there was enough love to go around. If the
Hereafter is anything like my Troy, I may be readier for it than I
thought. All that having been said, there was something carnival-
esque about the inhabitants. Just below the gentry and the "lace curtain Irish" swarmed a menagerie of drunkards, prostitutes, cowled
nuns, priests (both lapsed and repressed), widows, porky politicos,

head-breaking thugs, bootlickers, storytellers, and orphans. It was such a populace as Dickens might have drawn some fifty years earlier in London.

If I leave New Haven at eight in the morning, it is twelve-thirty when I drive up to the city limits. Each time, imagination swells. Just outside the ramparts, Trojan horsemen wheel and salute me on trumpets longer than themselves. Once I am inside the gates, every belfry starts quarreling with its fellows. "When the heir returneth, then shall ring out the bell. So the legend runneth, so the old men tell." That sort of thing. The city fathers who long ago chose the name Troy couldn't have foreseen that one day their small city would be "Iliized" by one of its sons.

It happened that a friend sent me an old edition of Shakespeare's *Troilus and Cressida* with the pages unslit. I would be the very first one to read this book. Reaching for my scalpel, I slit the first page, thrilling to the thought that by just such an act are Surgery and Literature made one. From the opening line, I was captured: "In Troy, there lies the scene . . ." The poem goes on to tell how the Greeks pitched their "brave pavilions" on the Dardan plain outside Troy. (The name of the yearbook at Troy High School is *The Dardanian*.) One by one, the pages of Shakespeare yielded to my scalpel. Nowadays, I suppose you wouldn't have to slit them. Just make two little holes in the cover, pump in some air, and read the book through a libroscope.

While naturally I have absolute allegiance to the Trojan side of that war, I must admit that Hector was a bit of a problem. When Ajax, the Greek hero, knocked him down in battle, Hector took it out on innocent bystanders, including his wife, Andromache, whom he "chid" strongly. Another victim was Hector's faithful armorer, whom he punched in the nose. Come to think of it, Hector sounds like any number of Trojans I used to know. Still, although I have, from time to time, strongly "chid" my city and its people, my love for them is undeniable, and it is requited. Whenever I go there, it is as the "Bard of Troy," and a good deal of bardolatry goes on. I can't even pay for my beer at Dempsey's Tavern. Next thing you know,

I'll be wearing a garland of violets in my hair. Never mind, I'd sooner be a poor shepherd in the hills above Troy than the Sultan of Brunei.

In the twenties and thirties, one still lived on the cusp of what was called "progress." There was, of course, electricity. But the smell of candle wax was everywhere. Automobiles, yes—frog-eyed, dash-boarded, and fendered—but in the streets, horse manure still gilded the cobblestones. Coal still had to be shoveled, the furnace stoked, and the mysteries of the damper solved. The Industrial Revolution had long since been born. We were but its delayed afterbirth. The Troy I have tried to remember is no myth of my invention, although I must be permitted the elaboration of other historians. Now and then, a reader will declare herself incredulous.

"That couldn't really have happened," she'll say. "I don't believe that for a minute." That person is *not* my reader. Who, after all, would have preferred that Herodotus tell nothing but the truth? The whole of my remembering is an effort to catch that time and place before night falls and the glass in the window shatters, and the pot cracks, like a heart.

At first glance, Troy has a two-dimensional look, rather like a picture postcard. But gaze long enough and slowly the city fills out, takes on perspective, begins to stir. I was born and raised here? you ask your-self. Imagine! Oh, I suppose that for those who live there, the beauty of the place must begin to fade. But for the Prodigal Son returning, there is a glow. Sparks fly up from the streets to make a constellation in the sky which, on certain celebratory nights, one is privileged to see. Almost at once, I am trafficking with ghosts. I feel them passing like a whiff of air. Look! There is Father, raised by my sighs, carrying his black doctor's bag on house calls. And Mother, with all the Some-body Elses she became during her long performance as Gertrude of Troy. There too, the ragpicker and the organ-grinder. I shouldn't be altogether surprised to come upon dog-faced Hecuba, maddened by the horror, who bit the stones and barked. Or Helen, the wastress of cities, encrusted with cosmetics, whose golden torch stayed lit all night long in her chamber.

—m—

In the early thirties, our block of Second Street was arguably the most sedate in the city, what with the Music Hall at one corner, and in the middle of the block, a white limestone mansion lived in by old Mr. Payne and his housekeeper (now a fraternity house), and farther on, the Hartt-Cluett house (now a museum). There was no street in Troy whose morals were more closely guarded. While the rest of the city was patrolled by streetwalkers, or soiled by bums, we were unstained. It was much to the regret of Billy and me. To us, it was less a city block than the aisle of a church. Voices lowered when people turned into our block. No car tooted, nor any dog barked. On Sunday, the silence deepened further. From the bay window, you might be forgiven for wondering if the entire city had been evacuated. The houses were three stories high and of either dignified red brick or brownstone. A certain formality prevailed. A screen door that might have permitted a fuzzy glimpse of an interior would have been considered a breach of architecture. I'm not sure we belonged there. From the minute I could see anything, I could see Mother arising from her bed like gray-eyed morn itself and leaning from the bay window in something pink that, from across the street, might have been taken for bare skin. She was "conspicuous," it was murmured. One might have thought that living on such a block would have encouraged a degree of tribalism among the neighbors. But such was not the *modus vivendi*. Nor, come to think of it, is it otherwise on St. Ronan Terrace in New Haven. About neighborliness, I would have to agree with Mother.

"It all depends," she said without further elaboration. Perhaps propinquity means very little unless you live in a hot climate—Ethiopia, say—where the actual people and not just their trash cans and newspapers are seen on the street. As it is, one sees only spoor and detritus. One hears not human speech, but the barking of each other's dogs.

Behind a lattice door, called the "area gate," a narrow alley led alongside the house to the back entrance. It was used by the trashman, breadman, milkman, fishman, and every other kind of "man" you can think of. When the iceman cameth, he had to carry a block of ice in his tongs, then chip away at it to get it to fit into the icebox. It wouldn't do to have any "manly" business conducted in the front vestibule, which was reserved for the patients. Once, one of Father's patients appeared at the front door with a large carp he'd just caught in the river. It hung still from the lethal hook. You can imagine how severely he was thanked by Mother, who told him to bring it down the alley to the kitchen door, but only after it had been scaled, boned, and gutted. That night, Father poached it in Fitzgerald's beer, then he and Grandpa feasted noisily. Since the passing of the gentry, the noble houses of Second Street are noble in a humbler way, but every remaining cobblestone in Washington Park is gravid with its former glory.

What was my horror on a recent visit to find that 45 Second Street had been destroyed by Philistines. A thousand years in Dante's Inferno to those who desecrated that house, covered the dignified red brick with a fake white brick applied in the wrong direction. The bay window was no more. It had been replaced by a deep raw slash across the face of the building that has all the charm of a machete wound. Only the high front stoop with its curved wrought-iron railing remains. Even now, I curse the troglodytes who soiled these premises. Surely they were not Trojans! Never mind, they know who they are.

It was in the not too distant past that I was once again in Troy. It was just before eight o'clock on a Sunday morning. The streets were still empty of life. Only the pigeons and I were abroad. At precisely the hour, every churchbell in the city rang out. There are only six working belfries, but like six roosters, they make enough noise for a hundred. This spooked the pigeons and sent them flapping. You'd think that by now they'd have gotten used to the uproar. Perhaps it isn't the noise so much as the air shaking inside their hollow bones. When the racket subsided, I found myself on Second Street in front of the Music Hall. With a full heart I gazed down the block that was my native land. All at once, the door to number 45 (my house!) opened, and a man emerged and came down the steps, his hand resting on the spiral ironwork railing. A man coming out of 45 Second Street? And it wasn't Father or Grandpa or Billy? A stranger! No, an intruder! Without thinking, I sprang like a mastiff.

"Wait! Wait!" I called out. The man turned, paused, then made as if to hurry on. But now I was blocking his way. "Do you live at forty-five?" There was a touch of menace in my voice. The man held up both hands as if to fend off an assailant. His face was a cold mask that would have none of me. "I used to live there," I said, "long ago. Before you were born." For a long moment, the man's face remained frozen, on guard. Then slowly recognition softened his features.

"You," he said accusingly, "are Richard Selzer." I toed the pavement and admitted it. "Would you like to come inside?" he asked. A simple invitation, you say, but to me it was what St. Peter might say to the blameless at the gates of Heaven. Thus it came to pass that on that fated morning in May, I was to reenter my homeland after sixty years of exile. I was an Israelite returning from Babylon to the Jerusalem of my dreams. Within moments I would pass through the vestibule and see once more the dear hallways, the cubbyholes, the stairwells of the past. Now, up the brownstone steps, my own hand resting on the filigree of ironwork, then through the glass double doors and into the front hall. There, on the right, was the door leading to Father's Waiting Room, and straight ahead, the steep staircase. The banister gleamed as though only moments ago it had been slid down. Up I was led, to the landing where I had sat listening to Father and his patients down below, and to Mother and her fluting up above.

But what was this! Once having crossed the threshold of the family rooms, I found myself in a place I had never seen before. Nothing in it so much as tugged at the sleeve of memory. Every wall had been taken down. What had been a cozy burrow of rooms was now a single large "modern" space, full of hanging plants, area rugs, and artificial flowers. Where was the ancient linoleum the feet of my dead once trod? Where the ancient doorways through which they had passed? Where was the massive mahogany bookcase that held *The Arabian Nights, Dr. Jekyll and Mr. Hyde*, and the novels of Rafael Sabatini? Where was the parlor itself with its large-print bilious wallpaper, its giant Philco console radio where we grouped listening to Lamont Cranston as the Shadow, or Gladys Swarthout and John Charles Thomas on *The Firestone Hour;* where we heard also the racist sermons of Father Coughlin? Where was the old upright piano where Mother and her friend Rae prepared for their musicales?

What had they done with the bowl of wax fruit that had sat in the center of the dining-room table? Where were the doilies, the antimacassar? Of the beloved furnishings, not a single plank or panel remained. And what was that live animal on the window ledge licking itself? Not a cat! Tell me that is not a cat, I implored silently. In our family cats were *personae non gratae*. We did not like cats. We were afraid of cats. We still are.

I went to look out a rear window to see the old garden. It wasn't there.

"Where is it?" I managed. "The backyard?"

"You're standing in it," I was told. And heard how the house had been extended all the way to the end of the lot, incorporating the garden. I could bear no more. Mustering all my deportment, I thanked my host and his genial roommate and made my way downstairs and out into the street. Meanwhile, the sky over Troy had turned cyanotic; a drift of rain blew in. In vain does one seek the grave of Lancelot.

The one-legged organ-grinder stood on the corner of Ferry and Third, his pants flowing around his wooden peg like antique drapery. It was what he had given for his country, said the Women of Troy. Nearby was his mendicant monkey in kepi and epaulets.

Ah, I have sighed to rest me,
Deep in the quiet grave,

—〰—

sang the doomed Manrico. It would have drawn tears from a brazen image. I have listened to my share of Bach, Beethoven, Brahms, and the rest, and all with the greatest pleasure. But in my heart of hearts, I prefer vaudeville, music hall, and Italian opera. My Trojan temperament craves vigorous emotion of a distinctly peasant sort. As the last notes of the "Miserere" from *Il Trovatore* were ground out, the little macaque held out his cap, and the organ-grinder waved his empty pants leg as if it were the American flag. Here is a man, we thought, who has not only shouldered his Cross, but is cheerful about it. Such pluck deserved a nickel. But I never saw the little anthropoid beggar without a blend of pity and shame. Pity for his ill luck to have been brought down from the forest canopy of Zanzibar to the cobblestones of Troy; shame at the degradation visited upon so close a relative. For the amputee too, pity. There is something about a man with a piece missing that stimulates the affections. Standing in the circle of his admirers, I would feel a tightening in my throat. It's the same at parades. Custom has never hardened me to the sight of men marching *en brigade* to fife and drum. I am all too likely to disgrace myself as the band goes by.

The chant of the ragman could be heard from blocks away, like the chant from a minaret. "Rags! Rags!" he intoned. The word was broken into two notes, the first longer than the second, as in "Rah-hags!" A perfect appoggiatura, Mother called it. To me it was the cry of a soul in Purgatory. Moments later, there was his rickety wagon with the ragman holding a whip above the bony haunch of his horse. I have said that the citizens of Troy were famous for their beauty. In such a town, homeliness was notable. What with his many jowls and chins, the ragman had a vast expanse of face that was but thinly populated by the features that clung there. His eyes wandered in their sockets, each bent on its own errand. It was said that he was "feebleminded," but I don't know about that. His gathering done, the ragman would sit in his cart among his "goods" and become a connoisseur, picking his way carefully, even daintily, through the heap of rags as though he were a chef boning a fish or a scientist using a vernier caliper.

The organ-grinder with his monkey and the ragman are long
since gone, nor shall we see their like again. "Age, thou hast lost thy
breed." Well fare the souls of those who riveted us when alive.

The Women's Exchange was a teahouse that occupied a storefront
on State Street. It was also a bakery to which impecunious widows
and genteel spinsters brought their angel food cakes and ladyfingers
for sale at a small percentage. The cakes and pies were the best in
town. No part of Troy has smelled that good since. Mother considered it a "privilege" to patronize the Women's Exchange.
    "It isn't charity," she insisted. "It's a benevolence." Every Sun-
day morning, I was dispatched to buy four freshly baked cinna-
mon buns. At the front of the shop there were half a dozen tables
each with its starched napery and vase of flowers. Tea and cake were
served on the premises. Once a month, Mother "invited" me to have
tea there. I made sure to pick a chair with its back to the windows so
that nobody I knew would see me eating ladyfingers at the Women's
Exchange. I needn't have bothered. What with the effusive greeting,
and all the compliments the Women Exchanged with Mother, the
whole town knew I was there. When I think of those women now,
I think of valor and grit. It was an early lesson that when you run
out of happiness, pride might just carry you through the rest of
the way.

When I was four, Father promised me a silver dollar if I learned to
read. Six months later, I read aloud to him the story of Jonah and
the Whale from my Bible book. For years I kept the silver dollar in
a cubbyhole of my rolltop desk until, at age sixteen and dying of
love, I spent it on a harmonica with which I hoped to win a kiss
from Emily Jane. Over and over, I played the only two songs I
knew—"Santa Lucia" and "Flow Gently, Sweet Afton."
    "Don't you know any others?" she asked. And that was that.
    "Just as well," consoled Mother. "A kiss given upon demand
gives no delight." I didn't believe that for a minute. Not then and
not now. What is sadder to the heart full of desire than "almost"? It

was hard news that unrequited love is hopeless. Even with the best of intentions, you can't command such inclinations. A year later, and still pining, I lured Emily Jane to the pergola in Frear Park and tried to kiss her. She tossed her head as though I were trying to slip a harness over it.

"No," she said and fussed inside her sweater to bring out a man's school ring on a leather cord. "Zeke and I are going out."

"I wouldn't, if I were you," I told her. "He's got strangler's thumbs." I should have cut out my tongue first. Next day, it was all over Troy High School. When Zeke vowed to exact revenge, Janie warned the strangler to keep away from me or face permanent dismissal. Such, such are the puzzling ways of women. Emily Jane—I loved her then. I love her now.

More than fifty years have gone by, and I've learned a thing or two about sex and about love, its romantic abstraction. Love hurts at least as much as it feels good, which doesn't stop us from searching for it over and over again. No sooner have the wounds of one love healed than we are abroad and hunting for another. It is the predicament of other species as well. Take the common garden slug, a hermaphrodite that possesses the reproductive organs of both genders. Despite such anatomical self-sufficiency, the snail insists upon lying with another of its kind. Only then will it release its eggs and sperm to commingle and fertilize. Now it happens that just inside the genital orifice of the snail is a glandular bag called the dart sac whose lining produces an exceedingly sharp calcareous weapon. At some point during copulation, this *spicula amoris* is thrust into the body of the other participant so as to inflict a wound in the region of the genital hole. Say what you will about the ecstasy of snails, this has got to hurt. But no scientist has reported that the anticipation of such discomfort has given a single snail the least hesitation once it has found a new partner. Then too, there is the guinea pig, whose penis bears a barbarous armature of horny spikes; the better to get a firm grip with, I suppose. Could this sort of inherent sadomasochism be an act of love?

While I have not enjoyed fame as a Don Juan, neither have I

loaded sex with the heavy baggage of morality. Any unforced act that does not abuse, misuse, or endanger the body and mind of another is acceptable. Sadism, rape, pederasty, molestation of any kind— these are all rejected along with sexual behavior among the immature and the irresponsible. By the eighth grade, two of the girls in my class had cracked a Commandment and had to drop out of school. Later they were spotted looking familial in the back courtyard of the House of Good Shepherd. The two fifteen-year-old sires had been whisked out of town never to be heard from again. Say what you will about prostitution and pornography, and there is plenty to say, they do fulfill a need that is often quite desperate in many people. I do not deplore either one. Nor do I share the disgust of Leonardo da Vinci for the sex act. "Love in its fury is so ugly . . . that the human race would die out [*la natura si perderebbe*] if those who practice it could see themselves." His sketches of copulation bear out that re- pugnance. It is strange that while the mechanics of the living body fascinated da Vinci, the sweating, panting, and groaning and the final transfiguration of humans into beasts that he saw in sex excited only his profound revulsion. Sir Thomas Browne, a physician of the six- teenth century, was also fastidious. He wrote that God should be ashamed of Himself for not having invented a more aesthetic manner of procreation. Such refinement did not keep "the little doctor of Norwich" from siring five children.

I am standing on the east bank of the Hudson, the same river that long ago carried away desire, and now carries away regret. One day, running like a cheetah (no one in Troy could catch me), I stopped abruptly at the river as though Apollo himself had suddenly appeared before me, making me tumble headfirst into the shallows. There it was lively with small fish, water weeds, and the glitter of light on pebbles. It was at this very place that I lay, turning this way and that, naked now and full of the rapture of my own swiftness. How the water boiled with my heat! The tendrils of a weeping willow brushed my thighs. And then came longing, for what I didn't know—some other, a naiad perhaps, perched on a rock, singing and combing her cold green hair. All that endless afternoon I lay there until my flesh grew spongy and transparent and took on the speckled pattern of the river. Toward evening, the water quieted, the slapping of the waves softened. I stood then, letting the muck flow between my toes, and cast my sperm into the river, then watched the small perch and sunfish rise to feed. By the time I reached home, it was late.

"Where in the world have you been?" asked Mother. "I was worried."

"He's been feeding the fish," said Billy, and he laughed. All that week, I wore the scent of the river on my skin. Little by little it dissipated until it was time to go back for more.

Now, more than fifty years later, I have crossed the bridge to the western bank. Perhaps, from here, I might catch a glimpse of someone lying in the shallows? Look! There he is! A boy, his skin tattooed with light and shadow, lying with his ears below the surface, listening to the stream. But my vision has gone dim. Is it a boy? Or something scintillant in a clear pool? I can't be sure. Still, I stand bewitched, for what is so entrancing as yourself as once you were? Overhead, gulls are tearing the sky to shreds with their screaming; the sunset has varnished the river red, and the clouds are piled up, gold-rimmed and smoldering, like the Halls of Valhalla. Just downstream from where I'm standing, a young couple draw together in the glamorous kindness of twilight. He bends above her, enamored as Adam bending above the newborn Eve.

As the first pale stars appear, a coolness filters through my sleeves. I cross the bridge back to Troy, where the river runs calmer, or so it seems, placid, monotonous, soothing. In the dusk, I can't say if it is Troy that floats along and the river that is still, or the other way around.

It has been my destiny always to live at the edge of a vacant lot. In the field behind the house on St. Ronan Terrace in New Haven, there is a brownish bedspread of chicory, Queen Anne's lace, and wild morning glory. This lot used to be the site of the Culinary Institute of America. Then there were dormitories, ovens, white-garbed chefs in tall hats, and a dining hall. But the school has long since moved away, taking its aprons and aromas. All but three of the buildings were torn down, and those three are boarded up—deaf, dumb, and blind. In the one directly behind the house, a family of raccoons procreates with terrifying ferocity. The snarls! The growling! Every summer, when their number grows insupportable, we must summon the exterminator to trap and "dispose of" as many as he can. This is not done without considerable breast-beating, but done it is. The road that winds through the lot is rich in potholes and almost covered by weeds. Mounding here and there is a herd of huge containers on wheels such as are pulled by the van of a truck. Who knows what these mastodons contain? They are never moved, nor opened, but stand in a prehistoric pattern like Stonehenge.

But the vacant lot of my dreams lay in Troy. The ancient Greeks believed that the Past lies in front of you, spread out for you to see and describe. The Future, unbeheld and unknown, lies behind you, awaiting its time. And so it is that I gaze ahead at that vacant lot of long ago that exists now only as the gray island of Ultima Thule. Just behind the fence at the back of the house on Fifth Avenue was a trapezoid of empty land. Every few hours, Grandpa would step out into the garden, open the back gate, and urinate. It was the sensible thing to do, as the only toilet downstairs was for the patients. What for Grandpa was a urinal was for Billy and me our south forty—the estate of so many acres that we patrolled each day. Vacant though it may have been, that lot was a prairie swarming with vitality. The prevailing trees were the ailanthus or stinkweed, of which there were many, and the catalpa with giant heart-shaped leaves and hundreds of droop-lipped flowers that gave off a sweetish odor that made me dizzy. Even now, the creamy blur of catalpa blooms unsettles my stomach. As for undergrowth, there were tall grasses that salaamed when you walked across the lot. Here too were chicory and Queen Anne's lace, as well as butter-and-eggs, clover, bladderwort, dandelion, thistle, jewelweed, goldenrod, moth mullein, and an infiltrate of wild morning glory and bittersweet. Any prelapsarian goat would find himself browsing in Paradise. For birds, we had pigeons and a pair of their aristocratic cousins, mourning doves. Starlings, grackles, robins, blue jays, cardinals, and several species of sparrow made up the rest. A squadron of crows on carrion patrol policed the lot. At dusk the air was sliced by bats and nighthawks. What with the cornucopia of garbage from the markets on King Street, and the deposition of rejectimenta by hoboes and drunks who used the lot for their shenanigans, there was always a surfeit of what to eat—chicken bones, hunks of spoiled meat. The crows just couldn't keep up.

"This place could use a buzzard or two," remarked Billy.

On the small leg of the trapezoid were the ruins of an old stone house. There, a clowder of feral cats sunned themselves between arguments. The whole place stank of them, lying in their bones, opening and closing their eyes just a little. Peaceful tabbies, you'd say, but I've seen them leap yowling from their repose to fasten tooth and claw into a rival. It was in the vacant lot that I learned to fear cats. (Right now, on the window ledge of my scriptorium, the neighbor's orange cat is yawning. In my notebook, I wrote in big capital letters CAT, GO AWAY! Then held it up for him to read. The insolence with which he stepped, paw after paw after paw, his tail meandering long after the rest of him was still. I am comforted by the knowledge that Chekhov too was afraid of cats.) Among the other fauna of the lot were rats, mice, squirrels, and a pickup band of stray dogs. The Hudson River was one block away; there was the croaking of frogs and the laughter of gulls.

The vacant lot was faced all around by the back fences of the houses on Fifth Avenue, the back doors of the markets on King Street, and the railroad tracks. Two cobbled and crooked alleys led into the open space, one from King Street, the other from the railroad tracks. Now and then there'd be a clatter as the key-maker or the ragman drove his horse and wagon down one of the alleys. In the center of the lot, there was a permanent stagnant pool that creamed and mantled like that standing pond in *The Merchant of Venice*. Then overnight would come rain, and the filthy suds would vanish, and the pool redeem itself by reflecting the sky. On sunny days, a carpet of glass shards caught the light so that the whole lot glittered and shook as though it were the smoking ruins of ancient Troy. With every step, you might find a bottlecap labeled Moxie, Nehi, or Hires—words that now seem strange and runic, with untranslatable power.

One summer, Billy and I built a shack under the biggest stink-weed tree, built it out of orange crates from the Mohican Market, and roofed it over with catalpa leaves. It was there that we went to read the novels of Rafael Sabatini, and the tales of Edgar Allan Poe, and listen to the crepitation of rain on the leafy roof. When the shed was finished, we invited Mother and Father to come and see. Mother had brought her fan made of the feathers of the Bolognese hawk, and she used it wildly.

"Germs!" she gasped.

"Not to worry," reassured Father. "No self-respecting germ would dwell here. Besides, I suspect they're immune by now." Not that we weren't scared—that strong presence of decay, the untamed proliferation. You could almost watch the nameless seeds germinating in the rot. To us, the vacant lot was a foreign city whose street signs were in an unknown tongue, Japanese say, and we would surely lose our way. Only with naming came a sense of security. You couldn't achieve mastery over the lot in any other way, not by prayer, surely, nor by any means spiritual. It had to be done by naming. Within months, Billy and I had identified every plant, insect, and creature in the lot. It was a case of taming by classification, and locating beauty, by the way. There was a low flowering plant with a narrow stem, three leaves, and a tight flower head, either pink or white. We brought one to the library and matched it leaf and flower with one in the botany book. It was a clover. "Clover," we said again and again, relishing the word.

What a *tabula rasa*! Anything could happen out there in the lot. The way it asked for and received our attention. From our bedroom window, we could hear the buzz and whine of insects that never ceased. At night, the humming of the insects became the humming of our own blood. Mornings, the birdsong was Thoreau's "infinite din." Only missing was Chanticleer's lusty brag. And all one unforgettable night, someone in one of the alleys plucked the strings of a guitar. No tune, only plaintive cascades of notes. Who could have done it?

Each time the fog rolled in from the river, there were lights and shadows of no human origin. Dare to step into the lot then and you left behind all streetlamps, sidewalks, bay windows, stoops, and fenced yards. There was the unknown and the unknowable, and all surely under some supernatural influence. Nor was the *genius loci* at all friendly. Trespass not, it seemed to say. You wouldn't dream of lying down in this lot. A meadow it was not. Nor would you think to mow it or swing a scythe, or tend it in any way at all. It was meant to be untamed. Such a vacant lot is the primordial wet ash pit from which all life first emerged. There was something else: Search and search as we might, we couldn't find the vacant lot on the map of Troy.

"You're not reading the map correctly," said Father. "Here, I'll show you." But he couldn't find it either. "Lousy map," he said. But I knew better. The vacant lot wasn't on the map because it wasn't of this world. Like Xanadu or the Domain of Arnheim, it had to be summoned, or conjured.

What with the ashes from bonfires set by the bums, the layers and layers of buried leaves, the garbage and the excrement of everything that scurried, slithered, or walked on it, the soil, lying heavy and undisturbed, had to be the richest in Rensselaer County. Any seed dropped was sure to become a seedling. Where two or more cobblestones had become dislodged, there was a sapling. One evening, the bats were already flying and the moon was "a ghostly galleon" when we, from the window, saw, or thought we saw, something mounding in the central ditch. We went out to make sure. It was a man, lying on his back, eyes open to the sky, his head half submerged in the turbid pool that had the texture of brocade. A bib of vomit covered his chin and chest. Had he staggered and tumbled backward? Or had he fallen forward, and with his last bit of strength rolled over to die in sight of the stars? Had he, I wondered, tried to stand up from the pool? Or had he yielded to the temptation to give up, let it go? Sometimes I've been that tired myself. Or had a grave yawned and yielded up its dead? How long had he been there? A cloud of flies rose and fell, rose and fell. A certain nude snail, tan and speckled, moved in and out of the ditchwater, laying down its glittering lunaqua. Already, two of the stray dogs were testing the air with their snouts. In the catalpa, a crow cawed loudly.

"I dare you to touch him," said Billy. "Touch him! Go ahead," urged Billy. "I dare you!" Never, never will I forget the feel of that cold moist forehead on my fingertip. We ran to get Father.

"Drunk," he diagnosed. "Vomited and aspirated. Both of you, get in the house pronto!" Minutes later, the ambulance from St. Mary's Hospital came and took it away.

Once, years later, and home from medical school, I went out into the vacant lot that was fen, compost heap, and graveyard. It was not without a certain voluptuous disgust, I confess, that I stooped and shoveled the heavy wet earth with my fingers. In the well of my palm lay all that I had been and all I was to become. All at once, I knew what the vacant lot was: It was me.

Let me tell you where I live now. St. Ronan Terrace in New Haven is a dead-end street, or, more politely, a cul-de-sac. We have occupied number 6 for thirty-six years. To move out would be unthinkable. The next occupants would find bits of my flesh stuck to the banisters and doorknobs. It's an old wooden Colonial, circa 1910, with black shutters and any number of architectural deformities. There has never been a time when the paint was not peeling. The decor is "world federalist," as no two objects appear to have originated in the same country. I am, I hope inoffensively, proud of it. Once it was filled with children and pets. In their place, we have creaks, slippered footfalls, and the whisper of pages being turned. It's a house that doesn't elbow you the way a good many in the neighborhood do. The "Saarinen house," as it is still called decades after the architect moved out of it, is English Tudor on the outside and, as you might expect, clear, bright, and pristine within. Number

12, at the top of the hill, is a bashful structure with a dense mantle of trees that keep it hidden for months at a time.

For thirty years, Janet and I looked after the house. Now it has turned itself into a bed-and-breakfast and looks after us. Scientists from all over the world have slept at 6 St. Ronan Terrace. I am the Assistant Hotel Manager and bellhop. I carry luggage up and down stairs, and do valet parking, which has caused any number of the Dents of Contention among the guests, and hilarity among my un-grateful relatives, who insist that I have never learned how to park and am a terrible driver. I also make coffee for breakfast, and since the visiting scientists are from all over the world, I carry on conver-sation in French, Italian, German, Japanese, and Korean, the last two at a distinctly pidgin level. My Korean consists mostly of medical phrases learned out of necessity during my Medical Corps years in the Far East. There is a certain shock value in saying at breakfast *Ore appumnikka*? (Where does it hurt?) and *Yom yoh masayoh* (You'll feel better soon). The guests, however, are under the impression that I am fluent enough to qualify for the job of Interpreter at Babel.

There is a shortcut to the science buildings. At the bottom of the garden, a wooden gate leads through a dense forest of bamboo planted twenty years ago by my son Jon. You emerge from the bam-boo and cross a vacant lot strewn with Queen Anne's lace and blue chicory. It resembles an old-fashioned bedspread. Soon you come to a park with a great weeping beech, cryptomeria, cedar, and linden trees, all of great age. And then there is Yale. All the beauty of the house lies in the garden, which blooms from March through Novem-ber, seducing twenty species of birds, butterflies, bees, and any num-ber of small mammals. At night, the squabbling of the raccoons lends a wild, jungly note to the yard.

St. Ronan Terrace is no more than five hundred yards long. It ascends steeply in a voluptuous curve to bury its head in the flank of the Yale Divinity School. From the window of my study, it looks for all the world like a pretty green snake lying on a hill. Seven houses constitute the neighborhood. Of these, one was for a time a residence for autistic children. Sometimes, at night, we could hear the melancholy sounds they made. Now they too are gone. Over the years, eminent men and women have lived on this street—the above-mentioned Eero Saarinen, Richard Ellmann, Robert Brustein, Ronald Dworkin, Brand Blanshard, and Robert Yerkes. The inhabitants of all the other houses have come and gone. Only we have stayed on. I prefer to think it is out of steadfastness and not a failure of the imagination. For a long time, all any of us knew about the name St. Ronan was that Sir Walter Scott had written a satirical novel entitled *St. Ronan's Well*. It is set in Scotland at a mythical mineral spring noted for its ability to redeem health and drive away care. Sir Walter peopled the spa with a clutch of eccentrics and odd outscourings of the human race, each with his own share of folly, vice or imprudence. It would not be a gross falsehood to suggest that some of us who have lived on this street might have stood as models for these characters.

Since it is the well itself that is the focus of Scott's novel, we are further entitled to our name by the existence of an underground stream or rill that flows down the terrace unseen until it surfaces in the garden of the house at the foot of the hill. There, by a clever combination of excavation and damming, the rill has been caught in the form of a pond. With time, the pond has become surfaced with lily pads and punctuated by tall reeds and grasses. A willow trails its tendrils over the bank, and the water teems with wildlife—goldfish, water bugs, and frogs predominate. Cardinals and blue jays are daily bathers. Once, I saw a small green heron feasting on the goldfish. A kingfisher too has his occasional way with them. Sharing the kindly fruits of the terrace with the humans is a tribe of raccoons, one of whom has learned to unscrew a mayonnaise jar to get at a chunk of apple. It had been placed there to give a lesson in humility to any arrogant child who might have supposed unscrewing to be an exclusively human talent.

It had been very heavenly to live on this street except for one mystery that nagged at the inhabitants, and that, from time to time, surfaced like an asp in a basket of fig leaves. It had to do with our name. Who, we died to know, was Saint Ronan? Where and when did he live? With all homage to Sir Walter Scott, we could not accept that our heritage was something concocted by a mere novelist. There had to be more to it. One day, while browsing in the stacks of Yale's Sterling Library, I came across a book entitled *Ancient Celtic Tales*. With a shiver of discovery, I saw that the opening chapter was called "The Story of Saint Ronan." I clutched the book to my breast. My hands trembled. At last, the mystery of St. Ronan was to be revealed.

It seems that somewhere in Druidic Gaul, there lived an old man named Ronan who was a Christian, the only one in that part of the world. (It is not explained how he came to this faith.) For whatever reasons, Ronan had chosen the severest kind of hermit's life, living alone in a mountain cave that was so small that his feet protruded from the entrance while he slept. Like most hermits, he ate only nuts and berries. His single garment was the skin of an animal. One day, the chieftain of a nearby pagan village, while hunting, caught sight of the old man's feet and dragged him forth to see. Ronan and the chieftain then embarked upon what was to be a long series of talks resulting in the secret conversion of the chieftain to Christianity. This was achieved at no small cost to the convert, who was castigated by his wife and ridiculed by his colleagues for neglecting his duties and spending altogether too much time sitting in front of a cave with an old man.

Now it came to pass that one day while the chieftain was visiting Ronan, a huge fierce wolf raided the village, laying it waste and killing the little son of the chieftain. When the grief-stricken father learned of this, he went back to the cave to seek solace from the old man. Whereupon Ronan rose and went down to the village with the chieftain. He asked to see the body of the boy. It was brought to him in a coffin, which Ronan opened. As the villagers watched, Ronan prayed and, bending over the corpse, breathed upon the face of the child. All at once, color returned to the boy's cheeks; he stirred, took a breath, then another, and sat up. Jumping out of the coffin, he ran to his happy father's side. It should come as no surprise that on that very day, the entire village converted to Christianity. When the old saint died, his body was placed in a cart drawn by six oxen and taken to the spot where he was to be buried. But before this could be accomplished, the whole cortege, cart, oxen, and saint, had been turned to stone. This rock formation can be seen to this day somewhere in what used to be Druidic Gaul.

All this I read, then replaced the book on its shelf at the library, wild to return to St. Ronan Terrace and spread the news of our namesake among the inhabitants. There was general rejoicing. A grand party was held that very night. For the first time, we felt ourselves bound together as a clan whose lost birthright had been found.

But the old order changeth. The original celebrants have long since moved away. New, skeptical people have moved in. Many times in the years that followed I have tried to find *Ancient Celtic Tales* again if for no other reason than to squelch the legions of disbelievers who accuse me of having made the whole thing up. But I never saw the book again. Search how I did for a misfiling, there was no sign of it. Had it been borrowed and not returned? It had not. Nor was it to be found listed in the card catalogue! But I read it. I swear I did. And will go to my grave in the unshakable certainty of having done so. Let those who will, doubt on. I know what really happened, and I take comfort in the conviction that Saint Ronan would agree with me. It is no easy job to convert the heathen.

The Surgeon
as Priest

—∿—

It is no great leap from the resuscitation by Saint Ronan to the forbidden dissections of that other outcast of society Vesalius. In the foyer of a great medical school there hangs a painting of the anatomist. Lean, ascetic, possessed, he stands before a dissecting table upon which lies the naked body of a man. The flesh of the two is silvery. A concentration of moonlight, like a strange rain of virus, washes them. The cadaver has dignity and reserve; it is distanced by its death. Vesalius reaches for his dissecting knife. As he does so, he glances over his shoulder at a crucifix on the wall. His face wears an expression of guilt and melancholy and fear. He knows that there is something wrong, forbidden, in what he is about to do, but he cannot help himself, for he is a fanatic. He is driven by a dark desire. To see, to feel, to discover is all. His is a passion, not a romance.

I understand you, Vesalius. Even now, after so many voyages within, so much exploration, I feel the same sense that one must not gaze into the body, the same irrational fear that it is an evil deed for which punishment awaits. Consider. The sight of our internal organs is denied us. To how many men is it given to look upon their own spleens, their hearts, and liver? The hidden geography of the body is a Medusa's head one glimpse of which would render blind the presumptuous eye. Still, rigid rules are broken by the smallest inadvertencies: I pause in the midst of an operation being performed under spinal anesthesia to observe the face of my patient, to speak a word or two of reassurance. I peer above the screen separating his head from his abdomen, in which I am most deeply employed. He is not asleep, but rather stares straight upward, his attention riveted, a look of terrible discovery, of wonder, upon his face. Watch him. This man is violating a taboo. I follow his gaze upward, and see in the great operating lamp suspended above his belly the reflection of his viscera. There is the liver, dark and turgid above, there the loops of his bowel winding slow, there his blood runs extravagantly. It is that which he sees and studies with so much horror and fascination. Something primordial in him has been aroused—a fright, a longing. I feel it, too, and quickly bend above his open body to shield it from his view. How dare he look within the Ark! Cover his eyes! But it is too late; he has already *seen* that which no man should; he has trespassed. And I am no longer a surgeon, but a hierophant who must do magic to ward off the punishment of the angry gods.

I feel some hesitation to invite you to come with me into the body. It seems a reckless, defiant act. Yet there is more than dread reflected from these rosy coasts, these restless estuaries of pearl. And it is time to share it, the way the catbird shares the song which must be a joy to him and is a living truth to those who hear it. So shall I make of my fingers, words; of my scalpel, a sentence; of the body of my patient, a story.

One enters the body in surgery, as in love, as though one were an exile returning at last to his hearth, daring uncharted darkness in order to reach home. Turn sideways, if you will, and slip with me into the cleft I have made. Do not fear the yellow meadows of fat, the red that sweats and trickles where you step. Here, give me your hand. Lower between the beefy cliffs. Now rest a bit upon the peritoneum. All at once, gleaming, the membrane parts . . . and you are *in*.

It is the stillest place that ever was. As though suddenly you are struck deaf. Why, when the blood sluices fierce as Niagara, when the brain teems with electricity, and the numberless cells exchange their goods in ceaseless commerce—why is it so quiet? Has some priest in charge of these rites uttered the command "Silence"? This is no silence of the vacant stratosphere, but the awful quiet of ruins, of rainbows, full of expectation and holy dread. Soon you shall know surgery as a Mass served with Body and Blood, wherein disease is assailed as though it were sin.

Touch the great artery. Feel it bound like a deer in the might of its lightness, and know the thunderless boil of the blood. Lean for a bit against this bone. It is the only memento you will leave to the earth. Its tacitness is everlasting. In the hush of the tissue wait with me for the shaft of pronouncement. Press your ear against this body, the way you did as a child holding a seashell and heard faintly the half-remembered, longed-for sea. Now strain to listen *past* the silence. In the canals, cilia paddle quiet as an Iroquois canoe. Somewhere nearby a white whipslide of tendon bows across a joint. Fire burns here but does not crackle. Again, listen. Now there *is* sound—small splashings, tunneled currents of air, slow gaseous bubbles ascend through dark, unlit lakes. Across the diaphragm and into the chest . . . here at last it is all noise; the whisper of the lungs, the *lubdup, lubdup* of the garrulous heart.

But it is good you do not hear the machinery of your marrow lest it madden like the buzzing of a thousand coppery bees. It is frightening to lie with your ear in the pillow, and hear the beating of your heart. Not that it beats . . . but that it might stop, even as you listen. For anything that moves must come to rest; no rhythm is endless but must one day lurch . . . then halt. Not that it is a disservice to a man to be made mindful of his death, but—at three o'clock in the morning it is less than philosophy. It is Fantasy, replete with dreadful images forming in the smoke of alabaster crematoria. It is then that one thinks of the bristlecone pines, and envies them for having lasted. It is their slowness, I think. Slow down, heart, and drub on.

What is to one man a coincidence is to another a miracle. It was one or the other of these that I saw last spring. While the rest of nature was in flux, Joe Riker remained obstinate through the change of the seasons. "No operation," said Joe. "I don't want no operation."

Joe Riker is a short-order cook in a diner where I sometimes drink coffee. Each week for six months he had paid a visit to my office, carrying his affliction like a pet mouse under his hat. Every Thursday at four o'clock he would sit on my examining table, lift the fedora from his head, and bend forward to show me the hole. Joe Riker's hole was as big as his mouth. You could have dropped a plum in it. Gouged from the tonsured top of his head was a mucky puddle whose meaty heaped edge rose above the normal scalp about it. There was no mistaking the announcement from this rampart.

The cancer had chewed through Joe's scalp, munched his skull, then opened the membranes underneath—the dura mater, the pia mater, the arachnoid—until it had laid bare this short-order cook's brain, pink and gray, and pulsating so that with each beat a little pool of cerebral fluid quivered. Now and then a drop would manage the rim to run across his balding head, and Joe would reach one burry hand up to wipe it away, with the heel of his thumb, the way such a man would wipe away a tear.

I would gaze then upon Joe Riker and marvel. How dignified he was, as though that tumor, gnawing him, denuding his very brain, had given him a grace that a lifetime of good health had not bestowed.

"Joe," I say, "let's get rid of it. Cut out the bad part, put in a metal plate, and you're cured." And I wait.

"No operation," says Joe. I try again.

"What do you mean, 'no operation'? You're going to get meningitis. Any day now. And die. That thing is going to get to your brain."

I think of it devouring the man's dreams and memories. I wonder what they are. The surgeon knows all the parts of the brain, but he does not know his patient's dreams and memories. And for a moment I am tempted . . . to take the man's head in my hands, hold it to my ear, and listen. But his dreams are none of my business. It is his flesh that matters.

"No operation," says Joe.

"You give me a headache," I say. And we smile, not because the joke is funny anymore, but because we've got something between us, like a secret.

"Same time next week?" Joe asks. I wash out the wound with peroxide, and apply a dressing. He lowers the fedora over it.

"Yes," I say, "same time." And the next week he comes again.

There came the week when Joe Riker did not show up; nor did he the week after that, nor for a whole month. I drive over to his diner. He is behind the counter, shuffling back and forth between the grill and the sink. He is wearing the fedora. He sets a cup of coffee in front of me.

"I want to see your hole," I say.

"Which one?" he asks, and winks.

"Never mind that," I say. "I want to see it." I am all business.

"Not here," says Joe. He looks around, checking the counter, as though I have made an indecent suggestion.

"My office at four o'clock," I say.

"Yeah," says Joe, and turns away.

He is late. Everyone else has gone for the day. Joe is beginning to make me angry. At last he arrives.

"Take off your hat," I say, and he knows by my voice that I am not happy. He does, though, raise it straight up with both hands the way he always does, and I see . . . that the wound has healed. Where once there was a bitten-out excavation, moist and shaggy, there is now a fragile bridge of shiny new skin.

"What happened?" I manage.

"You mean that?" He points to the top of his head. "Oh well," he says, "the wife's sister, she went to France, and brought me a bottle of water from Lourdes. I've been washing it out with that for a month."

"Holy water?" I say.

"Yeah," says Joe. "Holy water."

I see Joe now and then at the diner. He looks like anything but a fleshly garden of miracles. Rather, he has taken on a terrible ordinariness—Eden after the Fall, and minus its most beautiful creatures. There is a certain slovenliness, a dishevelment of the tissues. Did the disease ennoble him, and now that it is gone, is he somehow diminished? Perhaps I am wrong. Perhaps the only change is just the sly wink with which he greets me, as though to signal that we have shared something furtive. Could such a man, I think as I sip my coffee, could such a man have felt the brush of wings? How often it seems that the glory leaves as soon as the wound is healed. But then it is only saints who bloom in martyrdom, becoming less and less the flesh that pains, more and more ghost-colored weightlessness.

It was many years between my first sight of the living human brain and Joe Riker's windowing. I had thought then, long ago: Could this one-pound loaf of sourdough be the pelting brain? *This,* along whose busy circuitry run Reason and Madness in perpetual race—a race that most often ends in a tie? But the look deceives. What seems a fattish snail drowsing in its shell in fact lives in quickness, where all is dart and stir and rapids of electricity.

Once again to the operating room . . .

How to cut a paste that is less solid than a cheese—Brie, perhaps? And not waste any of it? For that would be a decade of remembrances and wishes lost there, wiped from the knife. Mostly it is done with cautery, burning the margins of the piece to be removed, coagulating with the fine electric current these blood vessels that course everywhere. First a spot is burned, then another alongside the first, and the cut is made between. One does not stitch—one cannot sew custard. Blood is blotted with little squares of absorbent gauze. These are called patties. Through each of these a long black thread has been sewn, lest a blood-soaked patty slip into some remote fissure, or flatten against a gyrus like a starfish against a coral reef, and go unnoticed come time to close the incision. A patty abandoned brainside does not benefit the health, or improve the climate of the intelligence. Like the bodies of slain warriors, they must be retrieved from the field, and carried home, so they do not bloat and mortify, poisoning forever the plain upon which the battle was fought. One pulls them out by their black thread and counts them.

Listen to the neurosurgeon: "Patty, buzz, suck, cut," he says. Then "Suck, cut, patty, buzz." It is as simple as a nursery rhyme.

The surgeon knows the landscape of the brain, yet does not know how a thought is made. Man has grown envious of this mystery. He would master and subdue it electronically. He would construct a computer to rival or surpass the brain. He would harness Europa's bull to a plow. There are men who implant electrodes into the brain, that part where anger is kept—the rage center, they call it. They press a button, and a furious bull halts in mid-charge, and lopes amiably to nuzzle his matador. Anger has turned to sweet compliance. Others sever whole tracts of brain cells with their knives, to mollify the insane. Here is surgery grown violent as rape. These men cannot know the brain. They have not the heart for it.

I last saw the brain in the emergency room. I wiped it from the shoulder of a young girl to make her smashed body more presentable to her father. Now I stand with him by the stretcher. We are arm in arm, like brothers. All at once there is that terrible silence of discovery. I glance at him, follow his gaze and see that there is more brain upon her shoulder, newly slipped from the cracked skull. He bends forward a bit. He must make certain. It *is* her brain! I watch the knowledge expand upon his face, so like hers. I, too, stare at the fragment flung wetly, now drying beneath the bright lights of the emergency room, its cargo of thoughts evaporating from it, mingling for this little time with his, with mine, before dispersing in the air.

On the east coast of the Argolid, in the northern part of the Peloponnesus, lies Epidaurus. O bury my heart there, in that place I have never seen, but that I love as a farmer loves his home soil. In a valley nearby, in the fourth century B.C., there was built the temple of Asclepius, the god of medicine. To a great open colonnaded room, the abaton, came the sick from all over Greece. Here they lay down on pallets. As night fell, the priests, bearing fire for the lamps, walked among them, commanding them to sleep. They were told to dream of the god, and that he would come to them in their sleep in the form of a serpent, and that he would heal them. In the morning they arose cured. . . .

Walk the length of the abaton; the sick are in their places, each upon his pallet. Here is one that cannot sleep. See how his breath rises and falls against some burden that presses upon it. At last, he dozes, only to awaken minutes later, unrefreshed. It is toward dawn. The night lamps flicker low, casting snaky patterns across the colonnade. Already the chattering swallows swoop in and out among the pillars. All at once the fitful eyes of the man cease their roving, for he sees between the candle-lamp and the wall the shadow of an upraised serpent, a great yellow snake with topaz eyes. It slides closer. It is arched and godlike. It bends above him, swaying, the tongue and the lamplight flickering as one. Exultant, he raises himself upon one arm, and with the other, reaches out for the touch that heals.

On the bulletin board in the front hall of the hospital where I work, there appeared an announcement. "Yeshi Dhonden," it read, "will make rounds at six o'clock on the morning of June 10." The particulars were then given, followed by a notation: "Yeshi Dhonden is Personal Physician to the Dalai Lama." I am not so leathery a skeptic that I would knowingly ignore an emissary from the gods. Not only might such sangfroid be inimical to one's earthly well-being, it could take care of eternity as well. Thus, on the morning of June 10, I join the clutch of whitecoats waiting in the small conference room adjacent to the ward selected for the rounds. The air in the room is heavy with ill-concealed dubiety and suspicion of bamboozlement. At precisely six o'clock, he materializes, a short, golden, barrelly man dressed in a sleeveless robe of saffron and maroon. His scalp is shaven, and the only visible hair is a scanty black line above each hooded eye.

He bows in greeting while his young interpreter makes the introduction. Yeshi Dhonden, we are told, will examine a patient selected by a member of the staff. The diagnosis is as unknown to Yeshi Dhonden as it is to us. The examination of the patient will take place in our presence, after which we will reconvene in the conference room, where Yeshi Dhonden will discuss the case. We are further informed that for the past two hours Yeshi Dhonden has purified himself by bathing, fasting, and prayer. I, having breakfasted well, performed only the most desultory of ablutions, and given no thought at all to my soul, glance furtively at my fellows. Suddenly, we seem a soiled, uncouth lot.

The patient had been awakened early and told that she was to be examined by a foreign doctor, and had been asked to produce a fresh specimen of urine, so when we enter her room, the woman shows no surprise. She has long ago taken on that mixture of compliance and resignation that is the facies of chronic illness. This was to be but another in an endless series of tests and examinations. Yeshi Dhonden steps to the bedside while the rest stand apart, watching. For a long time he gazes at the woman, favoring no part of her body with his eyes, but seeming to fix his glance at a place just above her supine form. I, too, study her. No physical sign nor obvious symptom gives a clue to the nature of her disease.

At last he takes her hand, raising it in both of his own. Now he bends over the bed in a kind of crouching stance, his head drawn down into the collar of his robe. His eyes are closed as he feels for her pulse. In a moment he has found the spot, and for the next half hour he remains thus, suspended above the patient like some exotic golden bird with folded wings, holding the pulse of the woman beneath his fingers, cradling her hand in his. All the power of the man seems to have been drawn down into this one purpose. It is palpation of the pulse raised to the state of ritual. From the foot of the bed, where I stand, it is as though he and the patient have entered a special place of isolation, of apartness, about which a vacancy hovers, and across which no violation is possible. After a moment the woman rests back upon her pillow. From time to time, she raises her head to look at the strange figure above her, then sinks back once more. I cannot see their hands joined in a correspondence that is exclusive, intimate, his fingertips receiving the voice of her sick body through the rhythm and throb she offers at her wrist. All at once I am envious—not of him, not of Yeshi Dhonden for his gift of beauty and holiness, but of her. I want to be held like that, touched so, *received*. And I know that I, who have palpated a hundred thousand pulses, have not felt a single one.

At last Yeshi Dhonden straightens, gently places the woman's hand upon the bed, and steps back. The interpreter produces a small wooden bowl and two sticks. Yeshi Dhonden pours a portion of the urine specimen into the bowl, and proceeds to whip the liquid with the two sticks. This he does for several minutes until a foam is raised. Then, bowing above the bowl, he inhales the odor three times. He sets down the bowl and turns to leave. All this while, he has not uttered a single word. As he nears the door, the woman raises her head and calls out to him in a voice at once urgent and serene. "Thank you, Doctor," she says, and touches with her other hand the place he had held on her wrist, as though to recapture something that had visited there. Yeshi Dhonden turns back for a moment to gaze at her, then steps into the corridor. Rounds are at an end.

We are seated once more in the conference room. Yeshi Dhonden speaks now for the first time, in soft Tibetan sounds that I have never heard before. He has barely begun when the young interpreter begins to translate, the two voices continuing in tandem—a bilingual fugue, the one chasing the other. It is like the chanting of monks. He speaks of winds coursing through the body of the woman, currents that break against barriers, eddying. These vortices are in her blood, he says. The last spendings of an imperfect heart. Between the chambers of her heart, long, long before she was born, a wind had come and blown open a deep gate that must never be opened. Through it charge the full waters of her river, as the mountain stream cascades in the springtime, battering, knocking loose the land, and flooding her breath. Thus he speaks, and is silent.

"May we now have the diagnosis?" a professor asks.

The host of these rounds, the man who knows, answers.

"Congenital heart disease," he says. "Interventricular septal defect, with resultant heart failure."

A gateway in the heart, I think. That must not be opened. Through it charge the full waters that flood her breath. So! Here then is the doctor listening to the sounds of the body to which the rest of us are deaf. He is more than doctor. He is priest.

I know . . . I know . . . the doctor to the gods is pure knowledge, pure healing. The doctor to man stumbles, must often wound; his patient must die, as must he.

Now and then it happens, as I make my own rounds, that I hear the sound of his voice, like an ancient Buddhist prayer, its meaning long since forgotten, only the music remaining. Then a jubilation possesses me, and I feel myself touched by something divine.

Lessons
from the Art

With trust the surgeon approaches the operating table. To be sure, he is impeccably trained. He has stood here so many times before. The belly that presents itself to him this morning, draped in green linen and painted with red disinfectant, is little different from those countless others he has entered. It is familiar terrain, to be managed. He watches it rise and fall in the regular rhythm of anesthesia. Vulnerable, it returns his trust, asks but his excellence, his clever ways. With a blend of arrogance and innocence the surgeon makes his incision, expecting a particular organ to be exactly where he knows it to be. He has seen it there, in just that single place, over and again. He has aimed his blade for that very spot, found the one artery he seeks, the one vein, captured them in his hemostats, ligated them, and cut them safely; then on to the next, and the one after that, until the sick organ falls free into his waiting hand—mined.

But this morning, as the surgeon parts the edges of the wound with his retractor, he feels uncertain, for in that place where he *knows* the duct to be, there is none. Only masses of scar curtained with blood vessels of unimagined fragility. They seem to rupture even as he studies them, as though it is the abrasion of the air that breaks them. Blood is shed into the well of the wound. It puddles upon the banks of scar, concealing the way inward. The surgeon sees this, and knows that the fierce wind of inflammation has swept this place, burying the tubes and canals he seeks. It is an alien land. Now all is forestial, swampy. The surgeon suctions away the blood; even as he does so, new red trickles; his eyes are full of it; he cannot see. He advances his fingers into the belly, feeling the walls of scar, running the tips gently over each eminence, into each furrow, testing the roll of the land, probing for an opening, the smallest indentation that will accept his pressure, and invite him to follow with his instruments. There is none. It is *terra incognita*. Hawk-eyed, he peers, waiting for a sign, a slight change in color, that would declare the line of a tube mounding from its sunken position. There is no mark, no trail left by some earlier explorer.

At last he takes up his scissors and forceps and begins to dissect, millimetering down and in. The slightest step to either side may be the bit of excess that will set off avalanche or flood. And he is *alone*. No matter how many others crowd about the mouth of the wound, no matter their admiration and encouragement, it is *he* that rappels this crevasse, dangles in this dreadful place, and he is *afraid*—for he knows well the worth of this belly, that it is priceless and irreplaceable.

"Socked in," he says aloud. His language is astronaut-terse. The others are silent. They know the danger, but they too have given him their reliance. He speaks again.

"The common bile duct is bricked up in scar . . . the pancreas swollen about it . . . soup." His voice is scarcely more than the movement of his lips. The students and interns must strain to hear, as though the sound comes from a great distance. They envy him his daring, his dexterity. They do not know that he envies them their safe footing, their distance from the pit.

The surgeon cuts. And all at once there leaps a mighty blood. As when from the hidden mountain ledge a pebble is dislodged, a pebble behind whose small slippage the whole of the avalanche is pulled. Now the belly is a vast working lake in which it seems both patient and surgeon will drown. He speaks.

"Pump the blood in. Faster! Faster! Jesus! We are losing him."

And he stands there with his hand sunk in the body of his patient, leaning with his weight upon the packing he has placed there to occlude the torn vessel, and he watches the transfusion of new blood leaving the bottles one after the other and entering the tubing. He knows it is not enough, that the shedding outraces the donation.

At last the surgeon feels the force of the hemorrhage slacken beneath his hand, sees that the suction machine has cleared the field enough for him to see. He can begin once more to approach that place from which he was driven. Gently he teases the packing from the wound so as not to jar the bleeding alive. He squirts in saline to wash away the old stains. Gingerly he searches for the rent in the great vein. Then he hears.

"I do not have a heartbeat." It is the man at the head of the table who speaks. "The cardiogram is flat," he says. Then, a moment later . . . "This man is dead."

Now there is no more sorrowful man in the city, for this surgeon has discovered the surprise at the center of his work. It is death.

The events of this abdomen have conspired to change him, for no man can travel back from such darkness and be the same as he was.

As much from what happens *outside* the human body as within that place that for him has become the image of his mind, the surgeon learns.

It is Korea. 1955.

I am awakened by a hand on my chest, jostling.

"Sir Doc! Sir Doc!" It is Jang, the Korean man who assists me.

I open my eyes. Not gladly. To awaken here, in this place, in this time, is to invite despair.

"Boy come. Gate. Very scared. His brother bad sick. Pain belly. You come?"

O God, I think, let it not be appendicitis. I do not know how many more anesthesia-less operations I have left in me. Not many, I think. For I can no longer bear the gagged mouths, the trembling, frail bodies strapped to the table, round and round with wide adhesive tape from neck to ankles, with a space at the abdomen for the incision. Nor the knuckles burning white as they clutch the "courage stick" thrust into their hands at the last minute by a mama-

san. Nor the eyes, slant and roving, enkindled with streaky lights.
Something drags at my arms, tangles my fingers. They grow ponderous at the tips.

"Couldn't they bring him here?"

"No, Sir Doc. Too very sick."

It is midnight. I force myself to look at the boy who will guide
us. He is about ten years old, small, thin, and with a festoon of snot
connecting one nostril to his upper lip. It gives a harelip effect.

We are four in the ambulance: Jang, Galloway the driver, the
boy, and myself. A skinny bare arm points up into the mountains,
where I know the road is narrow, winding. There are cliffs.

"We'll go up the stream bed," says Galloway. "It's still dry, and
safer. Far as we can, then tote in."

I make none of these decisions. The ambulance responds to the
commands of the boy like a huge trained beast. Who would have
thought a child to have so much power in him? Soon we are in the
dry gully of the stream. It is slow. Off in the distance there is a torch.
It swings from side to side like the head of a parrot. A signal. We
move on.

The first cool wind plays with the hair, blows the lips dry, brightens the tips of cigarettes, then skips away. In a moment it returns.
Its strength is up.

"Rain start today," says Jang.

"Today?"

"Now," says Galloway. A thrum hits the windshield, spreads to
the roof, and we are enveloped in rain. A flash light floats morosely
off to one side, ogling. There is shouting in Korean.

Now we are suckstepping through rice paddies, carrying the
litter and tarps. We arrive at the house.

A sliding paper door opens. It is like stepping into a snail shell.
On the floor mat lies a boy; he is a little smaller than the other. He
wears only a loose-fitting cotton shirt out of which his head sticks
like a fifth limb. His face is as tightly drawn as a fist. Flies preen
there. His eyes rove in their fissures like a pendulum. I kneel. Heat
rises from the skin in a palpable cloud. The ribbed bellows of the

chest work above the swollen taut abdomen. Tight parts shine, I think. Knuckles and blisters and a belly full of pus. I lay my hand upon the abdomen. It helps me. I grow calm. Still, my fingers inform of the disease packaged there, swarming, lapping in untouched corners. For one moment, I long to leave it there, encased. To let it out, to cut it open, is to risk loosing it over the earth, an oceanic tide.

The abdomen is rigid, guarded. *Défense musculaire*, the French call it. You could bounce a penny on it. The slight pressure of my hand causes pain, and the child raises one translucent hand to ward me off. *Peritonitis*. Fluttering at the open lips, a single bubble expands and contracts with each breath. A soul budding there.

Outside, the sound of the rain has risen. There is anger in it. We place the boy on the litter, cover him with the tarpaulin. The door is slid open; twists of water skirl from the roof.

"Don't run," I say. "No jouncing."

The two men and the litter disappear like a melting capital H. I bow to the family of the child. Their faces are limp, flaccid; the muscles, skin, lips, eyelids—everything still. I recognize it as woe. The mother hunkers by the pallet gazing at the door. Fine colonies of sweat, like seed pearls, show upon her nose; strapped to her back, an infant twists its head away from hers in sleep. The father stands by the door. His breath is rich with kimchi; he seems to be listening. I am relieved to thrust myself into the rain.

Once again we are in the ambulance.

"The bumps," I say. "They hurt him." I need not have said that. The others know.

There is no longer a stream bed. Where it was, a river rushes. It has many mouths. It is maniacal. In the morning the fields below will be flooded. We drive into the torrent because . . . there is nothing else to do. We hear his little grunts, the "hic" at the end of each breath, and we enter the river. In a minute the water is at the running board, sliding back and forth on the floor. We move out to the middle. It is deeper there. In the back of the vehicle, Jang hovers over the litter, bracing it with his body. All at once, I feel the impact of the wave, like the slap of a giant tail. We are silent as the ambulance goes over on its side. We are filling with water. I push with my boots against Galloway's body and open the door. I climb out onto the side of the ambulance.

"Pass him out. Give him here."

The moaning white figure is held up. He is naked save for the shirt. I hold him aloft. I am standing on the red cross. The others climb out. We huddle as the water screens the surface around where we stand. Then we are *in*. Rolling over and over, choking. I see the boy fly from my hands, watch him rise into the air, as in slow motion, his shirt ends fluttering, the wind whipping the cloth. For an instant, he hangs there, his small bare arms raised, his fingers waving airily. Then he is a fish, streaking whitely, now ducking, now curving above. At last, he is a twig, turning lazily, harbored. When we reach him, he is on his back, the water rolling in and out of his mouth, his cracked head ribboning the water with blood.

All that night we walk, carrying the body in turns. The next day the father arrives. We give him the body, and I listen as Jang tells him the story of the drowning. We do not look at each other.

A man of letters lies in the intensive care unit. A professor, used to words and students. He has corrected the sentences of many. He understands punctuation. One day in his classroom he was speaking of Emily Dickinson when suddenly he grew pale, and a wonder sprang upon his face, as though he had just, for the first time, *seen* something, understood something that had eluded him all his life. It was the look of the Wound, the struck blow that makes no noise, but happens in the depths somewhere, unseen. His students could not have known that at that moment his stomach had perforated, that even as he spoke, its contents were issuing forth into his peritoneal cavity like a horde of marauding goblins. From the blackboard to the desk he reeled, fell across the top of it, and turning his face to one side, he vomited up his blood, great gouts and gobbets of it, as though having given his class the last of his spirit, he now offered them his fluid and cells.

In time, he was carried to the operating room, this man whom I had known, who had taught me poetry. I took him up, in my hands, and laid him open, and found from where he bled. I stitched it up, and bandaged him, and said later, "Now you are whole."

But it was not so, for he had begun to die. And I could not keep him from it, not with all my earnestness, so sure was his course. From surgery he was taken to the intensive care unit. His family, his students, were stopped at the electronic door. They could not pass, for he had entered a new state of being, a strange antechamber where they might not go.

For three weeks he has dwelt in that House of Intensive Care, punctured by needles, wearing tubes of many calibers in all of his orifices, irrigated, dialyzed, insufflated, pumped, and drained . . . and feeling every prick and pressure the way a lover feels desire spring acutely to his skin.

In the room a woman moves. She is dressed in white. Lovingly she measures his hourly flow of urine. With hands familiar, she delivers oxygen to his nostrils and counts his pulse as though she were telling beads. Each bit of his decline she records with her heart full of grief, shaking her head. At last, she turns from her machinery to the simple touch of the flesh. Sighing, she strips back the sheet, and bathes his limbs.

The man of letters did not know this woman before. Preoccupied with dying, he is scarcely aware of her presence now. But this nurse is his wife in his new life of dying. They are close, these two, intimate, depending one upon the other, loving. It is a marriage, for although they own no shared past, they possess this awful, intense present, this matrimonial now, that binds them as strongly as any promise.

A man does not know whose hands will stroke from him the last bubbles of his life. That alone should make him kinder to strangers.

I stand by the bed where a young woman lies, her face postoperative, her mouth twisted in palsy, clownish. A tiny twig of the facial nerve, the one to the muscles of her mouth, has been severed. She will be thus from now on. The surgeon followed with religious fervor the curve of her flesh; I promise you that. Nevertheless, to remove the tumor in her cheek, I cut the little nerve.

Her young husband is in the room. He stands on the opposite side of the bed, and together they seem to dwell in the evening lamplight, isolated from me, private. Who are they, I ask myself, he and this wry-mouth I have made, who gaze at and touch each other so generously, greedily? The young woman speaks.

"Will my mouth always be like this?" she asks.

"Yes," I say, "it will. It is because the nerve was cut."

She nods, and is silent. But the young man smiles.

"I like it," he says. "It is kind of cute."

All at once I *know* who he is. I understand, and I lower my gaze. One is not bold in an encounter with a god. Unmindful, he bends to kiss her crooked mouth, and I so close I can see how he twists his own lips to accommodate to hers, to show her that their kiss still works. I remember that the gods appeared in ancient Greece as mortals, and I hold my breath and let the wonder in.

Far away from the operating room, the surgeon is taught that some deaths are undeniable, that this does not deny their meaning. To *perceive* tragedy is to wring from it beauty and truth. It is a thing beyond mere competence and technique, or the handsomeness to precisely cut and stitch. Further, he learns that love can bloom in the stoniest desert, an intensive care unit, perhaps.

These are things of longest memory, and like memory, they cut. When the patient becomes the surgeon, he goes straight for the soul.

I do not know when it was that I understood that it is precisely this hell in which we wage our lives that offers us the energy, the possibility, to care for each other. A surgeon does not slip from his mother's womb with compassion smeared upon him like the drippings of his birth. It is much later that it comes. No easy shaft of grace this, but the cumulative murmuring of the numberless wounds he has dressed, the incisions he has made, all the sores and ulcers and cavities he has touched in order to heal. In the beginning it is barely audible, a whisper, as from many mouths. Slowly it gathers, rises from the streaming flesh until, at last, it is a pure *calling*—an exclusive sound, like the cry of certain solitary birds—telling that out of the resonance between the sick man and the one who tends him there may spring that profound courtesy that the religious call Love.

Fairy Tale

—◇—

Seventy years and three months old, and I still don't know what reality is. When I write something down on a page, it becomes as real as this morning's coffee and toast. The act of writing makes it so. There is a kind of writing that can foretell the future—myth, for one, and fairy tale, because, in them, time has been abolished. They do not take place in the past, present, or future, but are timeless. If that is so, I have only to write a Fairy Tale and put myself in it to find out what's to become of me. And so I shall begin.

Once upon a time, there was an old man, seventy years and three months of age, to be precise. To the outside world, he led a life of conventional, not to say tedious, morality, with no more than three or four uncharacteristic outbursts, which were met with stupefaction by those who "knew" him. The rest of the time, he played the role of paterfamilias, was even uxorious in his fashion, and had achieved respectability in the university town where he lived. Long ago, he had followed his physician father into medicine and had become a surgeon. But after thirty years, the city had come to seem like the Beast with a Thousand Gallbladders. And where was it written that one must stand at the operating table until the scalpel slipped from one's lifeless fingers? He had no wish to be like the old lion whose claws have long since gone blunt, but not the desire to use them. And so, the Doctor retired.

(No, I shall not exclude myself from the present tense. Let it be taking

place now. To send myself back into the past would be cowardly, as if I feared what will come next.)

In this city, which is not mine (my native land is to the north and west of here), there is a street corner, the intersection of York and Broadway. Here every afternoon at two o'clock, two old friends meet. One is a doctor, now retired after some three decades of surgery. He is also a writer of minor talent—essays, memoirs, short stories. The other is an emeritus professor of linguistics. Neither one can quite remember how it happened that they began to meet on this corner every afternoon, only that they have come to count on it more than they would like to admit. Theirs is a friendship conducted only out of doors. It never occurs to them to invite or visit each other indoors. Hardly what you'd call a luxuriant intimacy, but rather a jovial warmth that, at unexpected moments, might plunge deeper. If they were seven instead of seventy, they would show each other their penises. That sort of thing. But why the corner of Broadway and York? Because only there are the conditions for their friendship congenial, the way certain rare plants flourish only on the southern slope of a single mountain. That is the way with friendships between old men. They are fragile. Of course, there are separations occasioned by bad weather and by visits to their children, all of whom live at some distance, even so far away as France. While neither man is deficient in the paternal affections, they do express regret at being apart from one another.

"Now and then, parent and child are thrown together."

"I know what you mean. It can't be helped," says the Linguist.

They live at opposite ends of the University shuttle bus route and are discharged each afternoon from one of the two ancient black-and-white buses for which a shock absorber would be but a relic of a more golden time. They are by far the oldest passengers on the bus. The drivers, Pedro and Mario, were patients of the Doctor years before. Pedro has undergone appendectomy at the Doctor's hands, and Mario has had his inguinal hernia repaired. Both are convinced that the Doctor saved their lives, and now behave toward the two old men in the manner of solicitous sons, varying the engine speed, steering deftly to avoid the worst of the ruts and potholes, swinging the old bus this way and that as if it were a cradle.

"They care about our guts," says the Linguist.

"Why shouldn't they? I cared about theirs," replies the Doctor.

Had they wives? It has already been said that the Doctor is "uxorious in his fashion." The Linguist is a widower of some years. Truth to tell, they prefer each other's company to that of women. This, despite the occasional petty rivalry, the bit of braggartry, the bursts of antipathetic temperament that punctuate their meetings. The Doctor, for instance, clucks his tongue at the Linguist's habit of bestrewing his conversation with foreign words. Not that they are pretentious coming from a linguist. What piques is that he, a simple "sawbones," is expected to understand them. By and large, they respect and are grateful for each other's reticence. Women, they agree, have so little restraint; they spill out everything along with their tears. Who could stand it? Unaccountably, both men are considered by women to be paragons of charm and gallantry.

Also to the corner of Broadway and York comes a cadre of elderly Italian men to scatter breadcrumbs and stale bakery goods for the large number of pigeons that congregate there. To the Linguist, whose cataracts are ripening, the birds seem to hatch from the pavement itself. Should he remove his glasses, amorphous clumps flow this way and that like the pseudopodia of an amoeba by which its shape is in constant flux. At times, the sidewalk seems aboil. Mostly, the birds strut about, whitening the pavement. Suddenly, the whole colony will rise with a great clatter of wings, touched off by some imagined peril. About the birds, the two men are of differing minds. The Doctor is fond of them; the Linguist detests them.

"The eternal youthfulness of a flock of doves." It is the Doctor speaking. "They are the same year in and year out. Why, from appearances you can't say that these are not the very same ones that gathered here half a century ago." Not so, the two men who stand in their midst, with suits that are too loose, too comfortable, scuffed shoes worn down at the heel (lateral, posterior), aluminum hair that descends from under a beret in one, and in the other, a gray fedora.

The Linguist is distinguished by the mahogany, silver-headed cane he flourishes. They are never seen without neckties, or in shirtsleeves. Whatever the original color of their clothing, it has faded to the sepia of an old-fashioned daguerreotype.

"One can only hope for a plague of psittacosis," says the Linguist.

"You say these things, but you don't mean them. The words that dribble down your chin don't come from your heart. I know you better than that." The Linguist is a pale, top-heavy-looking man, short—only five feet six inches tall, with eyes the color of a blue shirt that has been washed a hundred times. A Lithuanian, after all—a study in academic nonchalance, with his hands clasped behind his back and a meditative expression.

"Like Napoleon Bonaparte," the Doctor teases. The Linguist has the habit of saying "No matter" after any mild disagreement as if to defuse ill will that might have arisen. To the Doctor, the phrase seems dismissive. The one time he brought this up, the Linguist laughed.

"Hardly. It merely suggests that we ourselves and what we say are without substance, or matter."

There is that about the Doctor which suggests frailty, nothing physical, although he is much the smaller of the two; it comes from inside him. As pale as is the Linguist, just so darkly ruddy is the Doctor, a Sephardic Jew by ancestry, which would account for the touch of mysticism. He is subject to lapses of attention that are not too different from the "absences" of the lesser form of epilepsy known as petit mal. The Linguist is annoyed by what he calls his friend's "visions," largely because he feels excluded. Their differences are most sharply revealed in their hands. Those of the Linguist are white and soft with tapering fingers, and shot through with delicate purple veins. They have an unused look. Surely, they have never been clenched into fists, not even in response to some Departmental outrage.

"Refinement always shows in the fingers," remarks the Doctor. "You have it. I don't."

"I'd rather they'd been put to some use, like yours." The hands of the Doctor, as one might expect, are red, from having been scrubbed with a wire brush half a dozen times a day for thirty years. The nails are neatly trimmed. But what is this? The center of each palm is occupied by a hard, yellowish, bunched scar, most obvious at the base of the fourth finger and extending up to involve the oracular creases. These are the scars of Dupuytren's Contracture, present for years and causing him no distress. One day, he knows, this will progress to pull his fourth finger down into full fixed flexion, making surgical division of the band of tissue necessary. But not now. He himself is given to running his fingers over the deformations, especially while trying to solve a problem in his writing. When the two old men shake hands, the Linguist feels the hardness in the Doctor's palm. In the beginning, he would turn the hand over to see.

"It's nothing," reassured the Doctor. "Dupuytren's Contracture. He was a nineteenth-century surgeon who first described the scarring of the tissues beneath the skin. It's doubtless hereditary." The Linguist, who is rather squeamish about matters pertaining to the body, quickly let go of his friend's hand.

"It isn't pleasant to touch."

"It's not contagious. You can't catch it by shaking hands. Once, I half convinced an elderly nun that they were the stigmata of the Crucifixion."

"You surgeons naturally have a streak of cruelty."

"It is what enables us to cut open the bodies of people like you, rummage around in your guts."

The prevailing tree in the neighborhood is the sycamore, with the ginkgo a close second. It has been established by the Forestry School that these two trees withstand pollution better than the elm, for which the city had earned the title Elm City and which have all succumbed to a plague of Dutch elm disease. In the fall, the leaves of the ginkgo turn a startling chartreuse. The bark of the sycamore undergoes a decorative peeling that resembles camouflage in the rain. You have to visit the Grove Street cemetery in order to see oak, linden, and dogwood. "I am so tired," announces the Linguist.

"It's because you don't do anything. Doing nothing is the most exhausting thing in the world."

"And you? How, may I ask, do you keep busy?"

"I can't tell you that right now."

"Aha!" cries the Linguist. "So you are writing yet another book! Reticence in the normally talkative is a sure sign of authority."

"I am not, I repeat *not*, writing a book." The Linguist bends his head, then looks shrewdly up from under it. What else could his friend be up to?

One summer, a restaurant with the pretentious name au bon pain moved into the space vacated by a failed stationery store. It is one of a large national chain of restaurants. Both men resented the intrusion. Especially the Doctor. He was a man who hated change. Then again, he reasoned, there would be plenty of one-day-old bread and rolls to feed the pigeons. Before long, au bon pain (note the stylish lowercase letters) set out half a dozen tables on the sidewalk for those who might prefer to have their coffee amidst the traffic of pedestrians, dogs, and pigeons. On any given afternoon, the Doctor and the Linguist can be observed sitting there side by side like enthroned mummies awaiting eternity. What do they talk about? In the beginning, the Linguist would ask a question about doctoring, to which the Doctor would pretend ignorance.

"Oh, that old stuff? I've forgotten everything I knew. I'm prehistoric, as far as that goes." And that was to be that. Soon enough, the Linguist understood that the Doctor was averse to talking about his former profession, as though he had disgraced himself by retiring from it to become a writer. From then on, he avoided the subject. On another occasion, he asked his friend about his writing.

"What's it like for a surgeon to write?"

"What do you mean what's it like? Besides, I'm not a surgeon. I only used to be one." The Doctor looked far off into the distance.

"It's like surgery," he said, as though the idea had just occurred to him. "Making incisions with a pen, exploring cavities, taking great pains, leaping from a promontory down into a deep cul-de-sac, opening a blocked right-of-way, disimpacting something stony, sucking, teasing away, pressing an ear to the membranous ground to listen for the drumming of blood. And returning with a prize, or else bloodshot and empty-handed. You never know."

"You still use a pen? Not a computer?"

"No, a pen. I cut with it." He looked away, embarrassed. "I don't like to talk about it. Don't ask me." What do they talk about now? Sometimes they continue ancient conversations begun years ago and left unfinished. Perhaps they are preferring one of the Psalms to the others? Perhaps they are unraveling the mysteries of the kabbala? Is this not an edifying sight? Two old philosophers deep in debate, and engulfed in pigeons? In fact, they are more apt to be gossiping or trying to outwit each other. What they have achieved is a rarity: privacy in a public place. One would hesitate to invade such isolation. Still, it happens that someone will do just that. On this day, a man approaches the table where the two are sitting. Will he interrupt them? No, he thinks better of it and walks by, only to return minutes later. He doesn't know that they have noticed him and are wagering over whether he will speak or not. At last, he does. It seems that the man has heard of the Doctor and cannot resist telling him about his own operation, performed by another surgeon. The operation was not a success. It is the surgeon's fault. He "botched" the procedure. Many details are given in rapid succession. It is an Iliad of woes, an endless lamentation. The Linguist is furious at what he sees as the vulgarity of the interloper. The Doctor is utterly bored. His eyes have glassed over as though he has departed for another world. He is only waiting for the ribbon of syllables issuing from the man's mouth to cease. Perhaps he dozes off. Not until he has vented his indignation does the man go away.

To discourage such invasions, the Doctor has taken to bringing a book, which he either reads or pretends to, depending upon the threat of just such an assault.

"What's that you're reading?" the Linguist wants to know.

"Gray's 'Elegy Written in a Country Churchyard.' "

"For goodness sake! Why are you reading that now?"

"For thirty-five years I read his *Anatomy*. This is better."

(*I can't imagine where this fairy tale is going. It seems a series of digressions rather than a tale. To be honest, I'm losing interest in what happens to the old Doctor.*)

"*Allerverdammte Vogel!*" cries the Linguist in annoyance at a pigeon who is standing on the table between them. He makes as if to knock the bird off.

"Wait!" cries the Doctor. "These are no mere birds; they are old dreams. This is the street corner of dreams, the place where they congregate." He holds out his hand, palm up in invitation. Much to the amazement of the Linguist, an especially plump bird obliges. It is of a soft purplish red color, mauve. There is a patch of black on the breast. The touch of its tiny pink feet on his palm sends a voluptuous wave through the body of the old Doctor. Moments later, the dove has rejoined the flock, all the rest of which consists of the common bluish-gray *Columba livia.*

"What is it?" exclaims the Linguist. "You are blushing!"

"It's nothing. Nothing, I assure you. Just a recollection of something, someone."

"Brought by your dream bird, I suppose? Come, come, in the interest of old friendship, tell me your dream."

"It was of Sonya, a woman I used to know." The face of the Doctor is suffused with what can only be amorous tenderness. The Linguist urges him on.

"An old lover, this Sonya? I'm jealous."

"You needn't be. Former lovers leave nothing behind, only the memory of their bodies—the texture, smell, taste, color, the sounds of their lovemaking." He is remembering the black beauty spot she used to wear on her cheek.

(This tale isn't going anywhere. I have a good mind to drop the whole thing. It's getting embarrassing. I'm a married man, remember? Besides, who wants to read about an old, burnt-out love affair. Well . . . burnt-out isn't quite true. Barely smoldering would be more like it. But far be it from me to blow the lone coal back to life.)

As I was saying a paragraph or so ago, neither one can remember how or even when they began to meet, nor even why they have chosen this street corner. (Perhaps it was the street corner that chose them?) If someone should ask how long they have been meeting here, one of them would reply: "We have always come here." But what about before? "There was no before." Now and then one of them, usually the Doctor, suggests a stroll. Then they amble as slowly as possible, arm in arm, European-style, to the corner of York and Grove, one block to the north. At such times, they seem welded into a single bulky quadruped, roughly buffalo-shaped, only with two heads. The Linguist, who prides himself on having no sense of direction, calls it the Corner of Consternation, declares it *terra incognita* on the map of his mind. Always, upon arrival, he looks about as if for the first time, and pretends that they are lost. At the Doctor's insistence, they will continue on for a short block eastward to the corner of Grove and High streets. Here there is a gleaming white marble building in the style of a Greek temple with roof, pillars, and pediments in the Classic mode. Although, unlike the Parthenon, say, this one is windowless and sealed, exclusive of all but the chosen few. It is further protected from municipal contamination by a tall wrought-iron fence in the form of coiled snakes, an allusion to the name of this Secret Society—Book and Snake. Directly across Grove Street is a massive brownstone arch with a strong Egyptian flavor. This is the gate to the walled Grove Street cemetery. Carved above the entrance are the words "The Dead Shall Be Raised." Here the two old men linger, between Egypt and Greece, savoring the twin whiffs of ancient civilizations before ambling back to the corner of Broadway and York. "Where we belong," they agree. Whereupon the buffalo divides itself in two like a paramecium in the act of binary fission, and settles contentedly at one of au bon pain's outdoor tables.

"Only missing is a fountain to transform Broadway and York into the Piazza Navona in Rome," sighs the Linguist.

"Why not let the birds take the place of a fountain," replies the Doctor. "They do give a liquid, flowing motion to the sidewalk, the way they rise and fall, rise and fall, and their cooing is an oddly watery sound, don't you think?"

"They are more like the Deluge," says the Linguist in a sour aside to no one in particular. "In my humble opinion, these birds carry the permission of pigeons to be disgusting rather too far. And how wild they are today—*con furioso*, to say the least." When the Doctor fails to retort, he taps his forehead, and breaks the silence. "Pay me no mind," he says. "It's my nature to growl at the world at large." Now the Linguist takes out a venerable pipe, scrapes it out, fills it with tobacco from a pouch, and lights up. The Doctor clucks his tongue.

"Why must you smoke?" he asks.

"To give it pleasure," the Linguist explains.

"You shouldn't smoke."

"I don't do it for myself. I do it for the pipe. It wants to be smoked. That's what it was made for."

It is not true that nothing memorable happens on the corner of Broadway and York. One day, they arrive at the corner to find an organ-grinder preparing to turn the handle of his apparatus. At his feet there mopes a small melancholy macaque monkey caparisoned as a bellhop. It is holding a tin cup. The small creature is limping. "Bitten by a dog," someone says. An organ-grinder! Such a phenomenon hasn't been seen on the streets of the city for half a century. Moments later, there comes an asthmatic rendition of the "Miserere" from *Il Trovatore*. No sooner has the music ended then the monkey hobbles toward the two men, holding up the tin cup.

"Disgraceful!" hisses the Linguist. "To make such ill use of a poor animal. There ought to be a law!" When the Doctor is silent, he goes on, "Of course, to you it's all the same, I suppose. You, who believe these pigeons are dreams." The Linguist turns away from the beggar, and taking out a handkerchief blows his nose loudly enough to make the monkey start in alarm. The Doctor cannot take his gaze from the little macaque. Once again, the strains of the "Miserere" are heard. It is the wrong opera, the Doctor thinks. His are the eyes of Tonio, singing "Ridi, Pagliaccio . . ." Whatever his other weaknesses, it can never be said of the Doctor that he turns away from the terrible wherever it presents itself. No matter the unspeakable fungations growing among the entrails of his patients, he has always faced them without flinching. But thirty years of surgery have not inured him to misery. Reaching into a pocket, he brings forth a coin and drops it into the tin cup with a dull unmusical noise. The dying monkey— he dies in every town to which he is brought—makes a deep formal bow, then hobbles around to force the Linguist to look at him. The

Linguist covers his eyes with his hands. Even in the utter desolation of being on display, the monkey shows an animal's instinct for camouflage, for feigning. Spurned again, the monkey gives three quick yips, each one like a sharp little bite.

"It makes me want to vomit!" says the Linguist. The Doctor says nothing, only smiles slightly as you do when a truth about someone has been unwittingly revealed. All at once, the Doctor knows how hostile the outside world is. Everything inside himself, he feels, is secret, sterile. He too is a furtive creature whose Fate it is to pretend congeniality. When, in fact, he is as untouchable as fire. He glances at his old friend. The whites of the Linguist's eyes are the color of sulfur around china blue at the center. His lips are moving in a whisper, the way they do when he is trying to remember something. This is the glory of old age? But years have passed and the organ-grinder has never been seen again.

On another occasion, it is a man with a guitar who appears at the corner of Broadway and York. The case lies open on the pavement, with a suggestive dollar bill and two quarters inside. It is summertime, and the musician is wearing a torn T-shirt which reads "Jesus Christ died for your sins." Soon enough, the musician has opened a camp stool. He sits and lays the guitar across his chest, then bows his head low until his eyebrows touch the instrument, as in prayer. At first slowly, then faster and faster, he strums. The Doctor is entranced, not by the music, not at all. But by the man's flying fingers. Back and forth, they work the strings that bridge the opening whose darkness the Doctor drinks up with his eyes, the darkness that inhabits the center of the guitar. Such a woman-shaped thing, a guitar, the way she turns on the man's knees and moans in answer to his clever fingers. Who would have thought the old Doctor to have so much heat in him?

The guitarist too has never come back to the corner. Is there nothing that will strike root for keeps in this sad gray pavement? No, only the two old men, and the birds.

Every Friday, immediately upon arriving at the corner, they make what for them is an expedition west on Broadway to a humble restaurant called the Educated Burgher, a misnomer, as the shelves along the walls are filled with fake books. There the two men partake of New England clam chowder, which they agree is the best chowder of their lives.

Come the middle of April, you can count on it, the Linguist will propose a different trek. A safari, he calls it.

"Shall we?"

"Is it that time, already?"

"It was last year on this very date, remember?" And so the two start out, not on one of their well-traveled paths, but across York, then across Broadway (which has abruptly changed its name to Elm). One block to the east brings them to High Street. A right turn south on High for thirty paces, and they arrive.

"Ah, there it is!"

"You are right, as usual." What they come here to see is an ancient wisteria closely applied to the stone wall of one of the college buildings. It consists of a single trunk that ascends gracefully some twenty feet before sending out two transverse branches giving the vine the shape of the Cross. Every April, these two "arms" are heavy-laden with lavender flowers. A sweet reek fills the air of High Street. What never fails to call forth marvel from the friends is that, for most of its length, the trunk consists of but a thin posterior rim of bark, the rest of the tissue having long since been ravaged by time, insects, whatever.

"How can so much nourishment pass across it? It is miraculous!" The voice of the Linguist is lowered in awe.

"It is the ferocity of the life force," proclaims the Doctor.

The months go by in seeming tranquillity. Now, every day there comes the moment when the Doctor stands, holds out his hand, and waits for the mauve dove to alight on his upturned palm. It is the touch of the dove's feet that brings on a resurgence of the past. When he feels them, weightless upon his scar, it is no longer a stigma of the Crucifixion, but the sign of a covenant. When the ecstasy comes, he cannot say if he is experiencing it at that moment or if it is a vivid memory of some delight of long ago. And each time, he dares to cup his hand, to make a nest into which the dove settles and coos. The sound is as welcome as if she were the dove of the Flood. Moments later, with a whirr of wings, she has flown to rejoin the others. How many times, in the years to come, he will roll these coos in his fingers as if they were wet clay, shaping, molding them, hoping to sculpt, to *carnify*, the dove from her call alone. For the old Doctor, the mauve dove has become the divine messenger, the revealer of mysteries, the instigator of passion. But how could he translate this to his friend? He could not. Translations cannot be trusted; one could give the wrong meaning. Nor could he describe to anyone else the voluptuous sensation she induces in him, when he couldn't describe it to himself. Other than to say that it is intensely limpid. But what does that mean?

Once, a small raptor, a shark-shinned hawk, he could tell from the long, square-tipped tail and the "furry" legs, stooped right down in the midst of the flock of pigeons, sank its talons into a frenzy of feathers, then lifted off with its prize. Within minutes, the rest of the birds were strutting and vying with each other as if nothing had happened. The Doctor had a moment of terror before he saw his dove among the survivors.

(Noon. I have just returned to the library after lunch [beef barley soup and a hot dog at the Educated Burgher]. Now I am sitting in a deep leather chair in an alcove of a reading room. The only other people in the vast room are three sleepers. Outside, in the courtyard, a soft rain is falling. The lights in the alcove are of hypnotically low wattage, ideal for the inducement of sleep. A person like me must be careful in a place like this, not to be swept into someone else's dream. My great fear is that the Doctor and the Linguist will wrest themselves free of the fairy tale before I have learned my fate. Only the rain and the lamplight give hope of keeping them in my imagination.)

Every summer it happens that the Doctor will not appear at the corner of Broadway and York for a period of four weeks. He will be in France, visiting his son, instead. On the day after his return, at two o'clock in the afternoon, he steps down from the shuttle bus to the corner. How delighted he is that the Linguist is there, waiting for him amidst the swirling pigeons. And how his pulse quickens in anticipation of the sensuous moment he knows is coming.

"You look younger each time I see you," remarks the old Linguist.

"How do you do it?" The Doctor smiles, and holds out his hand, palm up. Immediately, the mauve dove lifts from the sidewalk. There the Doctor stands, palm to the sky, the sun so bright its rays pass right through the bird in his hand. He can see her tiny heart throbbing. No sooner does she alight than he feels the same sweet surge followed by tristesse. (Yes, that's closer to the feeling—a sweet sadness). The next day, the dove comes to the Doctor's hand bearing a tiny twig in its beak. When it flies away, the twig is left behind.

"Look! It wants to build its nest in my hand!"

"That's nothing. I heard of an Irish saint, I forget his name. When a bird came to him like that, he held out his hand until the nest was built." But the Doctor has given in to one of his "absences" and makes no reply. The Linguist waits for him to come out of it, then cocks his head impishly. "If I didn't know your age, I'd say you were having a love affair."

"Old age takes each of us in a different way," the Doctor says. Anyone passing by and noticing the two old men sitting there would not know that one of them is alive with passion, a late flowering that knows to keep itself hidden. But what is this! Amongst the twenty or so pigeons, all of the livid blue-and-gray coloration of their kind, he cannot find the mauve dove. With mounting fear, he searches among the others, who will not stay still but continue in a hectic motion so that he cannot be sure. Where is the mauve dove! The Linguist sees that his friend is greatly disturbed.

"You are looking for the one you trained to sit on your hand? Over there." He points to what, through the haze of cataracts, is a soft smudge in the middle of the street. "Flew right into the side of a car. The driver mustn't have noticed, didn't stop. Been run over a couple of times since, I'm sure." All this he says in a voice that is like spitting. "There it is. Over there. Don't you see? Dead. *Morta. Finito. Geshtorben. Tot. Mort. Shinde. Mat. Termo. Fim. Muerto. Defunto. Dod. Livlos. Belifd. Mortuus est. Spento. Inanimato. Zmarty. Miortvyi.* Done for. Kaput." Each word strikes the Doctor like a blow to the midsection. With each synonym, pronounced in a mock funerary tone, the Doctor gasps at the flash of meanness. All at once, he knows which way the Linguist's words are flowing—downward, downward from his lips to join the mountain of spoken cruelties at the bottom of a deep canyon, like bones thrown there by those who meant no harm. Even before the Linguist has finished speaking, the Doctor hears him but indistinctly, as though he were speaking through a surgeon's mask. The heavy body of the Linguist has faded. The Doctor is apart, isolated. Blindly, he wades through the flock of birds, who scarcely part to make way. Straight to the middle of the street where lies the mauve dove. Crumbs, his own, go scattering. A wild thread of black blood laps at his shoe. He kneels and takes the dove in his hands. Its outline on the pavement so sharp it might have been drawn there with a brush made of sedge, like one of those bulls engraved on papyrus on the banks of the Nile. But no, the imprint is a blossom growing out of the stone—mauve, with a touch of red. Who knows how long he will have knelt there before the honking of horns drives him back to the sidewalk where the Linguist is waiting? In his hands lies the body of the dove.

"Pigeons," says the Linguist in disgust, expectorating the word. "They are dirty, crawling with lice. Feh! Put it down, will you? Suppose someone sees you, a man of your age, holding a dead pigeon. How would it look?" The Doctor searches his friend's face. The Linguist cannot be silly enough to care what people might think of it. But he is. He is.

"You have language beyond the human range," the Doctor murmurs. As for his age, he had grown old before, any number of times, sometimes in a matter of minutes. No one could tell him anything about old age.

"The tongue is my calling," says the Linguist. "A thought minus its word is unclothed, and unfit to be seen. Language is the clothing of ideas." But the Doctor is not listening. Holding the dove firmly in one hand, he pulls a feather out of its breast, then returns to the place in the middle of the street and relinquishes the dove to its imprint on the pavement. The Linguist waits for him to return. He sees the feather in the Doctor's hand.

"Bizarre!" he mutters, and looks about to see if anyone has seen what took place. "Why cling to the relics of the dead? They won't bring back what's been lost." Ah, but that's where you are wrong, the Doctor thinks. I can conjure a whole dove from one feather. It is what a dreamer can do that a scholar cannot. One feather is like an old family saying that can evoke the entire childhood to which it is bound for all time. From this one feather I could recognize her out of ten thousand doves. One feather is love. But, of course, he can't say this to the Linguist, from whom, for the first time, he feels utterly estranged.

All night long, the old Doctor lies still, watching the spiders bind up the rafters of the ceiling, and listening. While he lies awake, the bed sleeps. For all of the silence, he might be Tutankhamen inside the pyramid. It is the same silence that Orpheus heard after the last footfalls of Eurydice had died away. At dawn, he falls asleep. All at once, the mauve dove flies across his mind! Its passage is like a sharp intake of breath. He holds out his dreaming hand, palm up, and waits for the prickle of tiny talons. Every few minutes he sighs as if to relieve a pressure. Surely, the dove would come to him. It must! But no, there is no prickle, no surge. Only the beating of wings in his blood. After a while, his arm grows tired, he lets it fall to the bed and awakens to see irresponsible sunbeams dancing and waving on his pillow. It makes his eyes water. Minutes later he has forgotten all about it, the way you forget about an umbrella you've left under a chair at the library.

THE END

"The end? The end? Just a minute!"
(*Voices of protest are being raised. They seem to be drifting up from the page which I am writing. Like steam, only thicker and acrid. Listen!*)
"This is what you call a Fairy Tale? A Fairy Tale is supposed to have a happy ending. The mauve dove turns into Sonya, and they walk off hand in hand to live happily ever after. Or the Doctor becomes a dove and they fly away to build a nest. That sort of thing."
(*Oh, all right. I'll try again.*)

Da capo.

As time passes, the old Doctor begins to doubt himself. He can no longer remember exactly what the dove looked like. He tries to picture the black spot on her breast, the brightness of her eyes, her dainty pink feet, but cannot. Perhaps the Linguist was right. A man of seventy (and then some), frequenting a pigeon? Seventy, he is told by those wishing to console him about his age, is not so old anymore. There are men who marry at seventy! The damned fools! Minutes later, he has forgotten all about it, the way you forget about an umbrella you've left under a chair in the library. Only, now and then, his palm will itch so that he must rub it.

THE END

(*There they go again!*)

"Oh no you don't! You are not going to get away with that old literary stunt. Do it again!"

Da capo.

For the three months of winter, the Doctor does not appear at the corner of Broadway and York. All during his winter of exile, he tries to exorcise those horrible synonyms for "dead" from his mind, but they have been engraved there. And he has berated himself for not telling his friend just how deeply injured he was. Now it is April, and truth to tell, he longs for the companionship of his old friend. Habits are hard to break. One man's sorrow is not any other man's sorrow. One man's pleasure is not any other man's pleasure. Perhaps it wasn't meanness at all. Perhaps the Linguist was just being rambunctious in the way that emeritus professors are likely to be, once relieved of the classroom and the Department. Besides, it is time for his spring haircut, and Tony's barbershop is three doors from the corner of Broadway and York.

Stepping down from the shuttle bus, he sees that nothing has changed. There are the birds touching the corner to life, charging it with energy. *Con furioso*, as his friend would say. Here is the old Linguist coming to greet him. His glance is a searching appraisal.

"Why do you look at me like that?" asks the Doctor.

"I see that you've been ill over the winter. You're pale, and your hair has gone very white. You are using a cane!"

"I am merely acting my age," says the Doctor with a tiny smile.

"Let's speak of other things, while we may."

THE END

(*The voices again.*)

"Absolutely not! We will not be herded into an elegiac ending. You call yourself an author? You are a despot." Now the two old men get up from the table at au bon pain and turn to face directly up at the perpetrator.

"You don't belong on the corner of Broadway and York with us anymore. Go away!" cries the old Linguist. He has made a fist (for the first time) and is shaking it. "You should have known that remembering is dangerous. It brings pleasure, yes, but then comes the sorrow of loss."

"It is out of control," adds the Doctor with equal vehemence, "this Fairy Tale, or whatever you call it. He who writes too much makes many mistakes. Leave us to our destiny."

(The two voices grow muffled, as though heard through a layer of moss or dry leaves. They have trouble enunciating. A moment more, and they will fall silent.)

(*Wait! Don't go! I must think. By replacing the body of the dead bird, is the Doctor relinquishing his old lover at last? Then all that will be left is her smell, her softness. What did he have in mind when he first retrieved the dead dove from the middle of the street? Did he mean to keep it from the crows? Two of these are already perching in wait on the roof of au bon pain, watching with a kind of feline shrewdness. On second thought, crows would be best. If it weren't for crows, we would be knee-deep in rotting carcasses from road kill alone. All right, he will lay her out for the crows. When the rush-hour traffic has died down, the black scavengers will shake down and land with a horrid little bounce. The old Doctor shudders at the thought. He imagines them pecking and pulling at the corpse of the dove with their strong horny beaks until the diminishing puddle disappears entirely. No, wait! That's not what happens at all. He'll bury her in the Grove Street cemetery. He will ask the Linguist to help him. Look!)*

The two old men are strolling arm in arm toward the corner of York and Grove. "If we are caught . . ." whispers the Doctor.

"Be calm," murmurs the Linguist. "*Te calma. N'ayez pas peur. Shimpai-inai.*" "Don't, please," the Doctor wants to say. But he doesn't. To his amazement, the words are strangely calmative. When the Linguist falls silent, he is disappointed.

"More," he says.

"*Apaisez-vous. Shtill. Heshkeet. Zei ruhig.*" The Linguist continues, the words tumbling out, nimble, acrobatic, magical. Yes, for the first time, the Doctor has an inkling of the magical effect of certain words.

"Yes, yes," replies the Doctor. "We must be calm." Even so, they lock their arms tightly to still the trembling. Now they walk east as far as the Greek temple. They cross the street to stand in front of the Egyptian gate of the cemetery. In his free hand, the Doctor carries a shopping bag in which are two trowels and a cigar box sealed with Scotch tape. It bears the label PANATELA, and was obtained by the Linguist from his tobacco shop.

But now they have been caught up in the narrative. They are being manipulated in accordance with a will other than their own. They are not calm. Their two old hearts are pounding. The Linguist is huffing and puffing. At the cemetery gate, they pause to read the inscription, as if for the first time.

"The Dead Shall Be Raised," reads the Doctor aloud. A glance to the east, the west, the south. No one. With an agility that surprises them, they slip beneath the arch of the gate. They might be a couple being shooed into the Ark.

Inside the graveyard, the dusk of evening has deepened toward night. They pass an angel that has shed one wing. It lies on the ground near its feet. Some fifty yards along the path, they come to a place where a dark red dogwood tree is in full bloom. The two old men nod to each other. It will be here, at the foot of this tree. One by one, holding on to the trunk, they lower themselves to their knees. A flock of small birds, juncos, flies out of the tree. Quickly now! The trowels. The light is fading. They begin to dig. The soil is clayey, and hard. It is slow work. On and on, they hack at the ground, lifting out teaspoonfuls of earth until what there is, is a grave. The Doctor places the cigar box in the hole, PANATELA side up. They cover it up. In the darkness, the earth offers itself to the labor, accepting the little casket, enveloping it with a rich smell. It is a hopeful smell; there will be dawn. Once again bracing themselves against the tree, they pull upright. It is black night, only a sliver of moon. Arm in arm, they feel their way back toward the gate, or where they imagine the gate to be, each holding out his free hand as if to fend off the darkness. There! The gate! But what's this? It is closed and padlocked for the night. The gatekeeper's cottage too is dark and shut tightly.

"We will have to spend the night," says the Doctor.

"There is nothing else we can do," agrees the Linguist. "Let's find a bench. At least we can sit." Turning back, they feel their way along a gravel path by the crunch of their footsteps. It is a gallant white magnolia that holds up its white blossoms to light up an iron bench.

"Sit down. Take it easy," says the Doctor. "You're out of breath. How many times have I told you not to smoke!" The Linguist sits. He reaches for his pipe, shivers in the chill.

"Sit next to me," he says. The Doctor does so. "Closer." They put their arms around each other, hugging for warmth, whispering words that no one else can hear. All night long, they sleep as they have walked, arm in arm. At last, it is dawn. The Linguist is awakened by the first rays of the sun, and the twittering of sparrows. He disengages himself from the Doctor, shakes him gently awake. The Doctor looks around at the graves and statues.

"We're not dead!" he exclaims, as if surprised.

"We must have been raised," says the Linguist.

Now, once again, they are strolling arm in arm on York Street toward the corner of Broadway. Already, the tables have been set out on the sidewalk.

"I could use a cup of coffee and a hard roll," says the Linguist. "What about you?"

"I'm starved. Being dead makes you hungry. You sit here. I'll bring it to the table." For a moment they sit looking at each other. A tiny smile plays about the lips of the Linguist. The Doctor's face breaks into a grin that radiates and permeates his friend. They shake their heads in wonder.

The Doctor has brought coffee and rolls. The two old men dunk the rolls in the coffee, and suck them up with gusto. The sounds they make are delicious in their ears.

THE END

(*From the page comes the sound of the two voices, only now they are strong, even youthful.*)

"And they lived happily ever after," says the Linguist.

"Yes," says the Doctor, "we did."

(*It seems that I have not yet rinsed my mind clean of them. Perhaps an epilogue would provide closure. But an epilogue is too grand a thing for a mere fairy tale. An afterthought would be more in keeping or, as the Linguist would say, an* arrière-pensée.)

It is one year later. Time to take leave of our two old friends. The Doctor is sitting at a table outside au bon pain on the corner of Broadway and York. He sees the Linguist approach, notes with affection and with rue his waddling gait and collapsed posture.

"Really, my friend, you must try to stand up straight. A man of your height cannot afford to waste so much as a single centimeter of it." The Linguist takes his seat rather more quickly than usual.

"Your hand!" he exclaims to the Doctor.

"What about my hand?" The Linguist takes it in his own, turns it to examine the palm. "I see that your fourth finger has been drawn farther toward the palm. You can't straighten it anymore. Good thing it's not the middle finger sticking up like that or you'd be arrested for public obscenity." The Doctor reaches into his coat pocket and takes out a pint of grappa. The Linguist produces two plastic cups.

"Now remember," warns the Doctor. "You're allowed only a single toast." The Linguist thinks for a long moment.

"*Chin-chin!*" he says. They touch cups. But before the Doctor can raise the cup to his lips, the Linguist lunges.

"*Bis hundert und zwanzig Jahr!*"

"That's two!" The Doctor is outraged, bristling.

"No matter," says the Linguist, and takes a first sip.

Phantom Vision

—∽—

1.

Among those who once were sighted but later become blind, there occurs the phenomenon of visual hallucination called phantom vision. It is not unlike phantom limb, in which the amputated limb is experienced. It occupies a position in space and can generate sensation such as pain and heat. This has something to do with the persistence of sensory pathways to which the brain has long become habituated. The mechanism, however, is not clearly understood. It is possible that the brain not only registers sensory events but contains the neural matrix in which externally and internally generated information flows. Dreaming and hallucination can be thought of as being parts of the same spectrum. Dreaming occurs during rapid eye movement sleep and appears to be the release of fantasy thought in a sequence of images. Visual hallucinations are most likely to be experienced when one is drowsy. They are often accompanied by sensations of moving, falling, or floating. A man will have the feeling that the chair in which he is sitting rises into the air and becomes enveloped in green foliage. The sightless person will "see" flashes of light and color, geometric patterns and pictures, both abstract and representational in wild profusion. Some are dramatic, religious, or archetypal. Others are of mundane objects. Rarely, sound may accompany the visual hallucination. Often these visions have some relation to events in life that are fraught with worry or emotion such as grief. Sometimes they simply burst upon the scene without premonitory cause. Some of these hallucinations are threatening, others are enjoyable, and even companionable. There is a tendency to fail to report, or to deny, these hallucinations so as not to be considered peculiar or even crazy. Perhaps Homer's white Ionian beaches and wine-dark sea were what he "saw." It follows, then, that blindness is the path to somewhere else.

2.

Not long ago I attended the memorial service for a twenty-one-year-old Yale senior. Six weeks before, he had disappeared. Ever since, we had been living in fear and hope. But then his body was found floating among the bulrushes of the Harlem River by a woman walking there. What was she doing by that stream contaminated with chemical waste and discarded tires and from which an entire rusted automobile emerges? Perhaps it had been the flash and slash, the ribaldry, of gulls that drew her attention to that place? The cause of death was suicide; he'd left a note. Battell Chapel was full of undergraduates, faculty, administration and library workers. Brilliant, handsome, amiable, witty, and kind he was and with a low chuckle, like water flowing over stones. Our friendship was conducted at the library, where he worked for the past three years at the circulation desk. Most days, we visited. His anguish had not been visible to me. Might there not have been an inkling, had I been made ready to receive it? A preternatural calmness of the features, a vacancy, the same stillness of a museum statue within its vitrine? My great regret is that he didn't confide. I could have whisked him away and out of sight until he felt better. Sitting in the chapel, I addressed the dead body. Did it have to be done? Couldn't it have been postponed or dismissed? For whose benefit was it? Where is the reason in such an act? Where is decorum? There is no decorum in committing suicide, no dignity. Behave yourself! I said aloud. But even alive, he would have been unreachable. To him, it was all as mercilessly clear as a primitive sacrifice. It wasn't a gesture, an "I'll show you!" For him, there was no other way.

"I do not feel joy," he had said once, said it out of the blue to a friend, who'd been a bit startled. But the next moment, Greg had laughed to show it was just a joke.

The service was presented as a "celebration." We were urged to be grateful for the gift of his life. And we were to take comfort in the knowledge that Greg was experiencing the joys of Heaven. I didn't believe any of that. Doves cooing on the window ledge offer more consolation. Or the scent of incense. His death had made survivors of us. Survivors have the habit of placing blame. It is a comfort to do so, but not yet. We were too deep in the moist delirium of grief. All about us, the vast, reverberant chapel echoed and vibrated. We heard the pounding of our own blood. Throughout the minutes of silent prayer, a telephone competed from somewhere in the chapel. I tried not to listen but heard each ring, the way you hear a snatch of music you can't get rid of—what the Germans call an *Ohrvurm*— earworm. Twenty times it rang—I counted, and had the wild thought that it was *he* phoning from anywhere but Heaven. I glanced in the direction of the sound, half intending to go and answer the phone.

Just then, the hush of prayer ended and the phone fell silent too. I imagined the boy coiled tightly inside his secretive mind, standing on a bridge over the polluted stream, his pocket stuffed with rocks, smoking a last cigarette, sending the butt in a melancholy arc, then the waning life that writhed inside him as he took the "revolting bliss" into his throat, and melted into the black, corrugated Harlem River that was to become his solution, the solution of him. Such an ingredient must surely turn the foulest water sweet, set its iridescent fetor aglow with the sumptuous light of rose windows. Down, down beneath the silvery aqualune, trailing bubbles, taking on the color of moonlight he descended in undulant chords like Debussy's cathedral, into the deep black pool beneath the bridge. Perhaps he had been dazzled into anesthesia by the light of a misshapen moon? (Let it be so.) Must I envision the hulk, weighted with stones, now swollen with gas, afloat and rolling a bit in semicircles, animated by the sluggish, cloacal current, bumping against tires, trash, the steely blades of reeds? It is merely a parcel afloat that no longer has anything in common with the boy. But is everything to me. Stop! That is the trouble with the imagination. It doesn't know when to leave off, but rollicks over into unbearable horror.

In my lap, the bones of my hands are visible. Can it be that these hands, which are only bones, performed surgery, labored to prolong life whether that was desirable or not? A knife would have been kinder, more fitting, somehow—to open his throat, then thrust a finger into the wound to make it larger, the blood leaping over my hand and down my arm. But no, never! Instead, I would hold his head still between my hands, and look into it the way children look at things forbidden. I would not be intimidated by the mysteries of the brain—the gyri and sulci, the pons and the medulla oblongata. I'd gaze and gaze until I could see the black creature that crouched at the bottom of his skull. I'd reach in and . . . pounce! Grab it just behind the neck (oh, I know the art of extirpation) and wrest it free. I have grown so old that I am young again, unburdened with wisdom, and with a head full of bloody fantasies. Let others celebrate his life; I cannot transform an apocalypse into a platitude. Death is the most absorbing event of life. I have watched so many throats straining to go or stay, you can't tell which. It is what comes of a preoccupation with the flesh. Surgery robs one of so much that might be consolatory. At the memorial service, tears spurted from the eyes of the distraught father. "Where is my son, and who is he now?" I asked myself. The breath began to flutter in my chest. A knot of sorrow closed my throat. Stricken classmates bore witness; we sang "Amazing Grace." Just behind me, a woman's voice put on feathers and rose to the stained glass. Tapes were played—of "Pearl Jam" and "Magenta," his favorites. The burr of two hundred candles softened the taut features of the mourners, and that was that. It is a tiny victory that he enjoyed smoking and didn't live long enough to pay for it with cancer or emphysema.

3.

It is weeks now since he discharged his fractured life like effluent into the river, and still, in a telepathy between the drowned boy and myself, his face goes swiveling on the current of my mind. I see his right hand raised, drawing over his head the shawl of water whose soft siffle might have been his last breath. I see him turning on his back as if to fasten upon the stars with eyes that were refracted for air, not water. I see the light of the aqualune shaking around him. I see the river dining on the bobbing flesh-wreck at whose flanks a froth of drool has gathered. If dead he knows no peace, then when? I see the Harlem running like drainage from a sore. This boy deserved a Nile. Or a Jordan. I know now that no one but himself could have saved him.

4.

It is the middle of October, almost ten months later. I lie awake in a bed that gleams with moonlight. I am submerged in it, as in a celestial river, like that sacred stream far away from human footsteps, in a clear meadow, under an open sky where, on the eve of battle, Jason the Argonaut reverently bathed his tender body. It is the Harlem, of course, only transformed by his presence in it, with all of his unhappiness skimmed from the surface. I see no discarded tires, nor any rusting contraptions in the deep black pool. Elsewhere the river runs two inches deep over a bed of gleaming pebbles. Trout pass beneath the fallen leaves. Not far upstream there is a waterfall. Nothing grand, mind you, but a falls nevertheless with a long drop of six feet and two shorter *cascatelli*. Listen! There is a gentle purling. The current churns into a voice. He chuckles.

Brain Death:
A Hesitation

—⁓—

Say that you have been walking in the mountains all day. You come upon a pool surrounded by trees. The water is perfectly still and inky black. The thought occurs that this pool is one of great depth. You don't know that it is, for you have not sounded it, nor have you the instruments to do so. You might dive into the pool and try to touch bottom, but if you don't . . . Even so, you sense that the depth is vast. You lean over until the pool invites your reflection. All at once, the water parts and there comes spurting up from the surface one gleaming fish that arcs, then plunges back down.

Not long ago, I stood at the bedside of a young man who had been declared brain-dead after a motorcycle accident. Within hours, his organs were to be removed and transplanted into others who were even then being made ready. His mother stood at the other side of the bed, one hand holding the boy's gingerly so as not to disturb the intravenous flow. Her other hand rested on the side rail, for which there was no need; he would not be stirring. A doctor from the transplant team visited.

"Just the sight of him lying there asleep . . ." The woman murmured so as not to awaken the boy.

"It isn't sleep," the doctor clarified. "It's coma."

"Yes. Yes, I know. But . . ."

"You must keep in mind the massive trauma to his head, the

hopelessness of it." The woman retreated into silence. All at once, the regular rhythm of the young man's respirations changed. He opened his mouth wide, drew in a deep shuddering breath, then slowly exhaled. He had yawned! The look on the mother's face announced it a miracle no less than the Raising of Lazarus. A moment later the breathing resumed its measured pace. But now, in the contagion of that phenomenon, I too yawned. It was as if the brain-dead man had sent forth a single spurt of energy, a message if you will, causing another human being to react. The doctor explained.

Yawning is the result of a buildup of carbon dioxide in the bloodstream. Such hypercarbia occurs in states of fatigue, sleepiness, or boredom. It's mediated at the very lowest level of the brain stem and so may occur even in the state of brain death. The deep breath with its large intake of oxygen and the ensuing exhalation of a large quantity of carbon dioxide would seem to be an attempt by the body to correct the imbalance of these gases in the blood.

"But boredom?" I asked.

"That part is still mysterious."

"And the contagiousness of a yawn?"

"Yawning," said the doctor, "must have a social as well as a bodily function, having to do with reciprocal stimulation."

"Reciprocal stimulation? What does that mean?"

"That too is not fully understood." In the silence that followed, the doctor tried again. "Maybe the extreme extension of the muscles of the jaw is like having a good stretch. Now do you see?"

"Oh yes," said the mother, just to be congenial. The transplant doctor left. The look on the woman's face said: "Well, go ahead and sleep, son. You need it." Then, aloud to me: "There've been times when I've been so tired myself I could have slept right through till the Resurrection." It was clear that for this woman, the young man in the bed was not a container of organs to be recycled but an utterly familiar and beloved son. There are those foolish romantics, sentimentalists really, who would say that a mother's love for her brain-dead child constitutes a kind of life. But of course, I'm not one of them.

"I wonder what he's thinking," said the woman. I could only shrug. But now it is my turn to wonder. Might there not be still some thoughts, like slow and aged fish, gliding about in the twilight of that deep coma? Not even the neurosurgeon who rummages in the very substance of the brain, who knows its every gyrus and sulcus as one knows his own handwriting, not even he can know the outer reaches of the mind. It would be arrogant to think so.

"I wonder what he is thinking," the boy's mother had said. But only in literature do the dead have a voice, and nowhere more powerful than in Noh, the traditional theatrical art of Japan. For a period of six hundred years, throughout the equivalent of the Middle Ages in Europe, Noh enjoyed enormous popularity, only to fall into relative obsolescence since World War II. In most Noh plays, the main character is the ghost of a dead person, often a warrior who died in battle or the heroine of a classic folk tale who reenacts some incident from life, and asks the audience what they think. Because the events have already taken place before the play begins, there is no dramatic incident, merely reflection on what happened and the posing of difficult questions as to right and wrong. The ghost invites the viewer into the past. Noh is distinct from and remote from this world. It escapes the usual notions of time and place and moves in the shadowy realm at the margins of life and death. The characters are poised at the point where the now and the hereafter touch. The events are faded, distant. Only the essence of the experience remains. To appreciate a Noh play, you have to rid yourself of all literality. The props are stripped of all but the merest *aperçu* of the objects. The audience departs the theater in a state of contemplation.

Until the spring of 1999, when a second operation was carried out, only a single heart transplantation had been performed in Japan, a country that dotes on technology. The first heart transplantation took place in 1968 in Sapporu, on the northern island of Hokkaido. The donor was a young man who had been "drowned" and sustained on a respirator. The recipient was a young man who died two months later. There followed a violent nationwide revulsion. All Japan rose up in indignation. How did the doctors know that the young man was really dead? Had all possible measures been taken to preserve his life? Where is it written that death and brain death are the same? Suspicion grew into accusation, and the surgeon was accused of murder, although never prosecuted. In Japan alone of all industrialized nations, there are societal, cultural, and religious reasons why the heart of one person may not be removed and placed in the body of another. Despite the secular nature of much of its society, a certain influence of animism persists in Japan. Animism states that the spirit, *tamashii*, resides in the body so long as it is warm. There is an age-old relationship between the living and the dead in which the dead must be assuaged and placated in order that they might advance upon the path to eternal peace. If not, they are doomed to everlasting discontent and resentment toward the living. Of course, this is scorned by the few brain-death protagonists as a peculiar relic of ancient paganism. According to Confucius, you have been lent your body by your parents and you are not free to give away parts of it. Nor can the next-of-kin, as they do not own the body. The idea of Judeo-Christian charity as it pertains to organ donation does not exist in Japan. Add to that a national mistrust of the medical profession, and you have a barricade to heart transplantation that shows little sign of being lifted. Besides, Japan is a society that requires consensus; everyone must be in agreement in matters that touch the fabric of life. The nail that sticks out must be hammered down.

Baffled and frustrated by the dilemma over the use of organs taken from the brain-dead, Tomio Tada, an eminent immunologist, wrote a Noh play, *The Well of Ignorance*, to ask the donor and recipient of a heart to tell their stories. His intention was to give them voice. As the play opens, a traveling priest comes upon a dried-up well in the midst of a barren moor. The well is a frequently used motif in Noh, symbolizing the source of rejuvenation and fruitfulness. A young woman approaches and tries to draw water. Suddenly a young man appears and tries to keep her from doing so. There is a brief struggle, after which these two figures withdraw. The priest seeks out a villager, who tells him the story of a rich man's daughter

with a failing heart. It was decided that she could be saved only by
a heart transplantation. It happened that there was a shipwreck after
which a sailor, all but drowned, was washed up on shore. At the
instigation of the girl's father, the doctors took the still-beating heart
of the "brain-dead" sailor and placed it in the girl's body. The operation was declared a success. The villager further tells of the young
woman's guilt when she learned that a "living" man had been sacri-
ficed for her sake. Her suffering was compounded when the well,
cursed by the spirit of the young man, went dry.

In Act II, the ghost of the sailor returns to bemoan his unhappy
fate. He relives the horror of the operation:

> *The doctors talk among themselves.*
> *A blade cold as ice.*
> *They rattle their metal scissors.*
> *They split open my chest.*
> *They take out my heart.*
> *How horrible! I hear their voices*
> *But my body is bound.*
> *I try to scream . . .*
> *If only a voice would emerge . . .*
>
> *Am I living or am I dead?*

At the end of the play, both characters plead for relief of their endless
suffering. The real struggle depicted in *The Well of Ignorance* is not
between the unfortunate sailor and the sick girl. It is between the
two of them on one side and the surgeon and the girl's father, who
remain offstage. The purpose of the play, then, is to let the dead
speak, and to ask the audience to dwell upon the justice or injustice
of heart transplantation. While the physician/playwright does not
openly condemn the practice, it is clear that he has misgivings. The
playwright's own scientific research has to do with overcoming the
natural rejection of foreign tissue by the "host." He, of all scientists,

should be ardent in his support of cardiac transplantation. But doubt has made this doctor "infirm of purpose." He has come to question the monopoly on decisions regarding brain death claimed as their right by the medical profession.

Look at a person in the state of brain death. His skin is warm to the touch; it is of good color. His lungs fill and empty; he is excreting urine. Should the room be too warm, he will perspire. If it is a woman, and she is pregnant, her fetus will continue to grow and develop until it might be delivered alive. If the brain-dead is a male, his sperm could be retrieved; he could father a child.

Now think of the harvester, the one who must take up a scalpel and lay open the body of a fellow human being, not for the sake of that person but as a means to an end. Even the most sophisticated surgeon must at first have had misgivings. I know, for once I harvested such organs. It was the only time that I used a knife upon another person for a reason other than to do him good. That is a line that the harvester must cross. To do so is to take a giant step away from the doctor/patient relationship of tradition. To do so is to remove yourself from the concept that every life is inherently valuable, that even the last few days of a life are as precious as any of the rest of it. If you believe that the body is sacred, then you cannot see it as a container of organs to be recycled.

Think of it! To reach in and pluck out the beating heart from a still-warm body, and to set it like a jewel of great price into the chest of another whose heart only moments ago was seen to be writhing ineffectually. It is thrilling! But does such an act lie within the precincts of civilized behavior?

What is life? What is death? If you cut out the heart of a dogfish and drop it into a beaker of warm saline, the heart will continue to beat for up to eight hours. Is that life? Or is it merely "technical life" or "virtual death"? Not long ago, some fossilized lotus seeds known to be two thousand years old were dug from a bog in Manchuria. A botanist chipped away the rocklike outer shell, incubated the seeds in damp cotton wadding. In time, delicate green shoots appeared. He set them out upon a lake. Behold! The lotus bloomed. Time was when one could say with King Lear as he cradled the body of Cordelia: "I know when one is living and when one is not." With the advent of medical technology, that distinction has become blurred. But death and brain death are not the same. In brain death the patient is mortally wounded but not yet dead. All you can say is that he will be dead. In harvesting his heart, you are removing a vital organ from a person who needs it to live out the rest of his life.

In recent years, scientists have retrieved certain neurons from the lining of the cerebral ventricles and grown them in tissue culture. These proliferated neurons show evidence of normal functioning potential. Will the time come when such cells can be infused into the injured brain of one in the state presently called brain death such that the person will no longer fit that diagnosis and prognosis? Will the time come when small implantable mechanical organs—heart, lungs, liver, kidney—will have been perfected, making the harvesting of organs obsolete?

Science speaks from the mountaintop with a deep masculine gravity. Science knows better than the rest of us. It's in the very word—"science," from the Latin *scire*, to know. But Science is not the true faith, and it must not be worshiped. Nor ought its feats to be dressed in gentle words so as slyly to mislead. "Harvest," "transplantation"—these are the soft words of husbandry and the soil, suggesting fecundity, fruition, renewal. The more precise word for what is done to the brain-dead is "evisceration" or "dismemberment." The synonym for "harvest" is "reap." But we do not refer to the taker of the organs as the "reaper," with the grim baggage of that term. Thus does language conspire to give organ transplantation a benevolent face. Nor is "donor" the right designation. In most instances, he has not given his organs; they have been taken with the consent of the next-of-kin. They don't own the brain-dead body in the sense that they can do with it whatever they wish—leave it unburied in the backyard, say, to be eaten by crows. There are some who believe it belongs only to God.

—ᴍ—

I don't pretend to know what is right and what is wrong. Often what looks like bad behavior has good results. It seems ungrateful and miserly to carp at the advances of technology that have made organ transplantation possible. The benefits of harvesting the organs of the brain-dead scarcely need iteration: relief of suffering, prolongation of life—these are the *raisons d'être* of medicine itself. Then why do I "hesitate"? It is that society is based on a belief in the self. Selfhood is what enables us to carry on our mental and physical commerce with each other. There is the self, and there is everyone else. Who is speaking? It is I. There is me, and there is the rest of my tribe. There is me, and there is the one I love. There is me, and there is God. In the literal, objective sense, the recipient of an organ is not the same as he was, not the same person. Part of him will have different genes, altered protein and other biochemical signatures. If it were not a heart but a testicle that is transplanted, he might father children who look like the original owner of that organ, not himself. And who can say that one day it will not be the brain that is transplanted? If, along with Descartes, you believe that the brain is where the person is, it would not be a brain transplant at all, but a body transplant. The person saved would be the donor, not the recipient. What with organ transplantation from other species, gene replication, cloning, the implantation of foreign tissue, to say nothing of sex-change surgery, the dazzled layman might wonder whether the function of Science is to distance mankind from its originality. Surely, there is a limit to personhood. Each of us is a single physical human being, uniquely so. If that is no longer true, what are we?

But what of the patient with a failing heart who lies in bed clinging to life while awaiting a suitable heart? Is it not without some guilt that he hopes there will be an automobile accident, or a shooting? After all, he is a decent human being. He expresses this to his doctor. The doctor hastens to assuage his guilt.

"It's a normal human reaction. Don't feel guilty. You just want to live. Nothing wrong with that."

Unlike the woman in the play, the recipient of an organ has no feeling of guilt that another had to die. By and large, he doesn't want to know who the donor was. Anonymity makes it easier. The recipient has enough to think about without becoming chummy with the donor family.

Once upon a time, there were three gods who were also brothers: Zeus, Poseidon, and Hades. The time had come to divide up the universe. Zeus chose to reign on Olympus, the home of the gods. Poseidon chose the kingdom beneath the sea. Hades took the underworld, that shadowy inn of numberless rooms to which all are welcomed. It was inherent in the nature of these three kingdoms that they be utterly distinct from one another, as though the separation had been made with two swipes of a giant blade. For any one of them to leave the earth and visit any one of the kingdoms would be unthinkable. But now what was this! One day, Zeus looked down to see his brother Hades coming to meet him for the first time on Olympus. Zeus knew that Hades wanted something. But what? He wanted a woman to share his throne. Not just any woman, but Persephone, the daughter of Zeus. Zeus could hardly protest. Hadn't he and Poseidon abducted earthly women again and again? Hadn't Zeus been known to meddle with the dead? It was inevitable that one day Hades would insist upon taking a living creature for himself. The "gift," he argued, would make the bond between the brothers much stronger.

It was a momentous decision, pregnant with consequence. For it ushered in a time of imbalance in Hell and on Earth. Hades had laid claim to something other than what existed in his dark and silent world. It was the earthly flower Persephone that he plucked and abducted. Or should I say harvested and transplanted? With her arrival in Hell, the marvelous was made real. Hades' kidnapping of a living woman upset the simple world order that had hitherto prevailed.

The living recipient's request that a part be handed back from the dead constitutes a kind of metamorphosis, or something veering close to it. Not only the life of the recipient, but the death of the donor has undergone transformation. There is confusion in the spirit world, a crisis of identity. In the case of Persephone, a live woman has entered the palace of death. In the case of heart transplantation, live tissue is handed back to remain on earth long after the rest of the donor has entered Hades.

It was in the nineteenth century that childbirth became "medicalized" and doctors took over the delivery room. Only lately, with the reappearance of the midwife, has that absurdity been partially dismantled. Uncomplicated childbirth is a normal process, and does not need, nor should it welcome, the presence of a doctor in the room. Now it appears that death too has been medicalized, that no one is permitted to die without the intervention of a physician. Doubtless the engine that drove society to this irrational pass is the denial of death that afflicts much of the human race. We cannot bear the thought of dying, and so devise newer and more ingenious ways of prolonging life. It is to be expected that a good part of the "heroic" attempt to stave off death is fueled as much by the pride of the physicians who do this work as by the benevolent wish to help the dying. What begins in sympathy can become prideful tinkering with the lives of others. "We must beware the danger which lies in our most generous wishes," wrote Lionel Trilling. What starts out as a lovely waltz may end in a lapse of virtue. History has shown that once you make human beings the object of your interest, you make of them objects for your pity, then of your wisdom, and ultimately of your coercion. Is this what has happened in the harvesting of the brain-dead? In persuading the next of kin to donate organs, the doctor is soothing. "That way, he will not really have died, but will live on." What the doctor does not say is that in time, the recipient, the next of kin, and the doctor himself will join the donor in death. "Live on"? There are other ways to live on than as a number of separate functioning organs. Parents live on in the genetic makeup of their children, as in their love; teachers in the minds of their students; artists in their works; scientists in their discoveries.

In the matter of religious faith, there are those who believe that on the Day of Resurrection, one's flesh, this very flesh, *ipso corpore*, will rise intact and one will *be* once again. So it is told in more than one place in the New Testament. If that is so, who, then, gets the heart on that Day? Donor or recipient? Nor are the next of kin permitted the hope of a miracle to return the loved one from the state of brain death. The physician, thank you, will perform his own miracle. Is our age then to be one in which the possibility of divine intervention is foreclosed?

Science will not love to ponder these questions, and surely my fellow surgeons will take umbrage. They have no need. These are contemptible pebbles I throw at Authority. I don't pretend to have David's arm or his aim with a slingshot. I come to praise Science, not to challenge it. Who am I to say what is good and what is evil? Sometimes, what seemed evil at first has good results, and what appeared to be for the good has turned out to be wickedness. One can, unbeknownst, perpetrate an evil deed. But I assure you that the men and women who do this work are honorable men and women. So are they all, all honorable men and women. Friends! Americans! Countrymen! Perhaps I have o'ershot myself to speak of it. I have no wish to set mischief in motion. Don't take me wrong. If I were disposed to stir your hearts and minds to horror at the harvesting of the brain-dead, I should do Science wrong and Technology wrong. I speak only lest it be said of us one day that we who removed the heart from one and placed it in another were barbarians. O Judgment!—I can hear them now—thou wert fled to brutish beasts and men had lost their reason.

If my hesitation is without substance, why then not to worry. A fresh gust of progress will soon blow it away. But if there is a kernel of reason herein, posterity will utter it again, and in a far more compelling way than I have. Our descendants will then learn that the late twentieth century was a time when all restraint was dropped, and human ingenuity given its head to do whatever it could and wanted to, like a brilliant spoiled child.

A Mask on
the Face of Death

—∞—

It is ten o'clock at night as we drive up to the Copacabana, a dilap-
idated brothel on the rue Dessalines in the red-light district of Port-
au-Prince. My guide is a young Haitian, Jean-Bernard. Ten years
before, J-B tells me, at the age of fourteen, "like every good Haitian
boy," he had been brought here by his older cousins for his *rite de
passage*. From the car to the entrance, we are accosted by a half-
dozen men and women for sex. We enter, go down a long hall that
breaks upon a cavernous room with a stone floor. The cubicles of
the prostitutes, I am told, are in an attached wing of the building.
Save for a red-purple glow from small lights on the walls, the place
is unlit. Dark shapes float by, each with a blindingly white stripe of
teeth. Latin music is blaring. We take seats at the table farthest from
the door. Just outside, there is the rhythmic lapping of the Caribbean
Sea. About twenty men are seated at the tables or lean against the
walls. Brightly dressed women, singly or in twos or threes, stroll
about, now and then exchanging banter with the men. It is as though
we have been deposited in Act II of Bizet's *Carmen*. If this place isn't
Lillas Pastia's tavern, what is it?

Within minutes, three light-skinned young women arrive at our
table. They are very beautiful and young and lively. Let them be
Carmen, Mercedes, and Frasquita.

"I want the old one," says Frasquita, ruffling my hair. The women
laugh uproariously.

"Don't bother looking any further," says Mercedes. "We are the prettiest ones."

"We only want to talk," I tell her.

"Aaah, aaah," she crows. "*Massissi*. You are *massissi*." It is the contemptuous Creole term for homosexual. If we want only to talk, we must be gay. Mercedes and Carmen are slender, each weighing one hundred pounds or less. Frasquita is tall and hefty. They are dressed for work: red taffeta, purple chiffon, and black sequins. Among them a thousand gold bracelets and earrings multiply every speck of light. Their bare shoulders are like animated lamps gleaming in the shadowy room. Since there is as yet no business, the women agree to sit with us. J-B orders beer and cigarettes. We pay each woman ten dollars.

"Where are you from?" I begin.

"We are Dominican."

"Do you miss your country?"

"Oh, yes, we do." Six eyes go muzzy with longing. "Our country is the most beautiful in the world. No country is like the Dominican. And it doesn't stink like this one."

"Then why don't you work there? Why come to Haiti?"

"Santo Domingo has too many whores. All beautiful, like us. All light-skinned. The Haitian men like to sleep with light women."

"Why is that?"

"Because always the whites have all the power and the money. The black men can imagine they do, too, when they have us in bed."

Eleven o'clock. I look around the room that is still sparsely peopled with men.

"It isn't getting any busier," I say. Frasquita glances over her shoulder. Her eyes drill the darkness.

"It is still early," she says.

"Could it be that the men are afraid of getting sick?"

Frasquita is offended. "Sick! They do not get sick from us. We are healthy, strong. Every week we go for a checkup. Besides, we know how to tell if we are getting sick."

"I mean sick with AIDS." The word sets off a hurricane of taffeta, chiffon, and gold jewelry. They are all gesticulation and fury. It is Carmen who speaks.

"AIDS!" Her lips curl about the syllable. "There is no such thing. It is a false disease invented by the American government to take advantage of the poor countries. The American President hates poor people, so now he makes up AIDS to take away the little we have." The others nod vehemently.

"*Mira, mon cher.* Look, my dear," Carmen continues. "One day the police came here. Believe me, they are worse than the *tonton macoutes* with their submachine guns. They rounded up one hundred and five of us and they took our blood. That was a year ago. None of us have died, you see? We are all still here. *Mira,* we sleep with all the men and we are not sick."

"But aren't there some of you who have lost weight and have diarrhea?"

"One or two, maybe. But they don't eat. That is why they are weak."

"Only the men die," says Mercedes. "They stop eating, so they die. It is hard to kill a woman."

"Do you eat well?"

"Oh, yes, don't worry, we do. We eat like poor people, but we eat." There is a sudden scream from Frasquita. She points to a large rat that has emerged from beneath our table.

"My God!" she exclaims. "It is big like a pig." They burst into laughter. For a moment the women fall silent. There is only the restlessness of their many bracelets. I give them each another ten dollars.

"Are many of the men here bisexual?"

"Too many. They do it for money. Afterward, they come to us." Carmen lights a cigarette and looks down at the small lace handkerchief she has been folding and unfolding with immense precision on the table. All at once she turns it over as though it were the ace of spades.

"*Mira, blanc* . . . look, white man," she says in a voice suddenly full of foreboding. Her skin too seems to darken to coincide with the tone of her voice.

"*Mira*, soon many Dominican women will die in Haiti!"

"Die of what?"

She shrugs. "It is what they do to us."

"Carmen," I say, "if you knew that you had AIDS, that your blood was bad, would you still sleep with men?"

Abruptly, she throws back her head and laughs. It is the same laughter with which Frasquita had greeted the rat at our feet. She stands and the others follow.

"*Méchant!* You wicked man," she says. Then, with terrible solemnity, "You don't know anything."

"But you are killing the Haitian men," I say.

"As for that," she says, "everyone is killing everyone else." All at once, I want to know everything about these three—their childhood, their dreams, what they do in the afternoon, what they eat for lunch.

"Don't leave," I say. "Stay a little more." Again I reach for my wallet. But they are gone, taking all the light in the room with them—Mercedes and Carmen to sit at another table where three men have been waiting. Frasquita is strolling about the room. Now and then, as if captured by the music, she breaks into a few dance steps, snapping her fingers, singing to herself.

Midnight. And the Copacabana is filling up. Now it is like any other seedy nightclub where men and women go hunting. We get up to leave. In the center a couple are dancing a *méringue*. He is the most graceful dancer I have ever watched; she, the most voluptuous. Together they seem to be riding the back of the music as it gallops to an unmistakably sexual beat. Closer up, I see that the man is short of breath, sweating. All at once, he collapses into a chair. The woman bends over him, coaxing, teasing, but he is through. A young man with a long polished stick blocks my way.

"I come with you?" he asks. "Very good time. You say yes? Ten dollars? Five?"

I have been invited by Dr. Jean William Pape to attend the AIDS clinic of which he is the director. Nothing from the outside of the low whitewashed structure would suggest it is a medical facility. Inside, it is divided into many small cubicles and a labyrinth of corridors. At nine in the morning the hallways are already full of emaciated silent men and women, some sitting on the few benches, the rest leaning against the walls. The only sounds are subdued moans of discomfort interspersed with coughs. How they swallow us with their eyes as we pass.

The room where Pape and I work is perhaps ten feet by ten. It contains a desk, two chairs, and a narrow wooden table that is covered with a sheet that will not be changed during the day.

The patients are called in one at a time, asked how they feel and whether there is any change in their symptoms, then examined on the table. If the patient is new to the clinic, he or she is questioned about sexual activities.

A twenty-seven-year-old man whose given name is Miracle enters. He is wobbly, panting, like a groggy boxer who has let down his arms and is waiting for the last punch. He is neatly dressed and wears, despite the heat, a heavy woolen cap. When he removes it, I see that his hair is thin, dull reddish, and straight. It is one of the signs of AIDS in Haiti, Pape tells me.

The man's skin is covered with a dry itchy rash. Throughout the interview and examination he scratches himself slowly, absentmindedly. The rash is called prurigo. It is another symptom of AIDS in Haiti. This man has had diarrhea for six months. The laboratory reports that the diarrhea is due to an organism called cryptosporidium, for which there is no treatment. The telltale rattling of the tuberculous moisture in his chest is audible without a stethoscope. He is like a leaky cistern that bubbles and froths. And, clearly, he is exhausted.

"Where do you live?" I ask.

"Kenscoff." A village in the hills above Port-au-Prince.

"How did you come here today?"

"I came on the tap-tap." It is the name given to the small buses that swarm the city, each one extravagantly decorated with religious slogans, icons, flowers, animals, all painted in psychedelic colors. I have never seen a tap-tap that was not covered with passengers as well, riding outside and hanging on. The vehicles themselves are little masterpieces of contagion, if not of AIDS then of the multitude of germs which Haitian flesh is heir to. Miracle is given a prescription for a supply of Sera, which is something like Gatorade, and told to return in a month.

"*Mangé kou bêf,*" says the doctor in farewell. "Eat like an ox." What can he mean? The man has no food or money to buy any. Even had he food, he has not the appetite to eat or the ability to retain it. To each departing patient the doctor will say the same words— "*Mangé kou bêf.*" I see that it is his way of offering a hopeful goodbye.

"Will he live until his next appointment?" I ask.

"No." Miracle leaves to catch the tap-tap for Kenscoff.

Next is a woman of twenty-six who enters holding her right hand to her forehead in a kind of permanent salute. In fact, she is shielding her eye from view. This is her third visit to the clinic. I see that she is still quite well nourished.

"Now, you'll see something beautiful, tremendous," the doctor says. Once seated upon the table, she is told to lower her hand. When she does, I see that her right eye and its eyelid are replaced by a huge fungating ulcerated tumor, a side product of her AIDS. As she turns her head, the cluster of lymph glands in her neck to which the tumor has spread is thrown into relief. Two years ago she received a blood transfusion at a time when the country's main blood bank was grossly contaminated with AIDS. It has since been closed down. The only blood available in Haiti is a small supply procured from the Red Cross.

"Can you give me medicine?" the woman wails.

"No."

"Can you cut it away?"

"No."

"Is there radiation therapy?" I ask.

"No."

"Chemotherapy?" The doctor looks at me in what some might call weary amusement. I see that there is nothing to do. She has come here because there is nowhere else to go.

"What will she do?"

"Tomorrow or the next day or the day after that she will climb up into the mountains to seek relief from the *houngan,* the voodoo priest, just as her slave ancestors did two hundred years ago."

Then comes a frail man in his thirties, with a strangely spiritualized face, like a child's. Pus runs from one ear onto his cheek, where it has dried and caked. He has trouble remembering, he tells us. In fact, he seems confused. It is from toxoplasmosis of the brain, an effect of his AIDS. This man is bisexual. Two years ago he engaged in oral sex with foreign men for money. As I palpate the swollen glands of his neck, a mosquito flies between our faces. I swat at it, miss. Just before coming to Haiti I read that the AIDS virus has been isolated from a certain mosquito. The doctor senses my thought.

"Not to worry," he says. "So far as we know there has never been a case transmitted by insects."

"Yes," I say. "I see."

And so it goes until the last, the thirty-sixth, AIDS patient has been seen. At the end of the day I am invited to wash my hands before leaving. I go down a long hall to a sink. I turn on the faucets but there is no water.

"But what about you?" I ask the doctor. "You are at great personal risk here—the tuberculosis, the other infections, no water to wash . . ." He shrugs, smiles faintly, and lifts his hands palm upward.

We are driving up a winding steep road into the barren mountains above Port-au-Prince. Even in the bright sunlight the countryside has the bloodless color of exhaustion and indifference. Our destination is the Baptist Mission Hospital, where many cases of AIDS have been reported. Along the road there are slow straggles of schoolchildren in blue uniforms who stretch out their hands as we pass and call out, "Give me something." Already a crowd of outpatients has gathered at the entrance to the mission compound. A tour of the premises reveals that in contrast to the aridity outside the gates, this is an enclave of productivity, lush with fruit trees and poinsettia.

The hospital is clean and smells of creosote. Of the forty beds, fewer than a third are occupied. In one male ward of twelve beds, there are two patients. The chief physician tells us that last year he saw ten cases of AIDS each week. Lately the number has decreased to four or five.

"Why is that?" we want to know.

"Because we do not admit them to the hospital, so they have learned not to come here."

"Why don't you admit them?"

"Because we would have nothing but AIDS here then. So we send them away."

"But I see that you have very few patients in bed."

"That is also true."

"Where do the AIDS patients go?"

"Some go to the clinic in Port-au-Prince or the general hospital in the city. Others go home to die or to the voodoo priest."

"Do the people with AIDS know what they have before they come here?"

"Oh, yes, they know very well, and they know there is nothing to be done for them."

Outside, the crowd of people is dispersing toward the gate. The clinic has been canceled for the day. No one knows why. We are conducted to the office of the reigning American pastor. He is a tall, handsome Midwesterner with an ecclesiastical smile.

"It is voodoo that is the devil here." He warms to his subject. "It is a demonic religion, a cancer on Haiti. Voodoo is worse than AIDS. And it is one of the reasons for the epidemic. Did you know that in order for a man to become a voodoo priest he must perform anal sodomy on another man? No, of course you didn't. And it doesn't stop there. These *houngans* tell the men that in order to appease the spirits they too must do the same thing. So you have ritualized homosexuality. That's what is spreading the AIDS." The pastor tells us of a nun who witnessed two acts of sodomy in a provincial hospital; she came upon a man sexually assaulting a houseboy and another man mounting a male patient in his bed.

"Fornication," he says. "It is Sodom and Gomorrah all over again, so what can you expect from these people?" Outside his office we are shown a cage of terrified, cowering monkeys, to whom he coos affectionately. It is clear that he loves them. At the car, we shake hands.

"By the way," the pastor says, "what is your religion? Perhaps I am a kinsman?"

"While I am in Haiti," I tell him, "it will be voodoo or it will be nothing at all."

Abruptly, the smile breaks. It is as though a crack had suddenly appeared in the face of an idol.

From the mission we go to the general hospital. In the heart of Port-au-Prince, it is the exact antithesis of the immaculate facility we have just left—filthy, crowded, hectic, and staffed entirely by young interns and residents. Though it is associated with a medical school, I do not see any members of the faculty. We are shown around by Jocelyne, a young intern in a scrub suit. Each bed in three large wards is occupied. On the floor about the beds, hunkered in the posture of the innocent poor, are family members of the patients. In the corridor that constitutes the emergency room, someone lies on a stretcher receiving an intravenous infusion. She is hardly more than a cadaver.

"Where are the doctors in charge?" I ask Jocelyne.

She looks at me questioningly. "We are in charge."

"I mean your teachers, the faculty."

"They do not come here."

"What is wrong with that woman?"

"She has had diarrhea for three months. Now she is dehydrated." I ask the woman to open her mouth. Her throat is covered with the white plaques of thrush, a fungus infection associated with AIDS.

"How many AIDS patients do you see here?"

"Three or four a day. We send them home. Sometimes the families abandon them, then we must admit them to the hospital. Every day, then, a relative comes to see if the patient has died. They want to take the body. That is important to them. But they know very well that AIDS is contagious and they are afraid to keep them at home. Even so, once or twice a week the truck comes to take away the bodies. Many are children. They are buried in mass graves."

"Where do the wealthy patients go?"

"There is a private hospital called Canapé Vert. Or else they go to Miami. Most of them, rich and poor, do not go to the hospital. Most are never diagnosed."

"How do you know these people have AIDS?"

"We don't know sometimes. The blood test is inaccurate. There are many false positives and false negatives. Fifteen percent of those with the disease have negative blood tests. We go by their infections—tuberculosis, diarrhea, fungi, herpes, skin rashes. It is not hard to tell."

"Do they know what they have?"

"Yes. They understand at once and they are prepared to die."

"Do the patients know how AIDS is transmitted?"

"They know, but they do not like to talk about it. It is taboo. Their memories do not seem to reach back to the true origins of their disaster. It is understandable, is it not?"

"Whatever you write, don't hurt us any more than we have already been hurt." It is a young Haitian journalist with whom I am drinking a rum punch. He means that any further linkage of AIDS and Haiti in the media would complete the economic destruction of the country. The damage was done early in the epidemic when the Centers for Disease Control in Atlanta added Haitians to the three other high-risk groups—hemophiliacs, intravenous drug users, and homosexual and bisexual men. In fact, Haitians are no more susceptible to AIDS than anyone else. Although the CDC removed Haitians from special scrutiny in 1985, the lucrative tourism on which so much of the country's economy was based was crippled. Along with tourism went much of the foreign business investment. Worst of all was the injury to the national pride. Suddenly Haiti was indicted as the source of AIDS in the western hemisphere.

What caused the misunderstanding was the discovery of a large number of Haitian men living in Miami with AIDS antibodies in their blood. They denied absolutely they were homosexuals. But the CDC investigators did not know that homosexuality is the strongest taboo in Haiti and that no man would ever admit to it. Bisexuality, however, is not uncommon. Many married men and heterosexually oriented males will occasionally seek out other men for sex. Further, many, if not most, Haitian men visit female prostitutes from time to time. It is not difficult to see that once the virus was set loose in Haiti, the spread would be swift through both genders.

Exactly how the virus of AIDS arrived is not known. Could it have been brought home by the Cuban soldiers stationed in Angola and thence to Haiti, about fifty miles away? Could it have been passed on by the thousands of Haitians living in exile in Zaire, who later returned home or immigrated to the United States? Could it have come from the American and Canadian homosexual tourists, and, yes, even some U.S. diplomats who have traveled to the island to have sex with impoverished Haitian men all too willing to sell themselves to feed their families? Throughout the international gay community, Haiti was known as a good place to go for sex.

On a private tip from an official at the Ministry of Tourism, J-B and I drive to a town some fifty miles from Port-au-Prince. The hotel is owned by two Frenchmen who are out of the country, one of the staff tells us. He is a man of about thirty, and clearly he is desperately ill. Tottering, short of breath, he shows us about the empty hotel. The furnishings are opulent and extreme—tiger skins on the wall, a live leopard in the garden, a bedroom containing a giant bathtub with gold faucets. We are followed by two small boys. Is it the heat of the day or the heat of my imagination that makes these walls echo with the painful cries of pederasty?

The hotel where we are staying is in Pétionville, the fashionable suburb of Port-au-Prince. It is the height of the season, but there are no tourists, only a dozen or so French and American businessmen. The swimming pool is used once or twice a day by a single person. Otherwise the water remains undisturbed until dusk, when the fruit bats come down to drink in midswoop. The hotel keeper is an American. He is eager to set me straight on Haiti.

"What did and should attract foreign investment is a combination of reliable weather, an honest and friendly populace, low wages, and multilingual managers."

"What spoiled it?"

"Political instability and a bad American press about AIDS." He pauses, then adds: "To which I hope you won't be contributing."

"What about just telling the truth?" I suggest.

"Look," he says, "there is no more danger of catching AIDS in Haiti than in New York or Santo Domingo. It is not what you are but what you do that counts." Agreeing, I ask if he had any idea that much of the tourism in Haiti during the past few decades was based on sex.

"No idea whatsoever. It was only recently that we discovered that that was the case."

"How is it that you hoteliers, restaurant owners, and the Ministry of Tourism did not know what *tout* Haiti knew?"

"Look. All I know is that this is a middle-class, family-oriented hotel. We don't allow guests to bring women, or for that matter men, into their rooms. If they did, we'd ask them to leave immediately."

At 5 A.M. the next day the telephone rings in my room. A Creole-accented male voice.

"Is the lady still with you, sir?"

"There is no lady here."

"In your room, sir, the lady I allowed to go up with a package?"

"There is no lady here, I tell you."

At 7 A.M. I stop at the front desk. The clerk is a young man.

"Was it you who called my room at five o'clock?"

"Sorry," he says with a smile. "It was a mistake, sir. I meant to ring the room next door to yours." Still smiling, he holds up his shushing finger.

This evening I leave Haiti. For two weeks I have fastened myself to this lovely fragile land like an ear pressed to the ground. It is a country to break a traveler's heart. It occurs to me that I have not seen a single jogger. Such public expenditure of energy while everywhere else strength is ebbing—it would be obscene. In my final hours, I go to the Cathédral of Sainte Trinité, the inner walls of which are covered with murals by Haiti's most renowned artists. Here are all the familiar Bible stories depicted in naiveté and piety, and all in such an exuberance of color as to tax the capacity of the retina to receive it, as though all the vitality of Haiti had been turned to paint and brushed upon these walls. How to explain its efflorescence at a time when all else is lassitude and inertia? Perhaps one day the plague will be rendered in poetry, music, painting, but not now. Not now.

A Question of Mercy

—⧃—

Almost two years ago, I received a phone call from a poet I knew slightly. Would I, he wondered, be willing to intervene on behalf of a friend of his who was dying of AIDS?

"Intervene?"

"His suffering is worthy of Job. He wants to commit suicide while he still has the strength to do it."

"Do you know what you're asking?"

"I know, I know."

"No," I told him. "I'm trained to preserve life, not end it. It's not in me to do a thing like that."

"Are you saying that a doctor should prolong a misfortune as long as possible?"

"There is society," I replied. "There is the law. I'm not a barbarian."

"You are precisely that," he said. "A barbarian."

His accusation reminded me of an incident in the life of Ambroise Paré, the father of surgery, who in the sixteenth century accompanied the armies of France on their campaigns. Once, on entering a newly captured city, Paré looked for a barn in which to keep his horse while he treated the wounded. Inside he found four dead soldiers and three more still alive, their faces contorted with pain, their clothes still smoldering where the gunpowder had burned them.

As Paré gazed at the wounded with pity, an old soldier came up and asked whether there was any way to cure them. Paré shook his head, whereupon the old soldier went up to the men and, Paré recounted in his memoirs, cut their throats "gently, efficiently and without ill will." Horrified at what he thought a great cruelty, Paré cried out to the executioner that he was a villain.

"No," said the man. "I pray God that if ever I come to be in that condition, someone will do the same for me." Was this an act of villainy, or mercy?

The question still resists answering. Not so long ago, a Michigan court heard the case of a doctor who supplied a woman with his "suicide machine"—a simple apparatus that allows a patient to self-administer a lethal dose of drugs intravenously. Since then, it seems that each day brings reports of deaths assisted by doctors. A best-selling book, *Final Exit,* written by the director of the Hemlock Society, now instructs us in painless ways how to commit suicide should the dreadful occasion arise. Even the most ideologically opposed must now hear the outcry of a populace for whom the dignity and mercy of a quick pharmacological death may be preferable to a protracted, messy, and painful end.

"But why are you calling *me*?" I asked my friend.

"I've read your books. It occurred to me that you might just be the right one."

I let the poet know that I had retired from medicine five years before, that I was no longer a doctor.

"Once a doctor, always a doctor," he replied.

What I did not tell him was that each year I have continued to renew the license that allows me to prescribe narcotics. You never know. . . . Someday I might have need of them to relieve pain or to kill myself easily should the occasion arise. If for myself, then why not for another?

"I'll think about it," I said. He gave me the address and phone number.

"I implore you," said the poet.

The conversation shifted to the abominable gymnastics of writing, a little gossip. We hung up.

Don't! I told myself.

~ DIARY. JANUARY 14, 1990

My friend's friend lives with a companion on the seventh floor of an apartment building about a ten-minute walk from my house. The doorman on duty is a former patient of mine. He greets me warmly, lifts his shirt to show me his gallbladder incision, how well it has healed.

"You can hardly see it," he says. That is the sort of thing that happens when I leave my study and reenter the world. The doorman buzzes me in.

At precisely 4 P.M., as arranged, I knocked on the apartment door. It is opened by Lionel, a handsome, perhaps too handsome, man in his late thirties. We recognize each other as presences on the Yale campus. He is an ordained minister. He tells me that he has made use of my writings in his sermons. In the living room, Ramon is sitting on an invalid's cushion on the sofa. A short, delicate man, also in his thirties, Ramon is a doctor specializing in public health— women's problems, birth control, family planning, AIDS. He is surprisingly unwasted, although pale as a blank sheet of paper. He gives me a brilliant smile around even white teeth. The eyes do not participate in the smile. Lionel and Ramon have been lovers for six years.

Ramon's hair is close-cropped, black; there is a neat lawn of beard. He makes a gesture as if to stand, but I stop him. His handshake is warm and dry and strong. There is a plate of chocolate chip cookies on a table. Lionel pours tea. Lionel's speech is clipped, slightly mannered. Ramon has a Hispanic accent; he is Colombian.

For a few minutes we step warily around the reason I have come. Then, all at once, we are engaged. I ask Ramon about his symptoms. He tells me of his profound fatigue, the depression, the intractable diarrhea, his ulcerated hemorrhoids. He has Kaposi's sarcoma. Only yesterday a new lesion appeared in the left naso-orbital region, the area between the nose and eye. He points to it. Through his beard I see another large black tumor. His mouth is dry, encrusted from the dehydration that comes with chronic diarrhea. Now and then he clutches his abdomen, grimaces. There is the odor of stool.

"I want to die," he announces calmly.

"Is it so bad?"

"Yes, it is."

"But how can I be sure? On Tuesday, you want to die, by Thursday, perhaps you will have changed your mind."

He nods to Lionel, who helps him to stand. The three of us go into their bedroom, where Ramon, lying on his side, offers his lesions as evidence. I see that his anus is a great circular ulceration, raw and oozing blood. His buttocks are smeared with pus and liquid stool. With tenderness, Lionel bathes and dresses him in a fresh diaper. Even though I have been summoned here, I feel very much the intruder upon their privacy. And I am convinced.

We return to the living room. Lionel and Ramon sit side by side on the sofa, holding hands. A lethal dose of barbiturates is being mailed by a doctor friend in Colombia. Ramon wants to be certain that it will not fail, that someone will be on hand to administer a final, fatal dose if he should turn out to be physically too weak to take the required number of pills. He also wants Lionel to be with him, holding him. He asks that Lionel not cry. He couldn't bear that, he says. Lionel says that of course he will cry, that he must be allowed to. Lionel is afraid, too, that it might not work, that he will be discovered as an accomplice.

"I am the sole beneficiary of the will," he explains. Lionel does not want to be alone when the time comes. He has never seen anyone die before. (A minister? Has he never attended a deathbed?) "It has just worked out that way," he says, as though reading my mind. Still, I am shocked at such a state of virginity.

We have a discussion. It is about death as best friend, not enemy. How sensible were the pagans, for whom death was a return to the spirit world that resides in nature. One member of the tribe vanishes forever, but the tribe itself lives on. It is a far cry from the Christian concept of death and resurrection.

Ramon passes a hand across his eyes as if to brush away a veil. His vision is failing; soon he will be blind. He coughs, shifts on the pillow, swallows a pain pill. He tells me that he has taken all of the

various experimental medicines without relief of the diarrhea. His entire day is spent medicating himself and dealing with the inconti-
nence. Despite chemotherapy, the tumors are growing rapidly. His
palate is covered with them. He opens his mouth for me to see.
Above all, he wants to retain his dignity, to keep control of his life,
which he equates with choosing the time and method of suicide.
Soon he will be unable to do it.

"But death," I say. "It's so final."

"I want it," he says again, on his face a look of longing. He wants
me to promise that I will obtain the additional narcotics that would
ensure death, if needed. I offer only to return in a few days to talk. Ramon urges me to think of myself as an instrument that he himself will
use for his rescue. An instrument? But I am a man.

The tone turns conspiratorial. Our voices drop. We admonish
each other to be secretive, tell no one. There are those who would
leap to punish. I suggest that Ramon arrange for a codicil to his will
requesting that there be no autopsy.

~ JANUARY 16

Four in the afternoon. Ramon answers the door. He has lost ground.
His eyes are sunken, his gait tottering. He is in great pain, which he
makes no effort to conceal. As arranged, he is alone. Lionel is to
return in an hour. The barbiturates have arrived from Colombia. He
shows me the bottles of tablets in the bottom drawer of the dresser.
A quick calculation tells me that he has well over the lethal dose.
The diarrhea has been unrelenting. The Kaposi's sarcoma is fulmi-
nating with new lesions every day.

"I have always counted so much on my looks," he says shyly
and without the least immodesty. "And now I have become something that no one would want to touch." Without a pause, he asks,
"What if I vomit the pills?" I tell him to take them at a regular
pace, each with only a sip of water so as not to fill up too
quickly. If necessary, would I inject more medication? "I have good
veins," he says, and rolls up a sleeve. I see that he does. There are

several needle puncture marks at the antecubital fossa—the front of
the elbow—where blood has been drawn. One more would not be
noticed.

"When?" I ask him. No later than one month from today. Do I
want to choose a date? Ramon rises with difficulty, gets a calendar
from the kitchen. We bend over it.

"Are you free on February 10?" he asks. "It's a Saturday."

"I'm free."

February 10! There is a date!

I ask Ramon about his life. He was born and raised in Medellín,
one of four sisters and three brothers. His mother had no formal
education, but she is "very wise." It is clear that he loves her. No,
she knows nothing; neither that he is gay nor that he is ill. He has
written a letter to be sent after his death, telling her that he loves
her, thanking her for all that she has done. In the family, only an
older brother knows that he is gay, and to him it is a disgrace. He
has forbidden Ramon to tell the others. His sisters live near his
mother in Medellín. There are twelve grandchildren. She will not be
alone. (He smiles at this.)

Had he always known he was gay? He discovered his attraction
to men at age eight, but of course it was impossible to express it.
Colombia is intolerant of homosexuality. At seventeen, he went to
Bogotá to study medicine. For six years he lived in an apartment
with four other students. There was close camaraderie but no sexual
expression. It was a "quiet" student's life. After one year of internship
in a hospital, he decided against clinical medicine.

It was while working toward a degree in public health at Yale
that he met Lionel. The year was 1983. After completing his studies,
he was separated from Lionel for two years, working in another city,
although he returned to visit Lionel frequently. There followed a
three-year period when they lived together in New Haven. Shortly
after they met, Ramon began to feel ill, thought he had an infection.
He suspected it was AIDS. He told Lionel at once and they agreed
to discontinue sex. Aside from mutual caressing, there has been no
sexual contact between them since.

"It was not sex that brought us together," he says. "It was love."
I lower my gaze, I who have always hesitated before expressing love.

Lionel returns. It is the first day of the semester at Yale. A
day of meeting with students, advising, counseling. He is impeccably dressed. He is accompanied by a woman, someone I know
slightly. He notices my surprise.

"This is Melanie," he announces. "She's all right." He places his
arm about her waist, explaining that they have been close friends
and confidants for many years. "She is the sister I have always
wanted." Lionel bends to kiss Ramon on the cheek.

"*Chiquito!* You are wearing your new shirt," says Lionel I am
alarmed by the presence of Melanie It is clear that she knows everything. We sit around the table drinking tea.

"Tell me about death," says Lionel

"What do you mean?"

"The details. You're a doctor, you should know. What about the
death rattle?"

"It has been called that." I explain about not being able to clear
secretions from the lungs.

"What sort of equipment will we need?"

"Nothing. You already have the diapers."

"Ramon has to die in diapers?" I explain about the relaxation of
the bowel and urinary sphincters, that it would be best.

"I shouldn't have asked." Lionel seems increasingly nervous. "I'm
terrified of the police," he says. "I always have been. Should I see a
lawyer? What if I'm caught and put in prison?" He begins to weep
openly. "And I'm losing Ramon. That is a fact, and there is not a
thing I can do about it!" When he continues to cry without covering
his face, Ramon reaches out a hand to console him.

"Look," I say. "You're not ready for this and, to tell the truth,
I'm not sure I am either."

"Oh please!" Ramon's voice is a high-pitched whine of distress.
"It is only a matter of a few minutes of misery. I would be dying
anyway after that."

Lionel pulls himself together, nods to show that he understands.

I begin to feel that my presence is putting pressure on him; it makes Ramon's death real, imminent. I tell him that I am ready to withdraw. How easy that would be. A way out.

"You are the answer to Ramon's prayers," he says. "To him you are an angel." But to Lionel I am the angel of death. "Of course, I agree to whatever Ramon wants to do," he says. It is Ramon who turns practical.

"If it is too hard for you, Lionel, I won't mind if you are not here with me." And to me: "Lionel simply cannot lie. If questioned by the police, he would have to tell the truth." I see that the lying will be up to me. All the while, Melanie has remained silent.

We go through the "script"—Lionel's word. In the bedroom, Ramon will begin taking the pills. I will help him. Lionel and Melanie will wait in the living room.

Lionel: "Will we be in the apartment all the time until he dies?"

Melanie (speaking for the first time): "Not necessary. We can go out somewhere and return to find him dead."

Lionel: "Where would we go?"

Melanie: "Anywhere. For a walk; to the movies."

Lionel: "How long will it take?"

Me: "Perhaps all day."

Lionel: "What if the doctors notify the police? Ramon has made no secret of his intentions at the clinic. They have even withheld pain medication because he is 'high risk.' "

Me (to Ramon): "Next time you go to the clinic, ask for a prescription for fifty Levo-Dromoran tablets. It's a narcotic. Maybe they'll give you that many. Maybe not."

Lionel: "I simply can't believe they would turn us in, but there's no way to be sure, is there?"

More and more we are like criminals, or a cell of revolutionaries. Lionel's fear and guilt are infectious. But then there is Ramon. I stand up to leave, assuring them that I will come again on Sunday at four in the afternoon. Melanie says that she will be there, too. Lionel hopes he has not shaken my resolve. He apologizes for his weakness.

"We'll talk further," I say. Ramon takes my hand. "You have

become my friend. In such a short time. One of the best friends of my life."

In the mail there is a note from Lionel in his small, neat handwriting. He thanks me. Enclosed is a copy of a lecture he gave in 1984 in which he cited an incident from one of my books, about a doctor who, entreated by a suffering patient who wants to die, stays his hand out of mercy. It is strangely prophetic and appropriate to the circumstances.

My nights are ridden with visions: I am in the bedroom with Ramon We are sitting side by side on the bed. He is wearing only a large blue disposable diaper. The bottles of pills are on the nightstand along with a pitcher of water and a glass. Ramon pours a handful of the tiny tablets into his palm, then with a shy smile begins to swallow them one at a time. Because of the dryness of his mouth and the fungal infection of his throat, it is painful. And slow.

"You're drinking too much water," I say. "You'll fill up too quickly."

"I will try," he says. What seems like hours go by. From the living room comes the sound of Mozart's Clarinet Quintet. Ramon labors on, panting, coughing. When he has finished one bottle, I open another. His head and arms begin to wobble. I help him to lie down.

"Quickly," I tell him. "We don't have much time left." I hold the glass for him, guide it to his lips. He coughs, spits out the pills.

"Hold me," he says. I bend above him, cradle his head in my arm.

"Let yourself go," I say. He does, and minutes later he is asleep. I free myself and count the pills that are left, calculate the milligrams. Not enough. It is too far below the lethal dose. I take a vial of morphine and a syringe from my pocket, a rubber tourniquet. I draw up ten cubic centimeters of the fluid and inject it into a vein in Ramon's arm. The respirations slow down at once. I palpate his pulse. It wavers, falters, stops. There is a long last sigh from the pillow.

All at once, a key turns in the door to the hallway. The door is flung open. Two men in fedoras and raincoats enter the bedroom. They are followed by the doorman whose gallbladder I had removed.

"You are under arrest," one of them announces.

"What is the charge?" I ask, clinging to a pretense of innocence.

"For the murder of Ramon C. . . . " I am startled by the mention of his last name. Had I known it? I am led away.

~ JANUARY 21

Melanie, Lionel, Ramon, and I.: Ramon's smile of welcome plays havoc with my heart. It is easy to see why Lionel fell in love with him. I offer an alternative: Ramon could simply stop eating and drinking. It would not take too many days. Neither Lionel nor Ramon can accept this. Lionel cannot watch Ramon die of thirst. There is a new black tumor on Ramon's upper lip. He has visited the clinic and obtained thirty Levo-Dromoran tablets. Suddenly, I feel I must test him again.

Me: "I don't think you're ready. February 10 is too soon."

Ramon (covering his face with his hands, moaning): "Why do you say that?"

Me: "Because you haven't done it already. Because you've chosen a method that is not certain. Because you're worrying about Lionel."

Lionel: "I feel that I'm an obstruction."

Me: "No, but you're unreliable. You cannot tell the lies that may be necessary."

Lionel: "I'm sorry, I'm sorry."

Me: "Don't apologize for virtue. It doesn't make sense."

Ramon: "There is one thing. I prefer to do it at night, after dark. It would be easier for me." That, if nothing else, is comprehensible. Youth bids farewell to the moon more readily than to the sun.

We rehearse the revised plan. Lionel, Melanie, and Ramon will dine together, "love each other," say goodbye. Lionel and Melanie will take the train to New York for the night. At 6 P.M. Ramon will begin to take the pills. At 8:30 I will let myself into the apartment.

The doorman may or may not question me, but I will have a key. I will stay only long enough to be sure that Ramon is dead. If he is not, I will use the morphine; if he is, I will not notify anyone. At noon the next day, Lionel and Melanie will return to discover the body and call the clinic. It is most likely that a doctor will come to pronounce death. Of course, he will ask questions, perhaps notice something, demand an autopsy. In that case, Lionel will show him the codicil to the will. Melanie asks whether the codicil is binding. At the end of the session we are all visibly exhausted.

~ FEBRUARY 3

Our final visit. Ramon is worried that because of the diarrhea he will not absorb the barbiturate. He has seen undigested potassium tablets in his stool. I tell him not to worry; I will make sure. His gratitude is infinitely touching, infinitely sad. We count the pills. There are 110 of them, totaling eleven grams. The lethal dose is 4.5. He also has the remaining Levo-Dromoran tablets. I have already obtained the vial of morphine and the syringe. Ramon is bent, tormented, but smiles when I hug him goodbye.

"I'll see you on Saturday," I tell him.

"But I won't see you," he replies with a shy smile. On the elevator, I utter aloud a prayer that I will not have to use the morphine.

~ FEBRUARY 7

Lunch at a restaurant with Lionel and Melanie

"It's no good," Melanie says to me. "You're going to get caught."

"What makes you think so?"

"Why would a doctor with a practice of one patient be present at his death, especially when the patient is known to be thinking about suicide?" She has contacted the Hemlock Society and talked with a sympathetic lawyer. She was told that there is no way to prevent an autopsy. By Connecticut law, the newly dead must be held for forty-eight hours before cremation, Ramon's preference. The

coroner will see the body. Because of Ramon's youth and the suspicion of suicide, the coroner will order an autopsy. Any injected
substance would be discovered. The time of death can be estimated
with some accuracy. I would have been seen entering the building
around that time. The police would ask questions. Interviewed sep-
arately, Lionel, Melanie, and I would give conflicting answers. I
would be named. There would be the publicity, the press. It would
be vicious. "No, you're fired, and that's that." I long to give in to the
wave of relief that sweeps over me. But there is Ramon.

"What about Ramon and my promise?"

"We just won't tell him that you're not coming."

"The coward's way," I say.

"That's what we are, aren't we?"

~ FEBRUARY 11

A phone call from Lionel: Ramon is "very much alive." He is at the
hospital, in the intensive care unit. They have put him on a respirator, washed out his stomach. He is being fed intravenously.

"I had to call the ambulance, didn't I?" he asks. "What else could
I do? He was alive."

~ FEBRUARY 15

The intensive care unit is like a concrete blockhouse. The sound of
twenty respirators, each inhaling and exhaling at its own pace, makes
a steady wet noise like the cascade from a fountain. But within
minutes of one's arrival, it becomes interwoven with the larger fabric
of sound—the clatter and thump, the quick footfalls, the calling out,
the moaning. Absolute silence would be louder.

From the doorway I observe the poverty of Ramon's body, the
way he shivers like a wet dog. The draining away of his flesh and
blood is palpable. The skin of his hands is as chaste and dry, as
beautiful, as old paper. I picture him as a small bird perched on an
arrow that has been shot and is flying somewhere.

"Ramon!" I call out. He opens his eyes and looks up, on his face a look that I can only interpret as reproach or disappointment. He knows that I was not there. Lionel the Honest has told him.

"Do you want to be treated for the pneumonia?" I ask. He cannot speak for the tube in his trachea, but he nods. "Do you want to live?" Ramon nods again. "Do you still want to die?" Ramon shakes his head no.

Twelve days later, Ramon died in the hospital. Three days after that, I met Lionel on the street. We were shy, embarrassed, like two people who share a shameful secret.

"We must get together soon," said Lionel.

"By all means. We should talk." We never did.

Liver

—⌇—

What is the size of a pumpernickel, has the shape of Diana's helmet, and crouches like a thundercloud above its bellymates, turgid with nourishment? What has the industry of an insect, the regenerative powers of a starfish, yet is turned to a mass of fatty globules by a double martini (two ounces of alcohol)? It is . . . the liver, doted upon by the French, assaulted by the Irish, disdained by the Americans, and chopped up with egg, onion, and chicken fat by the Jews.

Weighing in at three to four pounds, about one fiftieth of the total body heft, the liver is the largest of the glands. It is divided into two great lobes, the right and left, and two small lobes, the caudate and the quadrate, spitefully named to vex medical students. In the strangely beautiful dynamism of embryology, the liver appears as a tree that grows out of the virgin land of the foregut in order to increase its metabolic and digestive function. Its spreading crown of tissue continues to draw nourishment from the blood vessels of the intestine. Legion are the functions of this workhorse, the most obvious of which is the manufacture and secretion of a pint of bile a day, without which golden liquor we could not digest so much as a single raisin; and therefore, contrary to the legend that the liver is an organ given to man for him to be bilious with, in its absence we should become rather more cantankerous and grouchy than we are.

I think it altogether unjust that as yet the liver has failed to catch the imagination of modern poet and painter as has the heart and more recently the brain. The heart is purest theater, one is quick to concede, throbbing in its cage palpably as any nightingale. It quickens in response to the emotions. Let danger threaten, and the thrilling heart skips a beat or two and tightrope-walks arrhythmically before lurching back into the forceful thump of fight or flight. And all the while we feel it, hear it even—we, its stage and its audience.

One will grant the heart a modicum of history. Ancient man slew his enemy, then fell upon the corpse to cut out his heart, which he ate with gusto, for it was well understood that to devour the slain enemy's heart was to take upon oneself the strength, valor, and skill of the vanquished. It was not the livers or brains or entrails of saints that were lifted from the body in sublimest autopsy, it was the heart, thus snipped and cradled into worshipful palms, then soaked in wine and herbs and set into silver reliquaries for the veneration of the faithful. It follows quite naturally that Love should choose such an organ for its bower. In the absence of Love, the canker gnaws it; when Love blooms therein, the heart dances and *tremor cordis* is upon one.

As for the brain, it is all mystery and memory and electricity. It is enough to know of its high-topping presence, a gray cloud, substantial only in the bony box of the skull and otherwise melting into a blob of ghost-colored paste that can be wiped up with a sponge. The very idea of it, teeming with a billion unrealized thoughts, countless circuits breaking and unbreaking, flashing tiny fires of idea on and off, is too much. One bows before the brain, fearing, struck dumb. Or almost dumb, saying pretty things like "The brain is wider than the sky," or silly things like "The brain secretes thought as the stomach gastric juice, the kidneys urine." Or this: "Rest, with nothing else, corrodes the brain," which is a damnable lie.

It is time to turn aside from our misplaced meditation on the privileged brain, the aristocratic heart. Let the proletariat arise. I give you . . . the liver! Let us celebrate that great maroon snail, whose smooth back nestles in the dome of the diaphragm, beneath the lattice of the rib cage, like some blind wise slave, crouching above its colleague viscera, secret, resourceful, instinctive. No wave of emotion sweeps it. Neither music nor mathematics gives it pause in its appointed tasks. Consider first its historical role.

Medicine, as is well known, is an offshoot of religion. The predecessor of the physician as healer was the priest as exorciser. It is a quite manageable leap for me from demons to germs as the source of disease. It is equally easy to slide from incantation to prescription. Different incantations for different diseases, I gather, and no less mysterious to the ancient patients than the often mystic formulae of one's family doctor. The mystery was and is part of it. Along with the priest as exorciser was the priest as diviner, who was able to forestall illness by his access to the wishes of the gods, a theory that has since broadened into the field of preventative medicine. The most common method of divination was the inspection of the liver of a sacrificial animal, as is documented in cultures ranging from the Babylonian through the Etruscan to the Greek and Roman. Why the liver as the "organ of revelation par excellence"? Well, here it is:

In the beginning it was the liver that was regarded as the center of vitality, the source of all mental and emotional activity, nay, the seat of the soul itself. Quite naturally, the gods spoke therein. What a gloriously hepatic age! A man could know when and how best to attack his enemy, whether his amorous dallying would bring joy unencumbered with disease, whether the small would be great, the great laid low. All one had to do was to drag a sheep to the temple, flip a drachma to an acolyte, and stand by while the priests slit open the belly and read the markings of the liver, the position of the gallbladder, the arrangement of the ducts and lobes. It was all there, in red and yellow. This sort of thing went on for three thousand years, and, one might ask, what other practice has enjoyed such longevity? Even so recent a personality as Julius Caesar learned of the bad news of the Ides of March from an old liver lover, although that fellow used a goat instead of a sheep, and a purist might well have been skeptical. Incidentally, the reason the horse was never used for divination is that it is difficult to lift onto altars, and also does not possess a gallbladder, a fact of anatomy that has embarrassed and impoverished veterinarians through the ages.

It was only with the separation of medicine from the apron strings of religion and the rise of anatomy as a study in itself that the liver was toppled from its central role and the heart was elevated to the chair of emotions and intellect. The brain is even more recently in the money, and still has not quite overcome the heart as the seat of the intellect, as witness the quaint reference to learning something "by heart." Soon the heart was added to the organs used for prophecy by the Greeks and Romans, who then threw in the lungs, and finally, with an overdeveloped sense of organic democracy, the intestines. Since the liver was no longer *the* divine organ in the animal, out it transited along with Ozymandias and other sic glorias, which decline so dispirited the hepatoscopists that soon they gave up the whole damned rite and went off to listen sulkily to Hippocrates rhapsodize, tastelessly I think, about the brain and heart. As if that were not bad enough, Plato placed the higher emotions, such as courage, squarely above the diaphragm, and situated the baser appetites below, especially in the liver, where they squat like furry beasts even today, as is indicated in the term "lily-livered," or "choleric," or worse, "bilious." The assassination was complete. Still, there are memories, and the sense of history is a power and glory to all but the most swinish of men.

Today all that is left of the practice of divination is the unofficial cult of phrenology, in which character is interpreted from the bumps of the skull, and the science of palmistry, which is a rather ticklish business to get into, and seems to me merely a vulgar attempt to transfer divination to a more accessible part of the body. Nevertheless, my palmist always places great emphasis on the length and curve of the hand marking known as the "line of the liver."

The closest thing to liver worship still in business is the reverent sorrow with which the French regard their beloved *foie*. It is at once recalcitrant child and stern paterfamilias. This national preoccupation is entirely misunderstood, and thus held in ill-deserved contempt by the rest of the world, which regards such hepatism as a form of mass hypochondria. In fact, it is wholly admirable after the shallow insouciance and hectic swilling of the Americans, for instance. The French understand the absolute fairness of life, that if you want to dance you have to pay the fiddler. Nothing in our country so binds the populace into a single suffering fraternity, any of whose members has but to raise his eyebrows and tap himself below the ribs to elicit a heartfelt move of commiseration from a passing stranger. In the endless discussions of the relative merits of the various mineral waters, or whether the cure taken at Vichy or Montecatini effects a more enduring remission, class distinctions become as vague as mist. Princes of the Church, Communists at the barricade, légionnaires d'honneur, and chimney sweeps lock hearts and arms in the thrill of fellowship. Napoleon himself, wintering bitterly near Moscow in 1812, yearned not for Paris, or the Seine, or Versailles, or even for Josephine, but for Vichy and *the cure*. Obviously it is in the camaraderie of the liver and not in fragile treaties or grudging coexistence that the hope of the world lies—for ardently though one might wish to wash the brain of one's enemy, to bomb, bug, or hijack him, never would one sink to the infliction of harm upon his liver.

That these same French viciously funnel great quantities of grain into the stomachs of their geese in order to fatten the livers for pâté de foie gras, I consider simply a regrettable transference of their own hepatic anxiety onto their poultry. It is as though by bringing on such barnyard *crises de foie* they are in some way exorcised of their own. Ah, the power of insight! To gain it is to forgive and to love.

Deplorable is the constipated English view, delivered with nasal sanctimony, that the Continental liver phobia is an old wives' tale. One has but to glance at any recent map of the British Empire to know the folly of this opinion. Equally regrettable is the *que sera, sera* attitude in the United States, where the last homage to the liver was paid by the faithful users of Carter's Little Liver Pills, until the federal government invaded even that small enclave of devotion by ordering the discontinuance of the word "Liver." Now, oh, God, it's just plain Carter's Little Pills and we are the poorer.

Man's romance with alcohol had its origins in the Neolithic Age or earlier, presumably from the accidental tasting by some curious fellow of, let's say, fermented honey, or mead as it is written in *Beowulf*. The attainment of the resultant euphoria has remained a continuous striving of the human race with the exception of the perverse era of Prohibition, which presumed to tear asunder that which Nature had joined in absolute harmony. Even in the Scriptures it is implied that Noah had a lot to drink, and Lot could not say Noah. From its first appearance on the planet, alcohol has never been absent from the scene. An early hieroglyphic of the Eighteenth Egyptian Dynasty has a woman calling out for eighteen bowls of wine. "Behold," she cries, "I love drunkenness."

The human body is perfectly suited for the ingestion of alcohol, and for its rapid utilization. In that sense we are not unlike alcohol lamps. Endless is our eagerness to devour alcohol. Witness the facts that it is absorbed not only from the intestine, as are all other foods, but directly from the stomach as well. It can be taken in by the lungs as an inhalant, and even by the rectum if given as an enema. Once it is incorporated into the body, it is to the liver that belongs the task of oxidizing the alcohol. But even the sturdiest liver can handle only a drop or two at a time, and the remainder swirls ceaselessly about in the bloodstream, is exhaled by the lungs, and thus provides the state police with a crackerjack method of detecting and measuring the presence and amount of alcohol ingested. Along the way it bathes the brain with happiness, lifting the inhibitory context off the primal swamp of the id and permitting to surface all sorts of delicious urges such as the one to walk into people's houses wearing your wife's hat. Happily enough, the brain is not organically altered by alcohol unless taken in near-lethal amounts. The brain cells are not destroyed by it in any kind of moderate drinking, and if the alcohol is withdrawn from the diet, the brain rapidly awakens and resumes its function at the usual, if not normal, level. One must reckon, nevertheless, with the hangover, which retributive phenomenon is devised to make the drinker feel guilty. In fact, it is not more than a nightmarish echo of the state of inebriation brought on by excessive fatigue and the toxic effects of congeners, the natural products of the fermentation process that give distinction to the taste of the various forms of alcohol. In

The Adventures of Huckleberry Finn, we find Huck awakening to "an awful scream. . . . There was pap looking wild, and skipping around every which way, and yelling about snakes. He said they was crawling up his legs; and then he would give a jump and scream, and say one had bit him on the cheek—but I couldn't see no snakes. He started and run round and round the cabin, hollering. 'Take him off. Take him off; he's biting me on the neck!'; I never see a man look so wild in the eyes. Pretty soon he was all fagged out, and fell down panting; then he rolled over and over wonderful fast, kicking things every which way, and striking and grabbing at the air with his hands, and screaming, and saying there was devils a hold of him. He wore out by and by, and laid still awhile, moaning. Then he laid stiller, and didn't make a sound."

It was a French physician, quite naturally, who first described the disease known as cirrhosis of the liver, near the turn of the nineteenth century. His name, René Théophile Hyacinthe Laënnec. This fastidious gentleman was the very same whose aversion to applying his naked ear to the perfumed but unbathed bosoms of his patients inspired him to invent the stethoscope, which idea he plagiarized from a group of street urchins playing with rolled-up paper. The entire medical world continues to pay homage to Laënnec for his gift of space interpersonal. As if this were not enough, he permitted himself to be struck by the frequent appearance at autopsy of livers that were yellow, knobby, and hard. This marvel he named cirrhosis, from the Greek word for "tawny," *kirrhos*. The liver appears yellow because it is fatty, hard because it is scarred, and knobby because the regeneration of liver tissue between the scars produces little mounds or hillocks. It was suspected by Laënnec, and is known by all the rest of us today, that by far the most common cause of cirrhosis is the consumption of alcohol.

It is a matter for future anthropologists to ponder that the two favorite companions of business are Bottle and Board. More than one eminent literary agent, Wall Street broker, and vice president have died testifying affection for them. Deep drinking and intrigue are part of all the noble professions. These, combined with the studious avoidance of exercise, have conspired to produce a whole race of voluptuaries who, by twos and threes from noon till three, sit at tables in dim restaurants, picking at their sideburns and destroying the furniture with their gigantic buttocks. These same men can be seen after five years of such indiscretion transformed into "lean and slippered pantaloons," with scanty hair that is but the gray garniture of premature senescence.

In the city of New York such is the torrent of spirituous flow as to make the clinking of ice cubes and the popping of corks a major source of noise pollution. It is as though it had been purported by the Surgeon General himself that the best means of maintaining human life from infancy to extreme old age were by the copious use of the Blood of the Grape. It might with equal credibility be put forth that tobacco smoke purifies the air from infectious malignancy by its fragrance, sweetens the breath, strengthens the brain and memory, and restores admiration to the sight.

Counting every man, woman, and child in the United States, it is estimated that the average daily intake of calories is 3,300 a person. In this all-inclusive group, 165 calories are ingested as alcohol. Pushing on, if one were to divide these Americans into I Do Drinks and I Don't Drinks, the I Do's take in 500 calories from this same source. This alcohol is metabolized in the liver by a fiercely efficient enzyme called alcohol dehydrogenase, and transformed directly into energy, which would all be terribly nice were it not for the unjust fact that alcohol is poisonous to the liver, causing it to become loaded with fat. If enough is imbibed, and enough fat is deposited in the liver, this organ takes on the yellowish color noted by Laënnec. Still more booze, and the liver becomes heavy with fat, swelling so that it emerges from beneath the protective rib cage and bulges down into the vulnerable soft white underbelly. There it can be palpated by the examining fingers, and even seen protruding on the right side of the abdomen in some cases.

Even today, the progression from this fatty stage to the frank inflammation and scarring that are the hallmarks of cirrhosis is not well understood. Factors other than continued drinking pertain here. One of these is susceptibility. Jews, for instance, are not susceptible. One sees precious few cirrhotic Jews. It was formerly averred by somewhat chauvinistic Jewish hepatologists that Jews didn't get cirrhosis because they didn't drink much, what with their strong, dependable family ties, and their high motivation, and their absolute need to excel in order to survive. They didn't need to drink. But Jews are now among the most emancipated of drinkers and, with all the fervor of new converts, are causing such virtuosi as the Irish and the French to glance nervously over their shoulders. Still, the Jews do not get cirrhosis. This is not to say that they are not alcoholics. It has been reported by more than one visiting professor of medicine that noticeable segments of the population of Israel get and stay drunk for quite heroic periods of time. It is also reported that their livers remain enviably healthy.

Another measure of susceptibility is, brace yourselves, the absence of hair on the chest. In males, of course. Unpelted men of the sort idealized by bathing-suit and underwear manufacturers are sitting ducks for the onset of cirrhosis. All other things being equal, women, the marrying kind, would do well to turn aside from such vast expanses of naked chest skin and to cultivate a taste for the simian. It was formerly thought that cirrhotic men lost their chest hair. Not so. They never had any to begin with.

Lastly, it is said by some that climate is a factor: the closer to the equator, the more vulnerable the liver. Thus, a quantity of alcohol that scarcely ruffles the frozen current of a Norwegian's blood would scatter madness and fever into the brain of a Hindu.

There is a difference, I hasten to add, between imbibers of alcohol and alcoholics. Both develop fatty livers, true, but no one has shown conclusively that a fatty liver is the precursor of cirrhosis. One martini increases the fat content of the liver sufficiently so that it can be seen by the use of special stains under the microscope. In other words, a single martini increases the fat in a liver by 0.5 percent of the weight of the organ, above a normal percent. In the alcoholic this commonly reaches a death-defying 25 percent. But you don't have to be an alcoholic to get cirrhosis. Some quite modest drinkers get it. Nor does it matter the purity of the spirits consumed. Beer, wine, and whiskey equally offend, and he who would take comfort from the idea that he drinks only beer, or only wine, is to be treated with pity and contempt. One correlation that does hold water is the duration of time that one has been drinking. Cirrhosis is primarily a disease of the forties or fifties. Even here we cannot generalize, however, for great numbers of younger people are afflicted, and one patient within my ken was an eighteen-year-old girl whose voluminous liver could be felt abutting on her groin just eight months after she had retired to her room with a continuous supply of Thunderbird wine.

The state of nutrition is also a factor in the development of cirrhosis. It is no secret that boozers, the serious kind, stop eating, especially protein, either because they can't afford it—what with the cost of a bottle of bourbon these days—or because the sick liver just can't handle the metabolism of protein well, and the appetite is warned off.

The nitrogenous material of protein passes directly through the diseased liver and exerts a toxic effect on the brain. If one restricts protein in the diet of cirrhotics, the brain improves. A case in point is Sir Andrew Aguecheek of *Twelfth Night*, whose fervent wish to cut a dash was aborted by stupidity, cowardice, and social gaucherie. His eccentricity, emotional lability, and restricted vocabulary were almost certainly due to the organic brain syndrome of liver disease due to intolerance of nitrogen. Sir Toby Belch assesses Sir Andrew rather highly. Still, Sir Toby cannot resist the clinical judgment that "for Andrew, if he were opened, and you find so much blood in his liver as will clog the foot of a flea, I'll eat the rest of the anatomy." Such as Sir Andrew Aguecheek are thrown into mental confusion, confabulation, and even coma by no more than a single ounce of beef. Thus their medical nickname, "one meatballers."

In an analysis of the inhabitants of Chicago's Skid Row, it was observed that a customary diet consisted of alcohol in any form and jelly doughnuts. Yet in the cases of 3,900 such folk whose death certificates were signed out as cirrhosis, only 10 percent were actually found to have the disease at autopsy. Thus it might be stated that alcoholics exceed cirrhotics by nine to one—or that only 10 percent of alcoholics get cirrhosis.

What is clearly needed is a test to find out which are the 10 percent that are going to get it, so that the rest of us can enjoy ourselves. At the moment I prefer to take comfort from the example of such valiant topers as Winston Churchill, who swallowed a fifth of whiskey a day all the while leading Great Britain in her finest hour, and went on to die in his nineties, still holding his fingers up like that. It is also true that if one, moved by some transcendental vision or goaded by ill-conceived guilt, abstains from further drinking, in short order all the excess fat departs from the liver and it once again regains its pristine color and size. In this way do spree drinkers inadvertently rest their livers and avoid the cirrhosis we slow but steadies risk. Thus something can be said for periodic abstinence, a wisdom one would hesitate to translate into other vices.

Before enumerating the signs and symptoms of cirrhosis, and thus running the risk of offending sensibility, it should be unequivocally affirmed that he is no gentleman, in fact a very milksop, of no bringing up, that will not drink. He is fit for no company, for it is a credit to have a strong brain and carry one's liquor well. Saith Pliny, " 'Tis the greatest good of our tradesmen, their felicity, life and soul, their chiefest comfort, to be merry together in a tavern."

Envision, if you will, a house whose stones are living hexagonal tiles not unlike those forming the bathroom floors of first-class hotels. These are the hepatocytes, the cellular units of the liver. Under the microscope they have a singular uniformity, each as like unto its fellow as the antlers of a buck, and all fitted together with a lovely imprecision so as to form a maze of crooked hallways and oblong rooms. Coursing through this muralium of tissue are two arborizations of blood vessels, the one bringing food and toxins from the intestine, the other delivering oxygen from the heart and lungs. Winding in and among these networks is a system of canaliculi that puts to shame all the aqueductal glories of Greece and Rome. Through these sluice the rivers of bile, gathering strength and volume as the little ducts at the periphery meet others, going into ones of larger caliber, which in turn fuse, and so on until there are two large tubes emerging from the undersurface of the liver. Within this magic house are all the functions of the liver carried out. The food we eat is picked over, sorted out, and stored for future use in the cubicles of the granary. Starch is converted to glycogen, which is released in the form of energy as the need arises. Protein is broken down into its building blocks, the amino acids, later to be fashioned into more YOU, as old tissues die off and need to be replaced. Fats are stored until sent forth to provide warmth and comfort. Vitamins and antibodies are released into the bloodstream. Busy is the word for the liver. Deleterious substances ingested, inadvertently like DDT or intentionally like alcohol, are either changed into harmless components and excreted into the intestine, or stored in locked closets to be kept isolated from the rest of the body. Even old blood cells are pulverized and recycled. Such is the old catfish liver snufflin' along at the bottom of the tank, sweepin', cleanin' up after the gouramis, his whiskery old face stirrin' up a cloud of rejectimenta, and takin' care of everything.

But there are limits. Along comes that thousandth literary lunch and—pow! the dreaded wrecking ball of cirrhosis is unslung. The roofs and walls of the hallways, complaining under their burden of excess fat, groan and buckle. Inflammation sets in, and whole roomfuls of liver cells implode and die, and in their place comes the scarring that twists and distorts the channels, pulling them into impossible angulation. Avalanches block the flow of bile and heavy tangles of fiber impede the absorption and secretion. This happens not just in one spot but all over, until the gigantic architecture is a mass of sores and wounds, the old ones scarring over as new ones break down.

The obstructed bile, no longer able to flow down to the gut, backs up into the bloodstream to light up the skin and eyes with the sickly lamp of jaundice. The stool turns toothpaste white in commiseration, the urine dark as wine. The belly swells with gallons of fluid that weep from the surface of the liver, no less than the tears of a loyal servant so capriciously victimized. The carnage spreads. The entire body is discommoded. The blood fails to clot, the palms of the hands turn mysteriously red, and spidery blood vessels leap and crawl on the skin of the face and neck. Male breasts enlarge, and even the proud testicles turn soft and atrophy. In a short while impotence develops, an irreversible form of impotence which may well prod the invalid into more and more drinking.

Scared? Better have a drink. You look a little pale. In any case, there is no need to be all that glum. Especially if you know something that I know. Remember Prometheus? That poor devil who was chained to a rock, and had his liver pecked out each day by a vulture? Well, he was a classical example of the regeneration of tissue, for every night his liver grew back to be ready for the dreaded diurnal feast. And so will yours grow back, regenerate, reappear, regain all of its old efficiency and know-how. All it requires is quitting the booze, now and then. The ever-grateful, forgiving liver will respond joyously with a multitude of mitoses and cell divisions that will replace the sick tissues with spanking new nodules and lobules of functioning cells. This rejuvenation is carried on with the speed and alacrity of a starfish growing a new ray from the stump of the old. New channels are opened up, old ones dredged out, walls are straightened, and roofs shored up. Soon the big house is humming with activity, and all those terrible things I told you happen go away—all except that impotence thing. Well, you didn't expect to get away scot-free, did you?

And here's something to tuck away and think about whenever you want to feel good. Sixty percent of all cirrhotics who stop drinking will be alive and well five years later.

Good old liver!

Bone

—m—

Bones. Two hundred and eight of them. A whole glory turned and tooled. Lo the timbered femur all hung and strapped with beef, whose globate head nuzzles the concave underpart of the pelvis; the little carpals of the wrist faceted as jewels and as jewels named— capitate, lunate, hamate, pisiform; the phalanges, tiny kickshaws of the body, toys fantastic, worn upon the hands and feet like fans of unimagined cleverness; the porcelain pile of the vertebrae atop which rides the domed palanquin of the very brain; the vast, the slumbrous pelvis, called to wakefulness by the sweet intrusion of sex or the stirring of an impatient fetus. Out of this pelvis, endlessly rocking, drops man. I agree with those African tribes who decorate themselves with bones. It is more to my taste than diamonds, which are a cold and soulless shine. Whilst bone, ah bone, is the pit of a man after the cumbering flesh has been eaten away.

Bone is power. It is bone to which the soft parts cling, from which they are, helpless, strung and held aloft to the sun, lest man be but another slithering earth-noser. What is this tissue that has double the strength of oak? One cubic inch of which will stand a crushing force of two tons? This substance that refuses to dissolve in our body fluids, but remains intact and solid through all vicissitudes of temperature and pollution? We may be grateful for this insolubility, for it is what stands us tall. How is it that in these rigid, massive pieces is the very factory of the blood, wherein each day, one million red blood cells are made and discharged into the circulation to course their threescore-and-one days, then die?

Stony and still though it seems, bone quickens; it flows. It is never the same at any two moments. The traverse of calcium from the blood to the bone and back again is a continuous thing, which ceaseless exchange of mineral is governed by hormonal potentates from glands afar. Fluid, too, is pressed into, then extracted from, the bone in a never-ending current, yet slow as Everglade.

In bone, as in other life, there are the givers and the takers. Twin races of cells, one the Blasts, whose function is oppositely named, for they march resolutely, all the while laying down bone, spinning out the hard stuff, each one an Atlas, born to most grittily uphold the world as he sees it. Moving steadily is the army of Clasts. These are the borers who tunnel through a bed of bone like moles through a lawn. No granitic femur is impervious to their chewings. It is not to destroy that they burrow, but to cleanse. No killers they, but peppy sweeps, clearing away old cells, all the detritus of age, the debris of ill usage. Even as they drill their winding canaliculi, scoop out their cavitations, the rival Blasts rush in to line the spaces with new bone. Thus Blast and Clast engage in a race between growth and decay, yet all to the single purpose of renewal. Still it must be told that it is the Clast, the devourer, that is triumphant in old age, for his energies persist, while the Blast grows weary, his deposition slow. Thus does old bone grow porous, light, and brittle. Thus does it easily break, and but slowly knit.

Cartilage earns the title Mother-of-Bone. Strategically placed in the bones of the young are belts of cartilage which are the growth centers of the bone. During the first twenty years of life, this cartilage is replaced by bone at its margins even as the center remains a fiery pit of new cartilage. It must not be too hungrily replaced, before full growth is attained, or we are too short. At maturity all of the cartilage in these centers has been transformed, save for that which remains to pad the joints or, charmingly, to ornament and hold aloft the ears lest they flop like a spaniel's. In these disks of cartilage are all our stature.

Break a bone, and almost at once the blood clot between the two fragments begins to carnify. Fibrous tissue and blood vessels invade it, turn it meaty. Now, with cast or screw or metal plate, immobilize the bone so that further disruption will not take place, and the jellied mass is entered by bone-forming cells, the Blasts. Calcium salts are accepted here, and in time there is a bridge of new bone between the fragments. It is the trauma itself, the fact of fracture, that triggers the restoration. It is a cellular call to arms, a furious mobilization, an act of drive and instinct. It is the wisdom of Bone.

Remove a rib, if you must, in order to enter the chest for surgery, but leave intact the periosteum, that sheath of the bone. Strip it back, and bite away only the naked rib, and that rib will grow again, fed by the lining of the sheath, until an X ray taken months later will reveal the marvel of the tissues. The thoracic arch has been shored up.

Bone can be grafted from one place to another to span the gap between two unhealed fragments or to fuse an unstable joint. This bone acts as a framework upon which the new bone is woven until all the pieces are joined in a single unbending whole.

No inert span this bone, but a fact of physical life each of whose parts holds a measure of electricity. Walk, and you change the electrical potential of your bones. Here it springs from positive to negative; there, from negative to positive. The strands of bone line up to follow the direction of force at any given time, seizing the position of greatest mechanical advantage, responding to each stress and shear and impact. So does it bend and relent; so does it not break; so are forgiven all the bangs and crashings of locomotion.

Like the flesh, bone is subject to defect and disease. Should the muscles attached to a bone cease to function, as in stroke or paralysis, almost half the bone served by those muscles is quickly resorbed, and disappears. Exceed the tensile strength of a bone, and it answers with the exclamation—*fracture!* Nowhere is this event more likely than in osteogenesis imperfecta, wherein the process of ossification is badly done. Instead of a continuing sheet of bone, there are only scanty nests of osteoblasts. An infant so afflicted may survive the trauma of birth but with half his bones broken. Merely to diaper such a child is to risk fracturing his thighs. In the aged, many small clots form in the nutrient vessels of the bone. The replenishing blood is here and there blocked, and the bone grows withered and fragile; it cracks, most often at the neck of the femur, there where the weight is borne. Such a hip fracture may be the harbinger of death for the old one forced to share his bed with Confusion and Pneumonia.

Ah, but there is more to the skull than helmet to the brain, to the sternum than shield to the heart, to the ribs than staves off the thorax. The rest of the flesh is transient, strung like laundry upon a lattice. To dwell upon bone is to contemplate the fate of man. Bone is the keepsake of the earth, all that remains of a man when the rest has long since melted and seeped and crumbled away. It endures for a million years and, if then dug up from the ground, suggests still to anthropologists the humps of meat that once it wore, and to poets the much that was from the little that remains.

What man does not ponder the whereabouts of his skeleton—the place where it will lie? Say what you will, all sanitary and pragmatic considerations aside, these jaunty saunterers that have held us upright, have stiffened us against the grate and grind of life, are dear to us. What stands closer to a man all his days than his bones?

A savage queen contrives from the skull of her young lover a wine bowl. Years later, as she lifts the kissed and polished calvarium to her lips, her old passion shudders anew, and licking an errant drop from one socket, she smiles in wild ownership. No thank you; not for me. Far better to tumble among the unnumbered treasures of the sea.

Of higher taste were the Ottawa Indians, friends of the explorer-priest Marquette. Upon learning the whereabouts of the body of their beloved visitor, the Ottawas journeyed there, to the eastern shore of Lake Michigan.

Journeyed eastward to the lakeside,
Where beloved pale-face rested.
Dug them up, the bones of Father,

Washed and dried them, Boxed in birch bark,
And the moon upon the waters
Lay a silver path to guide them.
Paddled chanting, in procession
Their canoes all draped in mourning,
To the chapel at the mission,
Neath the floorboards there they laid them.

Homage to Longfellow! One now understands why he wrote this way. Once you start, you can't stop.

I myself have confronted the hard fact of bone and have been changed by it. Listen.

A man named Barney died. He was my friend who sprawled facedown upon rocks at the foot of a cliff. The impact had flattened and spread Barney, so that when I could scramble to where he crashed, he seemed to me wider, larger, than he had been. All splayed of limb he lay, downhill, with his head lower than his feet, his arms and legs reaching out to grapple the rocks to him, the rocks that became him so. Eagerly he had leaped, and eagerly landed.

"When I die," he had said to me that morning, "take my ashes and scatter them in this woods. Add me to this place. Do it gladly or you shall be the less for it." Barney was a hard man.

A tin can such as might be expected to hold peanuts was what the undertaker gave me, after checking the name tag. In a small clearing in the forest, where the trees leaned and interlaced above, I pried off the lid, unfolded the embossed napkin, and saw . . . not silty ash drifting and banked, but chunks of white bone the size of almonds! Here was a groove where once had ridden the trunk of a nerve; there persisted an eminence, round and smooth, to which a muscle had attached. All together they had done some act for Barney. Raised his glass, perhaps. From the can rose the faint odor of scorch. I had been ready for ash; I was filled with dread by these staring bones. From the perpetuity of ash I could have departed in peace, but from these crusts and careless crumbs, I would take away no

memory of the banquet of friendship, only a nausea of the soul. Nor
am I alone in my terrors. Other anatomists have touched the bones
of a fellow and felt their own burial cloths winding about them.
Vesalius, driven by his passion and the interdictions of society to
scavenge after public hangings, poked among subgibbetal offal to
retrieve yet another tibia, one fibula more. And all the while, his own
heart grown ossified in his breast.

But to the task. Quickly, as though to rid myself of incriminating
evidence, I walked round and round the clearing, spilling Barney's
bones upon the oak leaves until there were no more. Then looked
down to see them strewn as by some wizard who would read Event
from the pattern in which they lay. Nearby was a small park with
benches and tables and tall trash cans painted green to blend with
the trees. Trembling, I went there to sit alone, for it is comforting to
sit beside the dead and measure the distance between them and us.

All at once, there was a noise, an *alive* sound. Less than a thump;
a scrabble perhaps. I looked behind me. There was no one, nor any
creature. Only the woods where, doglike, I had dropped the bones
of my friend. I sat back; again I strained toward respectful elegy.
Again! A whirring. I wheeled, and . . . nothing. But now I am terrified. Who's there, I called out, and the whiteness of my voice informed the forest of my vulnerability. I started to walk away, toward
the road, backing off. I must not be seized from the rear. And then
I heard it again, that soft thrashing. From the rim of my vision I saw
a movement. A jiggling. It was a *trash can* wobbling. Once more
there was the noise, and once more the jiggling of the trash can. Now
I am torn by the need to run from this demonic place and the need—
yes, I must—to learn what lurks and leaps within that can that is no
one-pound tin but a receptacle large enough to hold a *man*. Back
and forth I flopped between resolve and panic, from No-I-shall-run-
away to Stay-for-I-must. I stayed. And, stalking, crept until I had
circled and sidled that horrid can three times, and heard again and
again the challenge of its rattle. At last, I must act or die, and rising
from a crouch, I ran full tilt toward it, kicked it with my foot high
up near the top, with all my strength redoubled by fear. Over it

went, rolled half a turn, and lay still. And from its gape there slouched and snarled the thinnest slice of winter I have ever seen. A raccoon. Its ribs each one visible in its flanks; its tail hairless, ignoble. Slow, contemptuous, the creature walked from the barrel. Six paces, then stopped, and turned to glare at me with loaded eyes, and lips drawn back from mauve gums, from which hung yellow teeth like tines of the gates of Hell. As I watched, the raccoon tilted back its head and loosed from its throat a sound that I shall remember all of my days. A long hiss playing out into a pneumonic rattle. It was what is left of a sigh when the rue and regret is exhausted. I felt the rank whiff upon my skin. Abruptly then, the creature walked to the edge of the woods and disappeared in the direction of the clearing where I had not gladly, not reverently thrown down the bones of my friend. I was once again alone. Barney, Barney.

Ah, you say, and smile. Spooks and banshees—childish frights. An overheated brain undoes the solid mind. Come, come, you insist. Laugh with us. And I try to join. I think fiercely of politics, of theater, and all the stuff of daytime. But even now, years later, I start from my bed as I hear the hissing of those bones. And it does not matter what you say, or if you think that what I've told is true. It matters that I have been changed by it, that I am not the same as I was.

Does the haughty orthopedist swaggering by, tapping his boot with a pet ulna, does he pretend to a courage he does not own? Does he retreat by night to his closet quaking with fear, whilst all around his head the rumble of angry bones rolls and thunders? Or is it some fetish to which he is compelled, that he must see and touch again and again all those hard smooth strokables? For who could gaze hourly upon the bones of man and not shudder at the intimations of his mortality?

So, I have decided. No gourd, nor royal drinking cup, nor forest strew for me. Upon the wall of some quiet library ensconce my skull. Place oil and a wick in my brainpan. And there let me light with endless affection the pages of books for men to read.

Most commonly, bone is afflicted with that ubiquitous degeneration that is known as osteoarthritis, wherein the wear and tear of usage is expressed as the grinding down of the disks of cartilage that cap the ends of the bones like icing and that facilitate the movement of the joints. As the cartilage is worn thin, the joint undergoes inflammation, with resultant deformity and limitation of motion. Hummocks and spurs build upon the bony surfaces, pressing against the surrounding tissues to cause pain, and thus further immobilize until the joint itself is frozen, locked, its range a pitiful semicircle or less. Live long enough, and you will win a measure of this ailment which has, more than any other, come to be synonymous with the decay of aging. That it is most apparent in the spine and hips is no more than the wages we are made to pay for the sins of our forefathers.

Of all the imprudences dared by man in his brazen reach for ascendancy, the most arrogant was his decision to stand up, to eschew his all-fours, and, piling his vertebrae one atop the other, to thrust himself erect. Admittedly, there were prizes to be won by this recklessness. An apple, heretofore waggling from a branch just out of reach, could now be plucked with ease. Ledges and rocks which had, up to then, walled him in could now be overpowered. Prey could be seen advancing; enemies too, long before their arrival. And rocks could be flung farther from the new height. Most exhilarating was the discovery of front-to-front copulation, a stunning innovation that ushered in the process of selection of a mate, now euphemistically called love. Prior to his standing up, man, like the others, copulated front-to-back, nor did it matter whose front, whose back. Now, laughing himself sick at kine and behemoth, *Homo erectus* picked and chose. This one had nice furry breasts; that one was gimpy. This one was bald; that, one-eyed. Having chosen, and wishing to keep the good parts in view, bifrontal copulation seemed but the natural sequitur. Woman, in her turn, was rewarded with orgasm, a phenomenon unknown to most other species.

It all seemed like such a good idea.

But this man who thrust himself from the earth, who wore the stars of heaven in his hair, was guilty of overweening pride. An act most audacious, he had defied nothing less than the law of gravity. He was to pay dearly for such high imposture. The vertebrae, unused to their new columnar arrangement, slipped, buckled, and wore out.

Next, the arches of the feet fell. The hip joints ground to a halt. Nor was payment extorted only from the skeletal system. The pooling of blood in the lower part of the body distended the fragile blood vessels beyond their limits. Thus bloomed the fruitage of hemorrhoids; thus are we varicose. Worse still, our soft underparts have given way. Under the sag of our guts, we bulge into hernia. We turn to soft lump.

Alas, was there no pithecantropoid Jeremiah who, horrified at the vainglory of the young, would scramble to some lofty place and cry out against this swagger? Would cry out to his fellow man, "Down, you fools. Get down, before it is too late"? So we have come to our pretty pass. Better to have maintained our low profile, content to nose among the droppings of mastodons—for it is swollen, bunched, sacculent, hung down, gibbous, hummocky, knobbed, sagging, adroop, warped, tipped, and tilted that we are made to wage life, slouching toward our infernal copulations toward our eternal reward. Such is the revenge of bone.

Skin

—ᴍ—

I sing of skin, layered fine as baklava, whose colors shame the dawn, at once the scabbard upon which is writ our only signature, and the instrument by which we are thrilled, protected, and kept constant in our natural place. Here is each man bagged and trussed in perfect amiability. See how it upholsters the bone and muscle underneath, now accenting the point of an elbow, now rolling over the pectorals to hollow the grotto of an armpit. Nippled and umbilicated, and perforated by the most diverse and marvelous openings, each with its singular rim and curtain. Thus the carven helix of the ear, the rigid nostrils, the puckered continence of the anus, the moist and sensitive lips of mouth and vagina.

What is it, then, this seamless body-stocking, some two yards square, this our casing, our façade, that flushes, pales, perspires, glistens, glows, furrows, tingles, crawls, itches, pleasures, and pains us all our days, at once keeper of the organs within and sensitive probe, adventurer into the world outside?

Come, let us explore: there exists the rosy coast, these estuaries of pearl.

Gaze upon the skin as I have, through a microscope brightly, and tremble at the wisdom of God, for here is a magic tissue to suit all seasons. Two layers compose the skin—the superficial epidermis and, deeper, the dermis. Between is a plane of pure energy where the life force is in full gallop. Identical cells spring full-grown here, each as tall and columnar as its brother, to form an unbroken line over the body. No sooner are these cells formed than they move toward the surface, whether drawn to the open air by some proto-plasmic hunger or pushed outward by the birth of still newer cells behind. In migration the skin cells flatten, first to cubes, then plates. Twenty-six days later the plates are no more than attenuated wisps of keratin meshed together to guard against forces that would damage the skin by shearing or compression. Here they lie, having lost all semblance of living cellularity, until they are shed from the body in a continuous dismal rain. Thus into the valley of death this number marches in well-stepped soldiery, gallant, summoned to a sacrifice beyond its ken. But . . . let the skin be cut or burned, and the brigade breaks into a charge, fanning out laterally across the wound, racing to seal off the defect. The margins are shored up; healing earthworks are raised, and guerrilla squads of invading bacteria are isolated and mopped up. The reserves too are called to the colors and the rate of mitosis increases throughout the injured area. Hurrah for stratified squamous epithelium!

Beneath the epidermis lies the dermis, a resilient pad of elastic tissue in which glands, hair follicles, nerves, and blood vessels are arranged in infinitely variable mosaic. Within this rich bed three million sweat glands lie; these, in full sluice, can extract from the blood up to three kilograms of fluid in a single hour. Such a warm fall cools the body even as it evaporates from its surface and, incidentally, flushes from us the excess of salt that threatens to make of the body juices a pickling brine. In this, the sweat glands are helpmates to the kidney. Ah, but the skin *harbors* water and heat as well, containing our fluid and blood lest, one sunny day, we leak our way to dusty desiccation on some pavement or, bitten, bleed an hour or two, and die.

These sweat glands are most numerous on the palms and soles, and have their highest density at birth, decreasing steadily thereafter. Only the glans penis, clitoris, labia minora, and inner surface of the prepuce have no sweat glands, a curiously sexual deficiency that ought to tell us something, but for God's sake what?

Never mind. Exclusiveness, in no matter what context, is not without its charms.

Still other glands of the dermis yield odoriferous oils. In that they attract mates and repel enemies, these musky syrups, called phero-mones, engage in a kind of cutaneous communication. One may well deplore the perverse vanity which insists that we spray, roll on, and dab our flesh so as to deny these darling chemicals their true role. To banish our natural stink is to play havoc with no less than the procreative process itself, depriving it of its olfactory joys, at the very least. Such misguided fastidiousness will do us no good in the end. Keep in mind, a single sniff of pheromone can raise expectations to which a whole Pacific of perfume cannot pretend, nor an Atlantic of attar attain.

Besides, some of us need all the help we can get.

Ranking with the earlobes as our most adorable gewgaws are the nails that decorate the fingers and toes. One parts with the nails only under political duress and in great pain. Long since having retired their acquisitive and protective functions, they are more like the sweet hooflets of a yearling than the talons of a hawk. Still, among guitar players, certain Japanese weavers, and women with time on their hands, length is prized. For such specialists as for all who find it impossible to go on without knowing, it must be put abroad that nails grow faster in the dominant hand, grow 20 percent faster in the summer than in the winter, and grow twice as fast during the day as at night. Pregnancy, trauma, and nail-biting (mother's bane) are said to increase the rate of nail growth.

Four living paints, called biochromes, combine to give the skin its color at any given moment. There are brown, yellow, bright red, and purplish red. The bright red is called oxyhemoglobin and is carried by the blood to the skin. In the state of anemia or hemorrhage, there is less blood, thus less bright red, and the skin whitens, turns pale, until the line between pillowcase and patient is as indistinct as any horizon where sea and sky blend. Among those so afflicted were

Elizabeth Barrett Browning, Annabel Lee, and the Lady of the Camellias. It is all very nineteenth-century.

Melanin is the brown pigment, which, under the influence of
glands afar, gives to the skin what darkness it has. Without it we are
albinos—pink, wretched creatures whose oxyhemoglobin is not
masked by melanin, and for whom the sun's rays are no solace but
ten thousand cruel fires that anger and abrade the tissues to malignancy.

It is differences in the number and size of pigment granules
called melanosomes that account for whether your skin is naturally
black or white. If your skin is black, you own more and larger of
these organelles. But it happens that, for as yet unexplained reasons,
a man may turn piebald.

Think, if you will, upon one Henry Moss. In Goochland County,
Virginia, sprang he, black as an eggplant, from the loins of his mother
and father in the otherwise unremembered year of 1754. Farmers his
begetters were, and so did young Henry remain until the Revolu-
tionary War broke out. He was twenty-two, and with many other
free blacks, he enlisted in the Colonial Army, where he served for
six years. Upon his discharge, Henry moved to Maryland, married,
and took up once again his hoe and his plowshare. For ten years he
farmed in peaceful anonymity, and would have done so until he died,
had not Fate, in the year 1792, given him her most enigmatic smile—
for in 1792 Henry Moss began to turn white.

First from his fingertips did the rich blackness fade—to no mere
cocoa or tan, but to such a white as matched the fairness of a Dane.
Soon the snowy tide had flooded his wrists, his arms, his neck. Next,
his chest and abdomen and back undarkened in great irregular
patches. He was Holstein. He was Dalmatian. The blanching spread,
coalesced, until four years later Henry Moss was almost totally white.
Imagine the dismay of poor Henry Moss as he gazed into his mirror
and saw vanishing therefrom the last bits of his dermal heritage.
What face was this, what head, where the once kinky wool crisped
thick and full, and where now limp white hair hung lank and silky?
Was it some dread leprosy? Some awful spot presaging dissolution?

Not for long was Henry Moss to wander his little farm alone and palely loitering, for even as he gazed into that mirror, he felt the first fierce fetch of fame . . . and Philadelphia! To Philadelphia, Athens of America, city of culture and sophistication, came Henry Moss with his new whiteness upon him, and in his bosom the glory that transfigures, for Henry Moss had gazed deep into that mirror and seen reflected there his fortune and his destiny.

It was the practice of the innkeepers and hostelers of that time to maintain upon their premises for the enjoyment of their clients any of a number of oddities of natural history. There was a dead whale which had been caught in the Delaware River; a pygarg, which was a strange Russian beast, part camel, part bear; a learned pig that could tell the time of day and who transmitted this data in cunning little grunts; and Miss Sarah Rogers, who, born without arms or legs, still managed to paint elegant flowers and to thread needles with her lips and tongue and teeth. To these was added Henry Moss, the black man who was turning white! Scrub him hard, and see for yourself.

Overnight Henry Moss became a star. For his appearance at Mr. Leech's tavern on Market Street, the Sign of the Black Horse, handbills were passed out upon the streets. A GREAT CURIOSITY, the handbills proclaimed, a sight to open "a wide field of amusement for the philosophical genius."

But Henry Moss was no mere odd outscouring of the human race, suitable only for gawking. Henry Moss wore a message that rocked the very roofbeams of racial chauvinism so muscularly buttressed by our forefathers. Henry Moss was proof that the races were interchangeable, the skin reversible. As naught now, the vaunted difference. Black was white. Why not white . . . black? Why not, indeed!

In time Henry Moss was brought before a convocation of the leading physicians of Philadelphia, where the matter was discussed. Questions were raised, debates joined. Was the source of blackness to be found in the peculiar climate of Africa? If uprooted for a generation or two, would the black essence recede, to be replaced by the white? Would Henry Moss reblacken if transported to Africa?

Would the progeny of a white turn black over there? Or was it indeed some perverse chemistry of the skin?

No answers were given. And the celebrated case of Henry Moss faded as swiftly as had the color of his skin. Still, one is left to wonder. . . . Had the good doctors of Philadelphia been led to believe in the interchangeability of the races, might not the blot of slavery, the Civil War itself, have been overleaped? Do you think Henry's vitiligo (a disease in which the pigment cells mysteriously fail to produce melanin) might have changed the course of history? Well, it didn't.

And what of Henry Moss? He surfaced last in rural Georgia, where he earned a modest keep showing himself in the saloons of that back country. Like many a fading star, Henry ended playing the boonies.

The skin is the screen upon which the state of the other organs is cast. One can read their health in its condition and hue.

Ails the liver? Then the skin yellows into jaundice as the dislocated bile floods across it.

In the anemic state, the skin turns paper white as the enfeebled blood fails, until it would seem that a mere blush would divert blood enough to send the body into shock.

The first sign of certain cancers hidden deep within the body is itching of the skin or a painful rash.

Trouble in the brain is often heralded by the disappearance of feeling in a part of the skin.

In the poverty of oxygen lack, the skin leadens, is prinked with purple.

So it goes, as the skin reflects the occult mishaps of the marshy interior. It is upon the skin that the calamities of the flesh are made most brutally apparent. Here is all decay realized, all blight and blister exposed.

Awed and hurting, the diabetic watches his feet advance from beveled grace through sore and ulcer to the blunt black scab of gangrene, extrapolating, as he must, from the part to the sum of his parts, to the whole, and feeling for his sad sweet blood only the most anguished rue.

The youth whose face blazes with rubies and carbuncles would sell his birthright, mortgage his future, to peel his soiled mask from him and don another. But there is no other. Nor any acnesarium where he might hide his pimentoes, eschewing both the pleasures and the risks of new manhood. He is badly touched indeed.

And what heartbroken psoriatic, surveying his embattled skin, would not volunteer for an unanesthetized flaying could it but rid him of his pink sequins, his silver spangles?

I hold no grief for rosy, turgid youth. It does but stir envy and leave compassion unaroused. My sympathies lie with the aging— those, motley with spots, gypsy with plaques and knobs, in whom each misfeatured stain announces with grim certainty the relentless slouching toward . . . the end. Those in whom the elastica has so "given" that one is hung with dewlaps and is with wrinkled crepe empanoplied, in whom neither surgery, nor paints, nor other borrowed trumpery can anymore dissemble, they are the creatures that my heart and my feelings are tied to—those whose state of grace is marginal, the ragtag and bobtail, those in whom the difference from homely to comely is but a single freckle, one wart, a crease.

Yes, my sympathies lie with *us*.

Imagine God as tailor. His shelves are lined with rolls of skin, each with its subtleties of texture and hue. Six days a week He cuts lengths with which to wrap those small piles of flesh and bone into the clever parcels we call babies. Now engage the irreverence to consider that, either out of the tedium born of infinity or out of mere sly parsimony, He uses for the occasional handicraft a remnant of yard goods, the last of an otherwise perfect bolt, dusty, soiled, perhaps a bit too small or large, one whose woof is warped or that is cut on the bias. I have received many such people in my examination rooms. Like imperfect postage stamps, they are the collector's items of the human race.

Such were the sorrows of wife Margaret vergh Gryffith, who, in the year 1588, in the month of May, in the town of Llangadfan, in Montgomeryshire, in the country of Wales, awoke one morning, stretched, rubbed her eyes to clear them of sleep, and felt (*qual orrore!*) a growth upon her forehead. At first a scaly eminence, a small rising at the very center of her brow; soon a horrid excrescence that no amount of dedicated picking, scraping, or nailed excavation could dislodge, so firm were its rootings. Daily it grew longer and larger in its girth, as though all of the young matron's energies were concentrated and refined to this one wicked purpose. Through salve and unguent she passed. Through poultice and plaster, through the cook of cautery and the sizzle of scarification to the endless agitation of *concealment*. But there was no way to do it, no cap or snood, net or kerchief, hood or cowl to hide this . . . *horn*. Yes, at last it must be said. Margaret vergh Gryffith had grown a horn which stood priapically from her brow for a height of three inches, then curved downward toward her nose to crook just above her right eye—there, where there is nothing for it but to *see* it or shut forever her eyes and sit blind beneath her antler.

Imagine poor Margaret's shame, her altered sense of herself. See her devising more and more desperate articles and habits of concealment. It was of no use. As well hang a smoking brazier on the thing and walk abroad. The horn could not be hid! Wheresoever she faced, in whatever stance, however deep her crouch, it was the horn stood high and hard before her, rejecting all drapery, a lewd probe that announced to her Puritan contemporaries as the very cornified concretion of adultery, an adultery she did not commit.

Then were fiery sermons delivered in all the cathedrals of Wales, to which the people came, and listened, and trembled in their pews. As far away as London was Margaret vergh Gryffith "made readie to be seene" and led out upon platforms whilst men thundered and pointed; and alone in their boudoirs, women raised cold fearful fingertips to their foreheads, and shuddered.

Shame on you, London. Where was your bold surgeon in 1588 who would dare thrust to the fore of the lickerish crowd, to lead the horned woman away to his surgery, to amputate the hideous prong of packed and layered keratin from her head?

Ah, he jests at scars who never felt a wound.

How proud and easy we slide in our skin. Extensible, it stretches to fit our farthest reach, contracts to our least flicker, and all in silky silence. How our skin becomes us! Lucky is Man to have his hide.

Moreover, it is not the brain nor the heart that is the organ of recollection. It is the skin! For to gaze upon the skin is to bring to life the past.

Here, in the crook of this arm, where the loose skin lies in transverse folds, in this very place, she rested the back of her head, her hair so black and glossy I could see myself in the mass of it.

And from this lower lip she drew two drops of my blood, that I was glad to give her.

And look, this scar upon my cheek that marked the end of love between two brothers.

It is all here engraved, that which I was, that which I did, all the old stories, but now purified somehow, the commonplace washed away, rinsed of all that is ordinary, and glowing as they never did, even when they happened.

The Knife

—⋙—

One holds the knife as one holds the bow of a cello or a tulip—by the stem. Not palmed nor gripped nor grasped, but lightly, with the tips of the fingers. The knife is not for pressing. It is for drawing across the field of skin. Like a slender fish, it waits, at the ready, then, go! It darts, followed by a fine wake of red. The flesh parts, falling away to yellow globules of fat. Even now, after so many times, I still marvel at its power—cold, gleaming, silent. More, I am still struck with a kind of dread that it is I in whose hand the blade travels, that my hand is its vehicle, that yet again this terrible steel-bellied thing and I have conspired for a most unnatural purpose, the laying open of the body of a human being.

A stillness settles in my heart and is carried to my hand. It is the quietude of resolve layered over fear. And it is this resolve that lowers us, my knife and me, deeper and deeper into the person beneath. It is an entry into the body that is nothing like a caress; still, it is among the gentlest of acts. Then stroke and stroke again, and we are joined by other instruments, hemostats and forceps, until the wound blooms with strange flowers whose looped handles fall to the sides in steely array.

There is sound, the tight click of clamps fixing teeth into severed blood vessels, the snuffle and gargle of the suction machine clearing the field of blood for the next stroke, the litany of monosyllables with which one prays his way down and in: *clamp, sponge, suture, tie, cut.*

And there is color. The green of the cloth, the white of the sponges, the red and yellow of the body. Beneath the fat lies the fascia, the tough fibrous sheet encasing the muscles. It must be sliced and the red beef of the muscles separated. Now there are retractors to hold apart the wound. Hands move together, part, weave. We are fully engaged, like children absorbed in a game or the craftsmen of some place like Damascus.

Deeper still. The peritoneum, pink and gleaming and membranous, bulges into the wound. It is grasped with forceps, and opened. For the first time we can see into the cavity of the abdomen. Such a primitive place. One expects to find drawings of buffalo on the walls. The sense of trespassing is keener now, heightened by the world's light illuminating the organs, their secret colors revealed a maroon and salmon and yellow. The vista is sweetly vulnerable at this moment, a kind of welcoming. An arc of the liver shines high and on the right, like a dark sun. It laps over the pink sweep of the stomach, from whose lower border the gauzy omentum is draped, and through which veil one sees, sinuous, slow as just-fed snakes, the indolent coils of the intestine.

You turn aside to wash your gloves. It is a ritual cleansing. One enters this temple doubly washed. Here is man as microcosm, representing in all his parts the earth, perhaps the universe.

I must confess that the priestliness of my profession has ever been impressed on me. In the beginning there are vows, taken with all solemnity. Then there is the endless harsh novitiate of training, much fatigue, much sacrifice. At last one emerges as celebrant, standing close to the truth lying curtained in the Ark of the body. Not surplice and cassock but mask and gown are your regalia. You hold no chalice, but a knife. There is no wine, no wafer. There are only the facts of blood and flesh.

And if the surgeon is like a poet, then the scars you have made on countless bodies are like verses into the fashioning of which you have poured your soul. I think that if years later I were to see the trace from an old incision of mine, I should know it at once, as one recognizes his pet expressions.

But mostly you are a traveler in a dangerous country, advancing into the moist and jungly cleft your hands have made. Eyes and ears are shuttered from the land you left behind; mind empties itself of all other thought. You are the root of groping fingers. It is a fine hour for the fingers, their sense of touch so enhanced. The blind must know this feeling. Oh, there is risk everywhere. One goes lightly. The spleen. No! No! Do not touch the spleen that lurks below the left leaf of the diaphragm, a manta ray in a coral cave, its bloody tongue protruding. One poke and it might rupture, exploding with sudden hemorrhage. The filmy omentum must not be torn, the intestine scraped or denuded. The hand finds the liver, palms it, fingers running along its sharp lower edge, admiring. Here are the twin mounds of the kidneys, the apron of the omentum hanging in front of the intestinal coils. One lifts it aside and the fingers dip among the loops, searching, mapping territory, establishing boundaries. Deeper still, and the womb is touched, then held like a small muscular bottle— the womb and its earlike appendages, the ovaries. How they do nestle in the cup of a man's hand, their power all dormant. They are frailty itself.

There is a hush in the room. Speech stops. The hands of the others, assistants and nurses, are still. Only the voice of the patient's respiration remains. It is the rhythm of a quiet sea, the sound of waiting. Then you speak, slowly, the terse entries of a Himalayan climber reporting back.

"The stomach is okay. Greater curvature clean. No sign of ulcer. Pylorus, duodenum fine. Now comes the gallbladder. No stones. Right kidney, left, all right. Liver . . . uh-oh."

Your speech lowers to a whisper, falters, stops for a long, long moment, then picks up again at the end of a sigh that comes through your mask like a last exhalation.

"Three big hard ones in the left lobe, one on the right. Metastatic deposits. Bad, bad. Where's the primary? Got to be coming from somewhere."

The arm shifts direction and the fingers drop lower and lower into the pelvis—the body impaled now upon the arm of the surgeon to the hilt of the elbow.

"Here it is."

The voice goes flat, all business now.

"Tumor in the sigmoid colon, wrapped all around it, pretty tight. We'll take out a sleeve of the bowel. No colostomy. Not that, anyway. But, God, there's a lot of it down there. Here, you take a feel."

You step back from the table, and lean into a sterile basin of water, resting on stiff arms, while the others locate the cancer.

When I was a small boy, I was taken by my father, a general practitioner in Troy, New York, to St. Mary's Hospital, to wait while he made his rounds. The solarium where I sat was all sunlight and large plants. It smelled of soap and starch and clean linen. In the spring, clouds of lilac billowed from the vases; and in the fall, chrysanthemums crowded the magazine tables. At one end of the great high-ceilinged, glass-walled room was a huge cage where colored finches streaked and sang. Even from the first, I sensed the nearness of that other place, the Operating Room, knew that somewhere on these premises was that secret dreadful enclosure where *surgery* was at that moment happening. I sat among the cut flowers, half drunk on the scent, listening to the robes of the nuns brush the walls of the corridor, and felt the awful presence of *surgery*.

Oh, the pageantry! I longed to go there. I feared to go there. I imagined surgeons bent like storks over the body of the patient, a circle of red painted across the abdomen. Silence and dignity and awe enveloped them, these surgeons; it was the bubble in which they bent and straightened. Ah, it was a place I would never see, a place from whose walls the hung and suffering Christ turned his affliction to highest purpose. It is thirty years since I yearned for that old Surgery. And now I merely break the beam of an electric eye, and double doors swing open to let me enter, and as I enter, always, I feel the surging of a force that I feel in no other place. It is as though I am suddenly stronger and larger, heroic. Yes, that's it!

The Operating Room is called a theater. One walks onto a set where the cupboards hold tanks of oxygen and other gases. The cabinets store steel cutlery of unimagined versatility, and the refrigerators are filled with bags of blood. Bodies are stroked and penetrated here, but no love is made. Nor is it ever allowed to grow dark, but must always gleam with a grotesque brightness. For the special congress into which patient and surgeon enter, the one must have his senses deadened, the other his sensibilities restrained. One lies naked, blind, offering; the other stands masked and gloved. One yields; the other does his will.

I said no love is made here, but love happens. I have stood aside with lowered gaze while a priest, wearing the purple scarf of office, administers Last Rites to the man I shall operate upon. I try not to listen to those terrible last questions, the answers, but hear, with scorching clarity, the words that formalize the expectation of death. For a moment my resolve falters before the resignation, the *attentiveness*, of the other two. I am like an executioner who hears the cleric comforting the prisoner. For the moment I am excluded from the centrality of the event, a mere technician standing by. But it is only for the moment.

The priest leaves, and we are ready. Let it begin.

Later, I am repairing the strangulated hernia of an old man. Because of his age and frailty, I am using local anesthesia. He is awake. His name is Abe Kaufman, and he is a Russian Jew. A nurse sits by his head, murmuring to him. She wipes his forehead. I know her very well. Her name is Alexandra, and she is the daughter of Ukrainian peasants. She has a flat steppe of a face and slanting eyes. Nurse and patient are speaking of blintzes, borscht, piroshki—Russian food that they both love. I listen, and think that it may have been her grandfather who raided the shtetl where the old man lived long ago, and in his high boots and his blouse and his fury this grandfather pulled Abe by his side curls to the ground and stomped his face and kicked his groin. Perhaps it was that ancient kick that caused the hernia I am fixing. I listen to them whispering behind the screen at the head of the table. I listen with breath held before the prism of history.

"Tovarich," she says, her head bent close to his.

He smiles up at her, and forgets that his body is being laid open.

"You are an angel," the old man says.

—⚊—

One can count on absurdity. There, in the midst of our solemnities, appears, small and black and crawling, an insect: the Ant of the Absurd. The belly is open; one has seen and felt the catastrophe within. It seems the patient is already vaporizing into angelhood in the heat escaping therefrom. One could warm one's hands in that fever. All at once that ant is there, emerging from beneath one of the sterile towels that border the operating field. For a moment one does not really see it, or else denies the sight, so impossible it is, marching precisely, heading briskly toward the open wound.

Drawn from its linen lair, where it snuggled in the stream of the great sterilizer, and survived, it comes. Closer and closer, it hurries toward the incision. Ant, art thou in the grip of some fatal *ivresse*? Wouldst hurtle over these scarlet cliffs into the very boil of the guts? Art mad for the reek we handle? Or in some secret act of fornication engaged?

The alarm is sounded. An ant! An ant! And we are unnerved. Our fear of defilement is near to frenzy. It is not the mere physical contamination that we loathe. It is the evil of the interloper, that he scurries across our holy place, and filthies our altar. He is disease—that for whose destruction we have gathered. Powerless to destroy the sickness before us, we turn to its incarnation with a vengeance, and pluck it from the lip of the incision in the nick of time. Who would have thought an ant could move so fast?

Between thumb and forefinger, the intruder is crushed. It dies as quietly as it lived. Ah, but now there is death in the room. It is a perversion of our purpose. Albert Schweitzer would have spared it, scooped it tenderly into his hand, and lowered it to the ground.

The corpselet is flicked into the specimen basin. The gloves are changed. New towels and sheets are placed where it walked. We are pleased to have done something, if only a small killing. The operation resumes, and we draw upon ourselves once more the sleeves of office and rank. Is our reverence for life in question?

In the room the instruments lie on trays and tables. They are arranged precisely by the scrub nurse, in an order that never changes, so that you can reach blindly for a forceps or hemostat without looking away from the operating field. The instruments lie *thus*! Even at the beginning, when all is clean and tidy and no blood has been spilled, it is the scalpel that dominates. It has a figure the others do not have, the retractors and the scissors. The scalpel is all grace and line, a fierceness. It grins. It is like a cat—to be respected, deferred to, but which returns no amiability. To hold it above a belly is to know the knife's force—as though were you to give it slightest rein, it would pursue an intent of its own, driving into the flesh, a wild energy.

In a story by Borges, a deadly knife fight between two rivals is depicted. It is not, however, the men who are fighting. It is the knives themselves that are settling their own old score. The men who hold the knives are mere adjuncts to the weapons. The unguarded knife is like the unbridled warhorse that not only carries its helpless rider to his death, but tramples all beneath its hooves. The hand of the surgeon must tame this savage thing. He is a rider reining to capture a pace.

So close is the joining of knife and surgeon that they are like the Centaur—the knife, below, all equine energy, the surgeon, above, with his delicate art. One holds the knife back as much as advances it to purpose. One is master of the scissors. One is partner, sometimes rival, to the knife. In a moment it is like the long red fingernail of the Dragon Lady. Thus does the surgeon curb in order to create, restraining the scalpel, governing it shrewdly, setting the action of the operation into a pattern, giving it form and purpose.

It is the nature of creatures to live within a tight cuirass that is both their constriction and their protection. The carapace of the turtle is his fortress and retreat, yet keeps him writhing on his back in the sand. So is the surgeon rendered impotent by his own empathy and compassion. The surgeon cannot weep. When he cuts the flesh, his own must not bleed. Here it is all work. Like an asthmatic hungering for air, longing to take just one deep breath, the surgeon struggles not to feel. It is suffocating to press the feeling out. It would be easier to weep or mourn—for you know that the lovely precise world of proportion contains, just beneath, *there,* all disaster, all disorder. In a surgical operation, a risk may flash into reality: the patient dies . . .

of *complication*. The patient knows this too, in a more direct and personal way, and he is afraid.

And what of that *other,* the patient, you, who are brought to the operating room on a stretcher, having been washed and purged and dressed in a white gown? Fluid drips from a bottle into your arm, diluting you, leaching your body of its personal brine. As you wait in the corridor, you hear from behind the closed door the angry clang of steel upon steel, as though a battle were being waged. There is the odor of antiseptic and ether, and masked women hurry up and down the halls, in and out of rooms. There is the watery sound of strange machinery, the tinny beeping that is the transmitted heartbeat of yet another *human being*. And all the while the dreadful knowledge that soon you will be taken, laid beneath great lamps that will reveal the secret linings of your body. In the very act of lying down, you have made a declaration of surrender. One lies down gladly for sleep or for love. But to give over one's body and will for surgery, to *lie down* for it, is a yielding of more than we can bear.

Soon a man will stand over you, gowned and hooded. In time the man will take up a knife and crack open your flesh like a ripe melon. Fingers will rummage among your viscera. Parts of you will be cut out. Blood will run free. Your blood. All the night before you have turned with the presentiment of death upon you. You have attended your funeral, wept with your mourners. You think, "I should never have had surgery in the springtime." It is too cruel. Or on a Thursday. It is an unlucky day.

Now it is time. You are wheeled in and moved to the table. An injection is given. "Let yourself go," I say. "It's a pleasant sensation," I say. "Give in," I say.

Let go? Give in? When you know that you are being tricked into the hereafter, that you will end when consciousness ends? As the monstrous silence of anesthesia falls discourteously across your brain, you watch your soul drift off.

Later, in the recovery room, you awaken and gaze through the thickness of drugs at the world returning, and you guess, at first dimly, then surely, that you have not died. In pain and nausea you will know the exultation of death averted, of life restored.

What is it, then, this thing, the knife, whose shape is virtually the same as it was three thousand years ago, but now with its head grown detachable? Before steel, it was bronze. Before bronze, stone—then back into unremembered time. Did man invent it or did the knife precede him here, hidden under ages of vegetation and hoofprints, lying in wait to be discovered, picked up, used?

The scalpel is in two parts, the handle and the blade. Joined, it is six inches from tip to tip. At one end of the handle is a narrow notched prong upon which the blade is slid, then snapped into place. Without the blade, the handle has a blind, decapitated look. It is helpless as a trussed maniac. But slide on the blade, click it home, and the knife springs instantly to life. It is headed now, edgy, leaping to mount the fingers for the gallop to its feast.

Now is the moment from which you have turned aside, from which you have averted your gaze, yet toward which you have been hastened. Now the scalpel sings along the flesh again, its brute run unimpeded by germs or other frictions. It is a slick slide home, a barracuda spurt, a rip of embedded talon. One listens, and almost hears the whine—nasal, high, delivered through that gleaming metallic snout. The flesh splits with its own kind of moan. It is like the penetration of rape.

The breasts of women are cut off, arms and legs sliced to the bone to make ready for the saw, eyes freed from sockets, intestines lopped. The hand of the surgeon rebels. Tension boils through his pores, like sweat. The flesh of the patient retaliates with hemorrhage, and the blood chases the knife wherever it is withdrawn.

Within the belly a tumor squats, toadish, fungoid. A gray mother and her brood. The only thing it does not do is croak. It too is hacked from its bed as the carnivore knife lips the blood, turning in it in a kind of ecstasy of plenty, a gluttony after the long fast. It is just for this that the knife was created, tempered, heated, its violence beaten into paper-thin force.

At last a little thread is passed into the wound and tied. The monstrous booming fury is stilled by a tiny thread. The tempest is silenced. The operation is over. On the table, the knife lies spent, on its side, the bloody meal smear-dried upon its flanks. The knife rests.

And waits.

The Corpse

[*Homage to Sir Thomas Browne*]

—〰—

Shall I tell you once more how it happens? Even though you know, don't you?

You were born with the horror stamped upon you, like a fingerprint. All these years you have lived you have known. I but remind your memory, confirm the fear that has always been prime. Yet the facts have a force of their insolent own.

Wine is best made in a cellar, on a stone floor. Crush grapes in a barrel such that each grape is burst. When the barrel is three-quarters full, cover it with a fine-mesh cloth, and wait. In three days, an ear placed low over the mash will detect a faint crackling, which murmur, in two more days, rises to a continuous giggle. Only the rendering of fat or a forest fire far away makes such a sound. It is the song of fermentation! Remove the cloth and examine closely. The eye is startled by a bubble on the surface. Was it there and had it gone unnoticed? Or is it newly come?

But soon enough more beads gather in little colonies, winking and lining up at the brim. Stagnant fluid forms. It begins to turn. Slow currents carry bits of stem and grape meat on voyages of an inch or so. The pace quickens. The level rises. On the sixth day, the barrel is almost full. The teem must be poked down with a stick. The air of the cellar is dizzy with fruit flies and droplets of smell. On the seventh day, the fluid is racked into the second barrel for aging. It is wine.

Thus is the fruit of the earth taken, its flesh torn. Thus is it given over to standing, toward rot. It is the principle of corruption, the death of what is, the birth of what is to be.

You are wine.

SHE: Is he dead, then?

HE: I am sorry.

SHE: Oh, God.

HE: I should like to ask . . . because of the circumstances of your husband's death, it would be very helpful . . . to do . . . an autopsy.

SHE: Autopsy? No, no, not that. I don't want him cut up.

Better to have agreed, madam. We use the trocar on all, autopsied or merely embalmed. You have not heard of the suction trocar? Permit me to introduce you to the instrument.

A hollow steel rod some two feet in length, one end, the tip, sharp, pointed; to the other end there attaches rubber tubing, which tubing leads to the sink; near this end the handle, sculpted, the better to grip with; just inside the tip, holes, a circle of them, each opening large enough to admit the little finger or to let a raisin pass. This is the trocar.

A man stands by the table upon which you lie. He opens the faucet in the sink, steps forward, raises the trocar. It is a ritual spear, a gleaming emblem. Two inches to the left and two inches above your navel is the place of entry. (Feel it on yourself.) The technician raises this thing and aims for the spot. He must be strong, and his cheeks shake with the thrust. He grunts.

Wound most horrible! It is a goring.

The head of the trocar disappears beneath the skin. Deeper and deeper until the body wall is penetrated. Another thrust, and he turns the head north. First achieved is the stomach, whose stringy contents, food just eaten, are sucked into the holes. A three-inch glass connector interrupts the rubber tubing. Here one is spectator as the yield rushes by. Can you identify particular foods? Beets are easy, and licorice. The rest is merely . . . gray.

Look how the poker rides—high and swift and lubricious. Several passes, and then the trocar is drawn expertly back until the snout is barely hidden beneath the skin. The man takes aim again, this time for the point of the chin, he says. Then he dives through the mass of the liver, across the leaf of the diaphragm, and into the right chambers of the heart. Black blood fills the tubing. Thrust and pull, thrust and pull, thunking against the spine, the staves of the ribs, shivering the timbers, the brute bucking as it rides the magnificent forearm of the Licensed Embalmer in high rodeo.

The heart is empty. The technician turns the tool downward, into the abdomen once more. Now are the intestines pierced, coil upon coil, collapsing their gas and their juice to the sink. It is brown in the glass connector. Thunk, thunk, the rod smites the pelvis from within. The dark and muffled work is done: the scrotum is skewered, the testicles mashed, ablaze with their billion whiptail jots. All, all into the sink—and then to the sewer. This is the ultimate suck.

The technician disconnects the tubing from the sink, joins the tubing to a pump. He fires the motor; preservative fluid boils up, streams into the trocar, thence to thorax and abdomen.

The trocar is doubly clever.

HE: Urea combines with the phenol to make plastic. We, in effect, plasticize the body.

SHE: I do not want him plastic.

HE: It's only a word.

SHE: Jesus, words.

HE: There is the problem of the mouth.

SHE: Jesus, problems.

HE: It is all words, all problems. Trust me; I see. I . . . am . . . a physician. I really know, don't you see?

SHE: All right, then. The mouth. Tell me.

Our technician forces the mouth shut, holds it there, assessing. Buckteeth are a problem, he says. Sometimes you have to yank them to get the mouth closed. He removes his hand, and the mandible drops again. Now he takes a large flat needle. It is S-shaped, for ease of grasping. A length of white string hangs through the eye of this needle. He draws back the bottom lip with thumb and forefinger. He passes the needle into the lower gum. Needle and string are pulled through and out, and the lip allowed to rest. Next, the upper lip is held away, and the needle is passed up into the groove at the crest of the upper gum, thence to the left nostril, through the nasal septum into the right nostril, finally plunging back into that groove and once again to the mouth. This stitchery will not be seen. Pledgets of cotton are inserted to fill out a sag here, a droop there, lest the absence of teeth or turgor be noticed.

What? No penny enslotted here for Charon? No bite of honey cake for mad Cerberus?

No. Only cotton.

About this invented fullness the jaws are drawn to as the string is tied. One square knot is followed by two grannies. Prevents slippage, Death's tailor says. Gone is all toothy defiance. In its place, there is only the stuffed pout of anything filled too much. Now the plastic caps are inserted beneath the eyelids—pop, pop. And here— hold still—we are ready for cosmetics.

The case is opened importantly. It is of alligator hide, imitation of this. Within are shelves for the jars, slots for the brushes, as many as the vanity Death's whore requires. The technician selects three jars. Red, yellow, blue: daubs a bit of each on the palette; mixes, turns, and wipes—until the color of your skin is matched. More blue for Negroes, says he; less yellow and more blue for them. He has said something unarguable—and is now quiet. Many a sidelong glance later, he is ready. He steps to the head of the table and applies the paint, massages the color into the skin of face and hands. This is what shows, he says. And one must do, but not overdo, he says. At last our fellow approves. How lovely the morning, pockless glow! It is a wholesome look—a touch of evening blue in the hollows of the lids. Oh, yes, art is truly bottled sunshine.

Who, but a moment ago, was huffing rider of the belly is now artist, configuring Death, shaping it. He has rebuilt a ravaged chin, replaced an absent nose, he says. Give him enough plaster and a bit of paint and he can make a man, he says. I wait for him to lean over and blow into these nostrils. He can make anything except life, he says.

Thus combed and shaved (lemon-scented Colgate is nice) and powdered, the corpse gleams, a marquis upon ruched velvet, banked with fierce forced blossoms.

SHE: Embalming belittles death.

HE: On the contrary, art dignifies. It is the last passion. For both fellows, don't you know?

SHE: But there must be some other way. As for myself, mind you, I prefer to be of use. I have made arrangements that my body be given to a medical school for dissection. I carry this little card that so states. In case of accident.

HE: A gesture in the grand style. You join a gallant band. So many are concerned with the appearance of the flesh, leaving ill-considered its significance. Well . . . its usefulness.

Forty feet long, four wide, and seven deep is THE TANK. It is set into the ground at the very bottom of the medical school. If Anatomy be the firstborn of Medicine, then the tank is its sunken womb. Here at the very center of stench it lies; here is the bite of embalming fluid sharpest. Tears overwhelm the eyes. The tank demands weeping of this kind. It is lidded, covered by domed metal, handle at apex, like a casserole of chow mein.

Let me remove this lid. Behold! How beautiful they are, the bodies. With what grace and pomp each waits his turn. Above the fluid, a center rod, like a closet rod, suspends them in a perfect row; forty soldiers standing in the bath, snug as pharaohs, only heads showing, all facing, obediently, the same way.

Come, walk the length of the tank. We review these warriors who, by their bearing, salute us. Arteries have been pumped full of fluid. It helps the flesh to sink, lest feet float to the top in embarrassing disarray. Thus weighted, the bodies swim readily to erect posture. Upon each head, worn with a certain nonchalance, are the tongs, the headdress of this terrible tribe. The hooks of the tongs are inserted one into each ear, then sunk home by pulling on the handle. Each set of tongs is then hung from the center rod by a pulley. In this way the bodies can be skimmed back and forth during the process of selection or to make room for another.

We end skin overcoats on a rack.

A slow current catches the brine and your body sways ever so slightly, keeping time. This movement stirs the slick about your shoulders. Iridescent colors appear, and little chunks of melt, shaken off in annoyance, it seems, bob up and down.

Does some flame far below, at the center of the earth, thus bring this tank to lazy boil? Or is it the heat from hell? Look. A dead fly floats, one wing raised in permanent effort at extrication. A fly? Well, of course. There is food here.

It is wine.

> SHE: I want nothing done. Let him be put in the ground as he is.
> HE: You are distraught. Perspective. What you need is perspective. Listen. Outside the rain is falling, soft as hair. [A pause] No toilette, then?

Dead, the body is somehow more solid, more massive. The shrink of dying is past. It is as though only moments before, a wind kept it aloft, and now, settled, it is only what it is—a mass, declaring itself, an ugly emphasis. Almost at once the skin changes color, from pink-highlighted yellow to gray-tinted blue. The eyes are open and lackluster; something, a bright dust, has been blown away, leaving the globes smoky. And there is an absolute limpness. Hours later, the neck and limbs are drawn up into a semiflexion, in the attitude of one who has just received a blow to the solar plexus.

One has.

Even the skin is in rigor, is covered with goose bumps. Semen is forced from the penis by the contraction of muscle. The sphincters relax, and the air is poisonous with loosed sewage. Colder and colder grows the flesh, as the last bit of warmth disperses. Now you are meat, meat at room temperature.

Examine once more the eyes. How dull the cornea, this globe bereft of tension. Notice how the eyeball pits at the pressure of my fingernail. Whereas the front of your body is now drained of color, the back, upon which you rest, is found to be deeply violet. Even here, even now, gravity works upon the blood. In twenty-four hours, your untended body resumes its flaccidity, resigned to this everlasting posture.

You stay thus.

You do not die all at once. Some tissues live on for minutes, even hours, giving still their little cellular shrieks, molecular echoes of the agony of the whole corpus. Here and there a spray of nerves dances on. True, the heart stops; the blood no longer courses; the electricity of the brain sputters, then shuts down. Death is now *pronounceable*. But there are outposts where clusters of cells yet shine, besieged, little lights blinking in the advancing darkness. Doomed soldiers, they battle on. Until Death has secured the premises all to itself.

The silence, the darkness, is not for long. That which was for a moment dead leaps most sumptuously to life. There is a busyness gathering. It grows fierce.

There is to be a feast. The rich table has been set. The board groans. The guests have already arrived, numberless bacteria that had, in life, dwelt in saprophytic harmony with their host. Their turn now! Charged, they press against the membrane barriers, break through the new softness, sweep across plains of tissue, devouring, belching gas—a gas that puffs eyelids, cheeks, abdomen into bladders of murderous vapor. The slimmest man takes on the bloat of corpulence. Your swollen belly bursts with a ripping sound, followed by a long mean hiss.

And they are at large! Blisters appear upon the skin, enlarge, coalesce, blast, leaving brownish puddles in the declivities. You are becoming gravy. Arriving for the banquet late, of course, and all the more ravenous for it, are the twin sisters *Calliphora* and raucous *Lucilia,* the omnipresent greenbottle flies, their costumes metallic sequins. Their thousands of eggs are laid upon the meat, and soon the mass is wavy with the humped creamy backs of maggots nosing, crowding, hungrily absorbed. Gray sprays of fungus sprout in the resulting marinade, and there lacks only a mushroom growing from the nose.

At last—at last the bones appear, clean and white and dry. Reek and mangle abate; diminuendo the buzz and crawl. All, all is eaten. All is done. Hard endlessness is here even as the revelers abandon the skeleton.

You are alone, yet again.

HE: Come, come, we are running out of time. How, at last, would you dispose of your husband? You must make a decision.

SHE: Why must I?

HE: Because you are the owner of the body. It is your possession.

SHE: Oh, cremation, dammit. I'm sick of this business.

HE: Brava! Man is pompous in the grave, splendid in ashes.

SHE: A smaller package to mail.

HE: You are doing the right thing, I assure you. The physiognomy does not endure in the grave. There is no identity. Cremation is tidy. I can see that you abhor the slough of putrefaction. Who wouldn't?

To the prettiness again. . . .

The good fellow slides you into the oven and ignites the fire. If you are burned in your casket, an exhaust fan sucks away the wood ash, until there is only your body. He observes through a peephole at the back of the oven. Now he turns off the exhaust, and lets the flames attack the body. Three hours later, at two thousand degrees Fahrenheit, it is done. The oven is turned off, is let cool overnight. The next day a rear door is opened, and the ashes are examined.

Intact pieces of bone are pulverized with a mallet. With a little broom the residue is whisked into an urn. The operator is fastidious, down to smallest bits of dust.

The modern urn is no garnished ossuary, but a tin can indistinguishable from that which holds coffee by the pound. It is unadorned. Pry open the lid and see the expensive white doily, of the best embossed paper, creased like a priest's napkin. Unfold it, and gaze upon the contents. Shocking! They are not ashes but chunks of bone, and recognizable as such. Some as big as your thumbnail, chalky, charred. A tin of cinders. Coals and calx—with the odor of smoke and the semen-smell of cooked bone.

> SHE: How do I know that it is my husband's ashes that you give me? That they are his and not some other's—an old woman's, a dog's?
> HE: A vile and baseless suspicion. Now, in the matter of the cremains . . .
> SHE: The what?
> HE: Your husband's cremains.
> SHE: His ashes?
> HE: Yes. Many bereaved find it a soothing term, less harsh than . . . you know . . .

But you are right to question.

Who knows the fate of his bones? His ashes? To what purpose tamp them into sad sepulchral pitchers? I have seen the cremation of two, even three, together. Later, the ashes were shoveled into cans in equal amounts, and labeled. Why not? Great religions have flourished on more spurious assumptions. The idea is not new. Were not the ashes of Achilles mingled with those of his lover Patroclus? Ah, you say, it is one thing to burn lovers, then fondly stir their ashes together; quite another to have one's urn-fellows selected at random.

Yet are not all our greatest intimacies merest chance?

> HE: Have you considered the disposition of the ashes?
> SHE: The toilet?

HE: I am afraid, madam, that we have reached an impasse. You prefer neither cremation nor embalming. You are repelled alike by anatomical dissection and the moist relentment of putrefaction. Why don't you admit that you are ashamed of death? You think it is a disgrace to be dead.

SHE: That's it. Yes. A disgrace. That's it exactly.

HE: Exactly, yes.

SHE: If you know everything, then what is your choice? For yourself?

HE: That is not the point.

Ah, but it is the point. Listen. On the banks of the Hudson, midway between Manhattan and Montreal, squats the lizard town of Troy. In the back room of Moriarity's Saloon, the November meeting of the Druids of Eld is taking place. Harry Bascomb rises to deliver the invocation:

"From insomnia as from bad dreams, from lack of love, from waiting so long you forget why, from enlargement of the prostate, from running out of coal, from constipation, from a sniveling son and a daughter who flunks Deportment, from the pox and from the gout, from a grave full of worms—in Moriarity's, in the woes of day and the throes of night, O Lord, deliver us."

This is followed by the ineffably sad sound of men trying to laugh together.

"The subject for tonight is what to do with your mortal remains. You first, Georgie."

Georgie assumes a leprechaun stoop and a high Irish voice. "I want me heart cut out and placed in a little silver box," he says, "with napkins and red candle wax all around. The rest ye can cast on terra damnata, and piss on it."

"You're next, Doc. Surely you've learned from the dying whispers of your fellow men?"

"Nothing. Nothing."

"What? A physician? Sawbones? Nothing? We can endure your hideous facts."

The doctor shivers despite the warmth of the saloon, and hugs his chest with his arms. He is fresh from debate with next of kin, weary, weary. There is a stain on his vest more terrible than the Ancient Mariner's eye.

"I want," he begins, "to be buried—unembalmed and unboxed— at the foot of a tree. Soon I melt and seep into the ground, to be drawn up by the roots. Straight to the top, strung in the crown, answering the air. There would be the singing of birds, the applause of wings."

"Fed to a tree? All right, then. But a cow would do the tree more good."

Then all sing:

> O what shall be done with our dead, old boys?
> We'll run out of ground very soon.
> Why, pack 'em in straw for a bed, old boys,
> And freight 'em straight off to the moon.

> O what shall we do with our dead, old boys?
> It seems a shame to waste 'em.
> So after your tears are shed, old boys,
> Why, spit 'em and roast 'em and taste 'em.

Then all drink their wine.
Wine?

Bald!

—⁓—

What plague is this that so thrives in the night a whole forest is notoriously laid waste? It is a smoldering of the dark hours—infection! The bedroom air steams with pestilence. By dawn the rigor has passed, the fever broken, and cold gray light is witness to a rumpled pillow bestrewn with the Fallen and the Shed.

It is Baldness that rages thus.

O Scalp, Scalp, wilt thou not bleed, not scream from this murderous depilation? Behold, thou art scythed and give no sign save a silence from nape to brow.

To the mirror. Oh, God. The comb trembles! A pass, tentative, light, from occiput forward. Now you hold the comb aloft at the window, through which indifferent morning bestows light in whose lidless glare you see the carnage of the night. Desperate lips tell the mournful numbers. Twenty-eight! Twenty-eight corpselets hanging limp between the teeth. And even as you watch, twenty-nine and thirty, made airborne by some tardy gust, rock sinkward.

O wild punching of the air! O damn and damn!

Frantic fingers forage among the survivors. You search for tomahawk wounds, fissures, all the lacerations and gougings of assault. There is nothing. All is smooth. All is still. Barren. A curse has come and passed, leaving no trace. Ah, lion unmaned, cock uncombed.

Your fingertips speculate back and forth upon the apex of your noggin. It has an obscene feel. One is joyless playing with himself *here*. You incline your head forward; your eye strains: an impossible angle. A pinkness flashes into view, and the horror is confirmed. Pink!

A punishment, you think. One has gazed too long on low delights.

Hair today, gone tomorrow, you say, and give a soldierly little smile. Yet you know that it is the joke and not the hair that is on you. Steady. You *will* look on the bright side. Good riddance, you say. Think of Absalom hanging by his hair from a tree. No such infringement for you. And what of Samson? Oh, God, *Samson,* you say weakly, and read in the pattern of those hairs in the sink the clarion message of power failing.

But, come, come, worrier, won't you think of all the time to be saved? At least half an hour a day of primping? And money? No haircuts, no combs, no brushes. No soap.

It is no use. You are shorn, forlorn. Delilahed. You lurch to the telephone to sound the alarm: Dermatologist! Barber! Quack shop! There is no rescue, no Column of Light Brigade. You grow old. You get ugly. And you get it all figured out: You lose your hair, you lose your *mind*.

What is it, this snatching that pains worse than gout, hurts worse than hernia? It is called by doctors alopecia—fox mange, that is, for it comes to elderly foxes even as it does to us. Nor is it news. In ancient Egypt, Amenophis II, Rameses II, and even Nefertiti had it. Aristotle was bald, as was Julius Caesar. Let us learn:

Embedded in the deepest layer of the skin, the dermis, are nests of specialized cells: hair follicles. Here the bubbling of cell division is most intense, new cells forming along the periphery, crowding the older ones toward the center of the follicle. These flatten, attenuate, and turn into filaments of protein called *keratin*. It is this keratin, both the secretion of the follicle and that which it will become, that is the hair.

Lucky follicle. To have its destiny in its secretion. It is what the poet wants but seldom gets.

Longer and longer grows the hair. On and on spins the follicle gnome, its growth intermittent; for there are rest periods: The gnome nods, and the hair remains, in these respites, the same length.

The scalp of the young adult boasts between 100,000 and 150,000 of these strands. Ninety percent grow while 10 percent rest. At a hectic four tenths of a millimeter per day, the hair grows, accumulating unto itself its daily measure of keratin. Beard hair, if left intact, can reach a length of some thirty centimeters, that of the scalp, much longer. Just how long is still a matter of dispute among trichologists. George Catlin, artist, went west to draw Indians, and reported back to a breathless world that it was not uncommon among the Crow tribe for a warrior's hair to fall five feet, brushing his heels as he walked. Long Hair, chief of the Crows, possessed the bravest follicles of all. His unbound tresses not only reached the ground but trailed after him for several feet. Less heroic but more accessible to view were the seven legendary Sutherland Sisters, displayed from town to town by patent medicine men. The unslung manes of these ladies cascaded to the insteps of their high-button shoes.

Long hair has always been construed as prima facie evidence for virility and power, while the bare scalp is a mark of degradation. Thus was the topknot taken in battle as a trophy of war—for he who possesses the hair of his slain enemy takes unto himself all the strength and courage of that foe. Not by Indians alone was such bushwhacking done, but by Scythians, Visigoths, and, yes, Maccabees as well. And prisoners, novice soldiers, traitors, and adulteresses alike were shaved to announce their ignominy. Along came Christianity to change shame into humility by having its monks plow their manes into tonsures. Still, there is nothing to indicate that it made a single baldy feel one whit better.

Will you not be comforted by the knowledge that, balding, you lose not the possibility of hair? Will it help to learn that the follicles, for some reason as yet unknown, involute, close down only? That they bank the fires of their mitosis, but do not perish? On rare occasions they may be roused from their long sleep to thrive once more. One must cultivate such tiny hopes. They are all you have.

Numberless are the unguents and poultices, the stoups and

butters with which desperate man has rubbed his pate. Eau de Por-
tugal, d'Égypte, de Chine—all in vain. To no avail electricity, vibration, massage, frightening, and the wearing of all manner of strange
devices including hog's bladder, which folk wisdom was whispered
to me by an indebted witch whose instructions were to wear for seven
days and seven nights a fresh porcine urinary bladder as a yarmulke
or capulet.

Actually, the entire body is covered with hair, save for the palms
and soles, most of it being of the vellus type, that fine fuzz that can
be seen in a good light. These are like the hairs that we wore in our
embryonic life. It is only here and there that creatures affect a more
conspicuous display, for purposes of either sexual attraction or spe-
cific protection. The bristles of the warthog are, after all, a distant-
early-warning system, an exteriorized hypersense that instructs of
friend, foe, or food nearby. And the tail tuft of cattle? Despite the
biological cynicism that insists that the tuft was developed as a kind
of evolutionary fly whisk, anyone knows what a coy cow can do to a
bull with a flick—now here, now there.

Why not revise your thinking, adopt a Grecian Urn mentality?
Seen hair is nice, but that unseen is nicer still.

Nothing is known about the cause of baldness. At a seventeenth-
century symposium called *De Capelli e Peli,* on the scalp and hair,
air pollution (*miasmi pestiferi*) was blamed for it. That hair follicles
transplanted from another part of the body to the scalp flourish
would indicate that hair-fall owes not to any deficiency of the tissue,
nor is any impairment of the circulation thus suspected of fault. What
is known is that androgen, the male sex hormone, must be present
for baldness to develop, thus reinforcing the folk wisdom that baldness and virility go hand in hand. The replacement or addition of
androgen by ingestion, injection, or smearing does nothing to delay
or reverse the rate of balding. Only castration is effective. Thus did
bald Aristotle gaze in envy at the flowing locks of the eunuchs of
Athens. Nor is it known why, even as scalp hair is lost, otherwise
hairless areas wax jungly. Witness the winglets of hair that sprout
upon the shoulders of old men. Genes matter. As failed your father's,

so fail yours. It is upon the reef of heredity that the fragile barque of beauty founders.

Why then this grieving over plait and lock? Does it comfort to learn that baldness is the natural fate of the he-man? Come. With heart defiant, advance your naked pate proudly to the public eye. Hair is but a keepsake with sentimental value. We mourn its loss as we would any memento that must be surrendered to the earth. Therefore let your balditude be boldly proclaimed. Bald is beautiful!

There is comfort for man in the comradeship of the orangutan, the chimpanzee, the ouakari, and the stump-tailed macaque, for they share in this unthatching. Nor has any of these beasts ever been observed to utter the least oath of shame or sorrow at such a falling out. Is not the dolphin bald? The whale? The dugong? What is clearly needed is a change of heart. The heart of a dugong is what you needs must have. In lieu of hair, it is the brain must be washed.

All right then, try philosophy. Be persuaded that it is in our nudity lies our greatness. In our nakedness are we most admirable. Who needs feathers? Of what use plumage when a blush will do? Still unconsoled? Well, then, obtain, by any means practical, the bladder of a hog. . . .

Writer's Block

—∞—

The original tongue was composed only of vowels. It is what man learned from animals. Vowels carry a cry for help a long way. It was by vowels that a mate was attracted, or grief given voice. Vowelage is the means by which pain is exteriorized from the body, and grief relieved. Consonants were an afterthought. They hold back, modify, restrain our feelings. We hide behind consonants. Facts are best expressed with consonants. The writer who would depict not the factual but the revelatory must use a rich alluvial language, full of outcry. Modern literature has become altogether too solid, coagulated. In my next life, I'm going to learn Persian. Any language that has given us the words *scarlet, peach, azure, lilac, taffeta,* and *cummerbund* is essential to a writer.

There is an instinctive element to writing. It is the same instinct that causes a nursing mother's breasts to squirt milk when she hears her baby crying in the next room. But there are times when instinct alone cannot open the floodgates of the imagination. On such days, I can be found flopping from bed to ottoman, scarcely able to "raise my heart to a drooping syllable." I stare into my inkwell for minutes at a time, looking for something that is not to be found there. Should I insist upon writing anyway, the pen turns into a quill dropped from Satan's wing; it produces nothing good, only rubbish. At other times, I feel like the attendant in a gas station: plug in the pen, pour in a gallon of ink, and watch the jalopy rattle off. The danger then is not knowing when to stop. Homer wisely refused to follow Achilles after he returns the corpse of Hector to his father, Priam. Virgil, on the other hand, should have quit with the death of Dido. It's all downhill, after that. Some writers require the silence of the tomb. Rilke roosted in lonely castles, with the furniture arranged just so. Only there might the angel appear holding out a sonnet on a silver tray. For Kafka, the least noise—a cricket on the hearth—brought on an attack of nerves. Others, I'm one of them, can scribble no matter the hue and cry. Give me that stridulating cricket, the one abhorred by Kafka. It's what comes of having had children who leaned on my shoulder to read the words as they issued from the pen, and from having had to write catch-as-catch-can in operating rooms, emergency rooms, and intensive care units with flesh and blood swirling about.

Afflicted with Writer's Block, one is not helpless but can call upon a small regiment of influences. First, clear the desk of everything but a sheet of paper, a pen, and a candle. Now turn off all the lights, and light the candle. All at once, the room will have shrunk to the flickering space around you. Observe the play of the candlelight upon your naked forearm, the way the flame bows toward you as you inhale, bends away when you breathe out, conversing with you, using its tongue to give you courage, peopling the room with shadows. Should this fail, put on your most sympathetic article of clothing, your slippers say, or the beret of contentment. For me, that would be my corduroy writing pants, bought twenty years ago in Florence, Italy. Brown as the Arno they are, and voluminous. Having long since lost all elasticity, they swirl about my ankles like classical drapery. Only to draw them upon my legs and tie the cord about my waist is enough to persuade the Muse to relent. There is also the small skullcap I put on for no religious reason, but to keep my thoughts from flying off the top of my head like those four and twenty blackbirds, when the pie was opened.

There is nothing more conducive to writing than a long steady rain—the grammatical sound of it on the roof, on the leaves, on pavement. Listen! A horse-drawn buggy comes scraping on the cobblestones. Within minutes, you are riding inward, one ear cocked for the sound of laughter caught in the puddles. At the lake's edge, lanterns light up the mist in which a centaur is born. That sort of thing. I pity those writers who must scratch away in dry countries where the annual rainfall is measured in millimeters. How do they get anything done in Arizona or Arabia? For these wretches (short of emigration) I recommend a simple device that will mimic the sound of rain. It need be no more than a hose directed down upon a sheet of tin placed just outside the window, and a catch basin and pump for recirculation. For good measure, add the owlish sound of a train whistle at night and churchbells not so close as to fracture the air with their clangor nor so far off as to be devoid of earthly echoes. Certain odors too have the loveliest way with writing—the smell of horse manure in the morning and tobacco at dusk. So. All you have to do is rent a house midway between a church with a working belfry and a railroad crossing, turn off the electricity, pray for rain, keep a horse in the backyard, and plant nicotiana outside the window of your study. Such a program is of far more use than books on "How to Write Well" which only teach you how to write *rather* well.

It is no use to appeal directly to the Muse. Not long ago, I implored the pen itself.

"Come, Ariel!" I cried. "We have a lof of work to do today."

"Nothing doing," she replied. "I'm not getting up today." I tried it in French (she is partial to that language).

"Levez-vous! Levez-vous! Nous avons beaucoup à faire aujourd'hui."

"Jamais. Laissez-moi dormir."

"There, there," I soothed. "You'll feel better in an hour." Whereupon the wicked pen swooned among my fingers and discharged a large inkblot onto the page.

Of Nazareth and New Haven

—∾—

~ MARCH 9, 2000

I have just left the Yale Art Gallery, where I have been looking at a painting by Francisco de Zurbarán. It shows Mary and Jesus at home in Nazareth. The teenage Jesus, dressed in a pale lavender tunic and barefoot, has been weaving a circlet of thorns, and has just pricked his finger. He bends to examine his wound, his face nearly touching his hand. Mary, dressed in a voluminous scarlet robe, has paused in her sewing and is contemplating the boy with a look of infinite tenderness and sadness, as if she has foreknowledge of what is to come. The entire scene is still, motionless, otherworldly, mystical. This, despite such homely details as a large basket of white laundry on the floor, some pears on a table whose drawer is partially open, a vase of flowers. A shaft of celestial light descends upon the room. In it one sees cherubim treading air and looking down at the mother and son. While the boy is engrossed with his wounded finger, the mother's attention is upon her son to the exclusion of all else. At the bottom of the picture, two plump white doves gaze directly outward, as though acknowledging the presence of the viewer.

Outside the Art Gallery, there is a row of low stone benches, attached to the front of the building. On the last of these, a black man and woman sit, so close together as to seem engrafted the one upon the other. Her left hand emerges from beneath his right arm.

Their heads are pressed together at the temples. Passing by, I over-
hear a bit of dialogue:

> SHE: I love you more than you love me.
> HE: You can't possibly love me more than I love you.
> SHE: Yes, I do.
> HE: No, you don't.
> SHE: Yes, I do.

I had already turned the corner from Chapel Street into High
Street but now, out of curiosity, I confess it, I reverse my steps until
I can observe them from nearby. It is rude, I know. She is the older,
but by how much it is at first difficult to tell. She is wearing a
woolen cap that covers her hair, and a shapeless, bulky overcoat.
Aside from a few streamlets of oysterish, barely pigmented cloud,
the sky is deeply blue. I stop to talk. It's that kind of day, noontime
after all, when both hands of the clock are lifted in either supplication or hallelujah. All about them, on the cobblestones, pigeons
are boiling.

> ME: Are you lovers?
> SHE: Yes, we lovers. He, my son. I love him to death.
> ME: Do you love him more than he loves you?
> SHE: Yes, I do.
> HE: No, you don't.
> SHE: Yes, I do.
> [Et cetera.]
> ME: Are you having a fight?
> SHE: Yes, this is the way we fight.

The woman is perhaps fifty, with a broad somewhat tipsy grin,
her speech a little slurred. She is smoking a cigarette.

> SHE (speaking to me): Come on over here, man, and give
> me a shake.

She holds out her hand. I take it in mine. It is soft and dry. She raises my hand to her lips, kisses it. Her breath too is a warm dry softness. When she smiles, I see that she has only two mandibular teeth so widely spaced as to be useless for chewing. He is in his thirties, I decide, with a spruce black mustache, a gold necklace and ring, a baseball cap, tracksuit pants and jacket, and large-size running shoes. There is a bandage on his right index finger.

"How did you hurt your finger?" I ask.

"Pullin' up a dead rose bush at her house."

Now they resume their argument over the relative intensity of their love for each other. I cannot be sure but I think that my presence has spurred them on to even more vehemence in their tender reproaches. That is the effect of an audience on the players.

ME: You're the luckiest people in the city.
HE: We know it. We know it, don't we?
SHE: Uh-huh, we do.

On the next bench but one, a man is singing to himself. "Beautiful dreamer, Queen of my song. List while I woo thee with soft melody . . ." For a long time, I stand somewhere between her saying "I love you more . . ." and his denying it. Look! See how she turns to gaze at his left ear, studying the delicate whorl of cartilage, then reaches out to touch the earlobe that is as soft as love itself. Theirs is a unique happiness, with its own wisdom. But such happiness is too unlucky to last. It will end violently. All at once, I want to warn her. I open my mouth to cry out, but I can't speak. Besides, it wouldn't do any good. Die now! I want to say. Only, this time, you go first! I shiver in their warmth, and listen to my teeth chattering. I can smell their suffering to come.

Could such a scene have been received between mere eyelids, these two sitting on the bench, pressed into each other? The smoke from her cigarette encloses him in a uterine mantle. At the outer edge, New Haven itself is smoky, elastic, elusive. It seems to me that the *Sitzgruppe* has risen off the ground. I have to look up to see them atop the pedestals upon which they have placed each other and where they are blurred as in a celestial astigmatism. Above them, pigeons, plump and weightless, have gathered on a ledge. From beneath each lifted wing, light is released. They might be cherubim giving off incense and effulgence and music. What is that smell? Sandalwood, I think, or frankincense.

It is absurd, this kneeling down inside my soul. But already I have heated ink, dipped a scalpel, and carved a tear on my left cheek. It burns all the way down. The mother smiles, and there again are the two canine teeth.

"Open your mouth, Mother. This won't hurt. They're so loose. They waggle. There! It's done. Rinse with this. Now spit."

"Teeth of the Virgin." (Verified.) Just think! Wrapped in velvet and resting in a tiny reliquary of gold and lapis lazuli. Harvested and donated anonymously to the Yale Art Gallery where a river of adoring gazes will bathe them from now on, wearing them thin and translucent and all the holier for it.

From this bench, I walk away, while they remain, telling on, one bead after another in contrapuntal argument until the whole chain will have been recited, then begun anew. Hushed are the pigeons on the high ledges. Only when I have turned the corner do they resume their cooing until, as at a given sign, they flutter up, wings whirring, and escort me away. Blessed are the people who sit on benches in the city. Blessed are the mother and her son. In the middle of the block on High Street, I tumble headlong to the pavement in a pool of words.

Time and again, I have returned to the corner of Chapel and High to stand by the stone bench, now vacant, straining to see departed splendor. Sometimes I remove my glasses and gaze into the city's dust turned golden by the sun, and I have the faint sense that here, in this place, are things not ready to be seen. The full significance of the encounter lies in its echo which only I was privileged to hear. For a brief moment, eternity became visible, palpable, audible when, beneath a noonday sun, a stone bench occupied by two persons became an imperishable vision to which I am bound by invisible chains. It seems to me now that mother and son had been waiting there for my participation, the way a blank mirror waits for the image it is meant to reflect.

In the months to come, I shall think of it. Let me be at that place by the gallery. Let the noonday sun be warm and bright. Let there be sitting a woman and a youth. Let him be weaving a crown of thorns. Let him prick his finger, then bend to examine the wound. Let her be dressed in a scarlet gown. Let him wear a tunic of pale purple. Let him be barefoot. Let there be a basket of white linen by her feet. Let her be sewing. Let her gaze at him with tenderness and sorrow. Let her reach out to touch the lobe of his ear. Let her feel its softness as a wound in her heart. Let me feel her beatific breath upon my hand. Let there be doves on the ledge above them. Let the bench be inside me. Let me keep it there.

Textbook

—⟋⟍—

I send as your graduation present my father's old textbook of physical diagnosis. It was published in 1918. Lifted yesterday from a trunk in the attic, it is still faintly redolent of formaldehyde, and stained with Heaven only knows what ancient liquid. I love my old books—Longfellow, Virgil, *Romeo and Juliet,* and *Moby-Dick*—but I love this *Textbook of Physical Diagnosis* more. I can think of no better thing to give you as a reminder that all of Medicine is a continuum of which you are now a part. Within you is the gesture of the prehistoric surgeon who trephined his neighbor's skull on the floor of a cave. Within you, the poultice of cool mud applied to a burn by an old African woman. The work of all doctors before you is in your blood. Yours will enter the veins of whosoever comes after you.

The patients shown on the pages of this book are long since dead; so, too, the doctors and nurses who tended them; so, too, the photographer who peered at them from beneath the black curtain of his camera. Gone, the brilliant pink chancre that gave to one man all of his distinction; gone, too, the great goiter that made of the most ordinary woman a grinning queen; and the boyish bravado that rose above a huge scrotum infested with microfilaria. To read this book is to understand that disease raises the sufferer, granting him from out of his fever and his fret an intimate vision of life, a more direct route to his soul. Now he has the body of a poet.

You cannot separate passion from pathology any more than you can separate a person's spirit from his body. Think of a particular person's spirit and, Presto! it is immediately incorporated. It has the size and shape of his body. The flesh is the spirit thickened. Gaze long enough at your patients, and from even the driest husk there will fly upward a shower of sparks that, to him who gazes, will coalesce into a little flame. Look at the pictures in this book and learn that the sick are refugees who must be treated kindly and gravely, without condescension. In the beginning you will love their wounds because they give you the occasion for virtue; later you will love the sick for their own sake. Rendered helpless by their afflictions, they cherish the memory of fertile lands and cool green glades and the company of love—all the stuff of their former selves. These people know something you and I do not yet know—what it is to live with the painful evidence of your mortality.

Notice that in each picture the eyes of the subjects have been covered by a black band to conceal identities. But the eyes are not the only windows to the soul. I have seen sorrow more fully expressed in a buttocks eaten away by bedsores; fear, in the arching of a neck; supplication, in a wrist. Only last week I was informed by a man's kneecaps that he was going to die. Flashing blue lights, they teletyped that he was running out of oxygen and blood. As soon as I got their cyanotic message, I summoned his family for a last vigil. A doctor's eyes must not be blindfolded against the light.

My hat is off to the photographer of this book, who chose misery for his subject in order to endear it. If I were you, I would not show these pictures to the squeamish who will be threatened by the echoes of their own mortality. Nor to vulgar people who decree that what they think ugly or gross ought not to be photographed. It would offend them. But what some think of as ugliness can become beauty to others—an ulcer, a dwarf, blood spreading on a pillow. An amputated leg retains something of the character of the one from whom it has been severed. Much as does the broken-off handle of a Greek amphora. It could have been part of nothing else. Retrieved and held up to fit, the handle sings again its old amphoric song. Personally, I suspect that truth is more accessible in "ugliness" than it is in beauty.

The man who photographed the people in this book knew that in October, when the leaves fall from the trees, you can see farther into the forest.

Let us look through the book together. A quick glance might lead you to think these folk impoverished. My God! you say, a squirrel in his packed nuttery has more than they. Well, perhaps. But to me they seem the freest humans on earth. For while they stand on the narrow ledge of physical torment, no one would try to jostle them from their perch to take their place. Soon, you know, they will leap from that ledge to the plain where the bones of their ancestors lie strewn. The rest of us must still contend for a place in the sun, must face as best we can the dreadful future tense.

On one page there are two photographs of the same woman. She is naked save for her high-button shoes. In the first picture, she stands sideways to show her huge, pendulous umbilical hernia. It hangs to within six inches of her knees like an apron. In the second, she lifts the flap with her two hands as though to begin a dance. On the next page a man with a detachable collar and sleeve garters holds out a hand whose fingers are mummified from lack of circulation.

And here is a black man shown from the rear. His back is so wasted that he resembles a hanging bat—lax webs slung from the shoulder blades and cinched at the hips. His scapulae have scrambled to the top of the wreck, and crouch there in fright.

A young woman throws her head back to show her credential here, a thyroglossal duct cyst seen as a lump at the front of her neck. Her mouth falls open to reveal her small upper front teeth, each one separated by a cunning space. The interior of her mouth is dark, a receptacle. Her face is oddly corrupt. Perhaps she is kneeling . . . and those babyish sharp teeth.

Next, the reckless stare of a hyperthyroid, her eye showing too much white. She lives in a frenzy. Her pulse, respirations, appetite, everything is furious. Her gaze, too. Here, at last, is countenance befitting the mood of the body. Even the page trembles finely in my hand.

Now a congenital syphilitic intent that you should see his perforated palate. A triangular hole in that palate leads to an upper vault that is hidden from view, all but a bit of glistening membrane at one corner. It is a secret room at the very base of his brain. Of the man's face, you see only the nostrils and a Ubangi mouth stretched to accommodate the mirror inserted for the photography.

Here, the kyphotic, the scoliotic, the severely lordotic. Their faces are older by far than their S-shaped bodies, as though the curvature of a spine is associated with a compensatory prolongation of childhood. Childhood, it is said, ought to be prolonged by whatever means possible. But not at the cost of such crookedness.

And on this page, a youngish woman with cross-eyed breasts. A pouch of fatigue hangs beneath one nipple. The other breast is shrunken, turned inward in bewilderment. You cannot see her face or arms, which might allow you to draw some conclusions. But at her throat—a string of brave dark beads.

An old woman lies back in whorish recumbency, her knees flexed and having drifted apart. She wears white cotton stockings rolled below the knees and knotted there. Her hands reach down to open her vulva to show something beefy and red growing just inside. It has always been her role to be helpful.

All this famished flesh. Pale as a family of fatherless little boys. Saint Hildegard was right; God does not inhabit healthy bodies. Now, shut the book, close your eyes, and hear the crimson thump of your heart.

If, in a darkened room, a doctor holds a bright light against a hollow part of the body, he can see through the outer tissues to the structures within—arteries, veins, projecting shelves of bone. In such a ruby gloom, he can distinguish between a hernia and a hydrocele of the testicle, or he can light up a sinus behind the brow to find the tumor there. Unlike surgery, which opens the body to direct examination, this transillumination gives an indirect vision, calling into play only the simplest perceptions of the doctor. The pictures in this book are a kind of transillumination. They hold a camera before the human body and capture through the covering layers the truth within.

Dear to me as it is, the *Textbook of Physical Diagnosis* is only a book, and cannot make of you a doctor.

In the matter of Physical Diagnosis, greed is not a sin; it is a virtue. There can never be enough hearts and lungs to teach a doctor his business. Do not rely upon the X-ray machine, the electrocardiograph, or the laboratory to tell you what your hands, eyes, and ears can find out, lest your senses atrophy from disuse. The machine does not exist that can take the place of the divining physician. The physical examination affords the opportunity to touch your patient. It gives the patient the opportunity to be touched by you. In this exchange, messages are sent from one to the other that, if your examination is performed with honesty and humility, will cause the divining powers of the Augurs to be passed on to you—their last heir.

Before long, you will lay your palm upon the back of a patient's chest, first on one side, then the other, and you will detect any diminution in the transmitted vibration of his voice. You will know, then, that in that place beneath your hand, the drawn breath does not fill a part of the lung that has become collapsed or carnified. Now listen there with your stethoscope. It is your cocked ear. Are there wheezes? bubbles? Do they occur as the breath is drawn or expelled? Are the bubbles coarse or fine? They will be fine only in the air sacs of the lung, coarse only in the large tubes—bronchi or trachea.

Again lay your palm upon the patient's chest such that your fingers contact him everywhere. Now tap your middle finger with the middle finger of your other hand. Listen . . . no, feel, it is something between listening and feeling that you do here—for the note that is struck. It ought to have a certain echo, a timbre. If it is not resonant, but instead the sound is flat and dead, something—fluid, a mass—is interposed between the lung and your hand. Tap out the area of dullness. Does it shift as he changes position? Why, then, like all fluid, it seeks its own level. Tap your way up the patient's back. At what place does the dullness change to resonance? The ninth rib? The eighth? Now you know how much fluid is present. You know, too, between which ribs your needle must pass in order to draw it out so that the compressed lung may expand. Even as you diagnose, you have begun your therapy.

Place your hand over the patient's heart. Let your fingers receive its beat. Find the exact place where the thrust is strongest. If this impulse is beyond the anterior fold of the armpit, the heart is enlarged. Should there be no single clean beat but a "thrill," as though a wren is stirring beneath your hand, the heart is damaged by disease or made wrong from the beginning. Now listen with the stethoscope. What you felt as a thrill is heard as a murmur. The wren sings. Touch and hearing blend, confirm. If the murmur be no soft whisper, but a harsh grate, or a rumble up and down the scale, a valve of the heart is damaged. Do you hear the slap of its calcified leaflets? Soon you will know which valve is tight, which leaky. Listening to the heart is like learning the songs of birds. A song once heard and identified is your own from then on. It will never be confused with the songs of other birds.

Is the rhythm crazy, coming willy-nilly, irregularly irregular? Then you have heard "fibrillation." Are the beats too close together to count? Perhaps this is "flutter." A bruit is a thrill that is heard. Here blood eddies around a narrows. Learn the language of this craft. Bruit, murmur, thrill, flutter, fibrillation—these are simple nouns that will soon become infused with knowledge and implication. Rejoice in these words that are used only in the highest purpose and that bind you to the others who do this work.

The abdomen is perhaps the deepest of mysteries. The very word *abdomen* has no known origin. It comes down to us from ancient times. Perhaps, they say, it means a secret place where things are stowed. You must approach such a mystery with tact. It is more threatening for a patient to uncover his abdomen than his chest. It is a kind of surrender. The abdomen, unprotected by a cage of ribs or a thick hide, presents itself equally to the surgeon's knife and the assassin's dagger. The slightest roughness on your part is a breach of the Articles of Medicine. In palpating the abdomen, the pressure of your hand must be neither too heavy nor too light. Too heavy a touch produces a guarding—a defense of the musculature. You will feel nothing through such a barricade. Too light, and you will tickle. This yields only discomfort and embarrassment. It goes without saying that your hands must be warm and dry. The belly is sensitive to every shock. Once intimidated, it can be reassured only at some effort, and then never fully. If the abdomen be divided into four quadrants, it is best to begin in the left upper quadrant, which is the least likely to be the site of disease, although by no means immune. Request that the patient roll himself a bit toward you. Guide him until he is at an angle of forty-five degrees. This allows the spleen to fall forward. Press just below the rib cage while asking him to take a deep breath. Such a full inspiration will depress the diaphragm, and with it the spleen. If the spleen is enlarged beyond normal size, its lower pole will bump against your fingers. How far below the ribs do you feel it? Two finger-breadths? Three? From this, you may estimate its degree of enlargement. Beware! Many the spleen, outsized and therefore delicate, that has been ruptured by the undue pressure of the examining hand.

The most cerebral of all examinations is that of the brain. Encased as it is in a bony box, the brain cannot be approached directly, but its condition must be deduced from signals given at the most distant outposts. The navel, say, or the knee. Stroke the sole of a patient's foot. Stroke it firmly with a hard instrument, and see the toes of that foot rise and spread. This is the sign of Babinski. It tells, perhaps, of a blood clot or tumor in the motor cortex of the opposite side of the brain. Ask your patient to stand and close his eyes. "I won't let you fall," you assure him. Almost at once he sways to one side and would surely fall if you did not catch him. So! The cerebellum too is involved. You are closing in on the lesion. Soon you will know its exact location. Now you are happy in the way that a hunter is happy when, following the spoor of an animal, he comes upon fresh evidence.

Just so, in the name of Asclepius, do I invite you to begin the sacred process of divination called Physical Diagnosis. There is no more beautiful sight in the world than that of a kindly, efficient doctor engaged in the examination of the body of a fellow human being.

Letter to a
Young Surgeon I

—◊—

So. You have chosen Surgery. Have you thought long and hard upon it? How necessary is the practice of Surgery to you? Would you die if you were not to do it? If you perceive Surgery as the loftiest branch of Medicine, remember that it is the one most vulnerable to injury and ignominy. It is not the privet hedge that is uprooted in a hurricane; it is the royal palm.

If all Medicine be considered a religion, why, then, the psychiatrist is the cloistered nun, a contemplative whose pale hands are unused save for the telling of beads. The surgeon is burly, brawling Friar Tuck, out in the world, taking up his full share of space, and always at some risk of exposing rather too much of his free-swinging beef from beneath his habit.

As for myself, it was never for a moment given me to choose my vocation. I could hardly have engaged myself in the Future, since a converse with Physics and Mathematics is essential when plotting the trajectory of a spacecraft. From both of these mysteries I have been forbidden by the gods. In hands such as mine, orbits are likely to become obits. In Physics I claim for my own only Archimedes' principle, having over and again witnessed its reenactment in my house. A child of mine, having filled the bathtub to the rim absolute, leaps in, thereby displacing to the bathroom floor an amount of water which I do not dispute is equal to the volume of the creature.

As for immersion in the Past, History or Literature? No. I am ill set up for the studies, since I am incapable of distinguishing among the preceding three centuries. The seventeenth, eighteenth, and nineteenth are to me as one. All of their wars, pestilences, famines, artists, and writers wallow together in my unselective memory. Did Bacon precede Lamb? Or the other way around? There is a vegetarian of my acquaintance who forbears to read either one. As for the present, it is all a matter of Psychology, and I could not bear to listen to the secret urges of others when my own so outdo them in flamboyance. I have always preferred what people do alone or in the company of one like-minded companion to the shifts and rumble of the mob. The only thing left, you see, was Surgery. But there is another reason.

One spring, when my brother Billy was ten years old, and I eight, the Hudson River at Troy, New York, turned traitor and overflowed its banks. Fifth Avenue between Jacob and Federal was inundated. Ecstasy! Children understand floods. To a child it is proper and amusing that the arrogant pavement, the high-and-mighty bricks and mortar, and the malignant automobile should be humbled by the unexpected slap of a big water.

One morning Billy and I leaned out of the second-story bay window and looked out over a vast, gleaming sea. All at once we spied a rowboat rounding the corner from Federal Street. Up the block it beetled. A lone man pulled at the oars for all he was worth. Oh, how he rowed! Opposite our house, the man turned the rowboat in our direction and headed straight for the place where once our front stoop had been, and where now there raced a cold and filthy current. There was a confusion of bumps and scrapes, the sound of water splashing, the voices of men shouting. The next thing we saw was the little rowboat retreating from the house and making its way down the street. But now there were two men in it—the one who had come and . . . Father, perched in the stern. Wearing his gray fedora and long overcoat, he held his black medical bag on his knees. Father was making a house call in a rowboat! It was such a sight as the children of astronauts must have as their daily breakfast, lunch, and dinner.

What, we were dying to know, was he going to do? Deliver a baby? Set a broken leg? Take out an appendix?

"I bet it's an appendix," said Billy.

"I bet it's a broken leg," I said.

"Nah, an appendix," reiterated Billy. "Then he could use it for bait."

"Yeah," I said, hooked as usual by the metaphor. "I bet it's an appendix, too."

I do not remember, if ever I was told, what it was that Father did on that voyage. But I shall never forget the sight of him sailing down Fifth Avenue toward Federal Street to save a life. It was my first real proof that Father was a hero.

Father died five years later. I was thirteen.

In the interview prior to one's acceptance into medical school, one is asked the obligatory question: Why do you want to become a doctor? I don't know what you said, but my answer had to do with Virgil. In the *Aeneid,* there is an old doctor who arrives at the siege of Troy to tend the wound of Aeneas, who has been struck by an arrow. The doctor's name is Iapyx. Now it happened that when Iapyx was a boy, Apollo fell in love with him, and offered him, as a gift, music, wisdom, prophecy, or swift arrows. Iapyx chose none of these, and asked for Medicine instead. For he wished only to prolong the life of the father he loved. But as the battle for Troy raged all around him, Iapyx realized that he could not save Aeneas. All his skill was to no avail. He cried out to the gods to help him. Suddenly, the arrow, of its own accord, fell from the wound of Aeneas. Iapyx surmised that more than man had wrought this cure. Iapyx was right. Venus, the mother of Aeneas, had placed a healing herb in the water that Iapyx was using to bathe the wound of her son, and the arrow was miraculously extruded.

I became a doctor to prolong my father's life, and many times since, I have summoned the gods to my side for consultation.

You may as well be told right now that Surgery as a healing art is a passing phenomenon. It may already have seen its time of greatest glory. I should not be surprised to learn that news of this waning might give rise to some melancholy in one who is just now embarking on a career as a surgeon, for he will surely outlive his usefulness, to become master of a dead art.

But what a joy this same news will be to the rest of mankind, to him who harbors a stone in his gallbladder and needs not to be cut for it, to her who has a cancer in her breast and needs not come to mastectomy. To them it will be a blessing for which even the greediest, least altruistic surgeon must pray. Even now, the surgery that removes lung tissue infected with tuberculosis is largely a thing of the past. Operations for thyroid disease and peptic ulcer, which only two decades ago composed the bulk of any operating-room schedule, are rarities. The internist, cardiologist, and endocrinologist have grown more and more adept at controlling disease with medication, diet, and prevention. Soon we surgeons will be turned out to pasture, to graze out our days dreaming of old wars and trying to remember what exactly they were all about. Only in Plastic and Reconstructive Surgery and the transplantation of organs will remnants of surgery survive. *Grâce à Dieu*, I shall be safe in my tomb like an ancient king in moldered ermine, unmindful that the kingdom I once ruled vanished long ago.

What is the difference between a surgeon and an internist? The surgeon, armed to the teeth, seeks to overwhelm and control the body; the medical man strives with pills and potions to cooperate with that body, even to the point of making concessions to disease. One is the stance of the warrior; the other, that of the statesman. The more technologically oriented the internist becomes, the more like a surgeon he becomes, removing himself from the quiet resonances of the consulting room and bedside in order to flail away with his own machete. Heaven help the internist. He is not suited for such red labor. He is not blooded to it. And Heaven help his patient, who, instead of the touch and gaze of wisdom, will receive an endoscope in his throat or a catheter in his heart.

Tomorrow you are an intern. You will work both night and day. You will be tired, I know, and I don't want any more of that kind of tired. An intern, like a poet, is at the disposal of his night. The more one drinks of the night, the more one thirsts for the light of day. This is as true for the doctor as it is for the insomniac. Still, there is something to be said for working at night in a hospital. The external glare of daytime is gone, and one is permeated by a wave of darkness. Now the ritual of healing is more naturally practiced. For so many years I have been patrolling these night corridors with the lamplight creeping just ahead from room to room, illuminating wounds that are faces, faces that are wounds. As though I were a sentry pacing out the border between home and a wild country. You must remember when you are tired and it is late at night, when the patients ask whether you are a real doctor or an intern, that it is at night when most people make love. It is night that dismantles the barricade to the heart.

Some people live out their whole lives within earshot of bells. As though it were the sound of those bells, the chiming, that was necessary to life, an essential element like oxygen. But you have chosen to live out your life within the sound of sirens, and page operators and cardiac monitors. To be on duty in an Emergency Room and to hear the sound of a siren is to listen to the gathering of a storm, or a battle growing nearby. Soon, you know, you will be fully engaged. It is a sound that, even now, after so many years, causes me to tremble. There will be days when you will regret that you chose sirens over bells. At such times you will hate the hospital with its dreadful Emergency Room and its Operating Room and its Morgue. What a far cry from the snug lamplit hut of your boyhood dreams, with outside a raging snowstorm, and inside, a lovely fire in the grate. Here the storm is likely to whirl through the premises. The wolves know the way in, too. All the same, you will know that this hospital is your bones and your breath, without which you cannot live.

Tomorrow you will be an intern. Yours will be the glory of jotting down the conflicting orders of each one of your many superiors, and then carrying them out long after the rest have gone on to bed and other matters. You will be the tag end of Rounds, following, in single file, the First-Year Resident, the Second-Year Resident, the Third-Year

Resident, the Chief Resident, and far ahead, caparisoned and plumed and glowing like Saint George—the Professor. And all the while, straining to hear their orders, gashing frantically at your notebook. Never mind. In four years, you, too, will become Chief Resident, second in line. To you, then, will fall the privilege of squiredom to your Professor. You will carry his stethoscope, and you will be to him dresser, clerk, guide, bandage, splint, scissors. You, his scrivener, his scullion, his squirm.

I must warn you that in every surgical training program the severest burden may not be the fatigue gained from working day and night, nor the fretfulness that comes from worrying over your patients, but the gauleiter mentality of some of the surgeons. These martinets infest every hospital to some degree, like rats in a silo. They are recognizable even from the time of their internships, when they can be observed preying upon medical students or barking impolitely at nurses. Invariably these surgeons rise to positions of great authority—Chief Resident, Professor of Surgery, Dean. Here a malignant character can flourish unhampered. They are often superb technicians, each with unassailable credentials. To locate one of these surgeons, follow the sound of guffawing. You will come upon him, outside the room of a patient, surrounded by myrmidons, all taking their fun at the "crock" in the bed. Later, he will scold an elderly nurse for her unfamiliarity with the newest information revealed, if the truth be known, only the day before to him.

They are all big, good-looking fellows, given to wearing string ties and cowboy boots that can imply virility if need be. They own underdeveloped souls, the blighted wisps having slipped into their perfect frames at the moment of birth to live out their tenancy unacknowledged. These men tend to displace more air than they are allotted by body volume. Such a surgeon has a keen nose for misery, which he keeps plugged the way his forebears did their nostrils in a plague-struck city. Lest he be infected and suffer a pang of compassion. But observe him in the company of his superiors. Here he is all charm, all oiled congeniality at many decibels. Toward his peers he is wary; toward his intern, abusive or flippant.

Of these two, abuse or flippancy, you should hope for the former. Unlike flippancy, unvarnished cruelty does not interfere with the appetite, nor is it as likely to turn you murderous. Beware contagion from this surgeon. His pox are highly catching. Once so afflicted, you cannot be cured, but must depend ever after upon mere diligence and correctness to keep you out of the malpractice courts. Above all, do not yield to the temptation to punch him in the nose. Go instead to the bedside of one whose nightly fever is a hot red wind. Visit him again and see how the fever has receded beneath his skin to the deeper parts where it whines and spits and gathers itself for the next evening's eruption. See how in the morning he is rinsed of color like a blank page from which the most terrible words have been erased, but whose ghastly outline can still be seen. Do this, and you will have placed your cruel surgeon in his proper place. Still, there is redemption. Years later, I came upon an old Resident tormentor of mine. He was playing Mendelssohn on the violin. I watched his face take on the soft, unguarded tenderness of a man in love. And I marveled at the regenerative powers of the human spirit. But, then, Purgatory is on the way to Heaven, isn't it?

What! Your heart still dances toward Surgery? Why, then, welcome to the Fellowship of the Knife. And God help you. If not . . . if so much as one single seed of hesitation has fallen from my pocket to germinate in your brain, turn aside. Let Surgery be a road not taken and not rued. Only a flaming Torch reflected in water can exist where it dare not go. Remember that Surgery, like Poetry, is a subcelestial art. The angels disdain to perform either one of them.

Letter to a
Young Surgeon II

—⁕—

At this, the start of your surgical internship, it is well that you be told how to behave in an operating room. You cannot observe decorum unless you first know what decorum is. Say that you have already changed into a scrub suit, donned cap, mask, and shoe covers. You have scrubbed your hands and been helped into your gown and gloves. Now stand out of the way. Eventually, your presence will be noticed by the surgeon, who will motion you to take up a position at the table. Surgery is not one of the polite arts, as are Quilting and Illuminating Manuscripts. Decorum in the operating room does not include doffing your cap in the presence of nurses. Even the old-time surgeons knew this and operated without removing their hats.

The first rule of conversation in the operating room is silence. It is a rule to be broken freely by the Master, for he is engaged in the act of teaching. The forceful passage of bacteria through a face mask during speech increases the contamination of the wound and therefore the possibility of infection in that wound. It is a risk that must be taken. By the surgeon, wittingly, and by the patient, unbeknownst. Say what you will about a person's keeping control over his own destiny, there are some things that cannot be helped. Being made use of for teaching purposes in the operating room is one of them. It is an inevitable, admirable, and noble circumstance. Besides, I have placated Fate too long to believe that She would bring on wound infection as the complication of such a high enterprise.

Observe the least movement of the surgeon's hands. See how he holds out his hand to receive the scalpel. See how the handle of it rides between his thumb and fingertips. The scalpel is the subtlest of the instruments, transmitting the nervous current in the surgeon's arm to the body of the patient. Too timidly applied, and it turns flabby, lifeless; too much pressure, and it turns vicious. See how the surgeon applies the blade to the skin—holding it straight in its saddle lest he undercut and one edge of the incision be thinner than the other edge. The application of knife to flesh proclaims the master and exposes the novice. See the surgeon advancing his hand blindly into the abdomen as though it were a hollow in a tree. He is wary, yet needing to know. Will it be something soft and dead? Or a sudden pain in his bitten finger!

The point of the knife is called the *tang,* from the Latin word for "touch." The sharp curving edge is the *belly* of the blade. The tang is for assassins, the belly for surgeons. Enough! You will not hold this knife for a long time. Do not be impatient for it. Nor reckon the time. Ripen only. Over the course of your training you will be given ever more elaborate tasks to perform. But for now, you must watch and wait. Excessive ego, arrogance, and self-concern in an intern are out of place, as they preclude love for the patient on the table. There is no room for clever disobedience here. For the knife is like fire. The small child yearns to do what his father does, and he steals matches from the man's pocket. The fire he lights in his hiding place is beautiful to him; he toasts marshmallows in it. But he is just as likely to be burned. And reverence for the teacher is essential to the accumulation of knowledge. Even a bad surgeon will teach if only by the opportunity to see what not to do.

You will quickly come to detect the difference between a true surgeon and a mere product of the system. Democracy is not the best of all social philosophies in the selection of doctors for training in surgery. Anyone who so desires, and who is able to excel academically and who is willing to undergo the harsh training, can become a surgeon whether or not he is fit for the craft either manually or by temperament. If we continue to award licenses to the incompetent and the ill-suited, we shall be like those countries where work is given over not to those who can do it best, but to those who need it. That offers irritation enough in train stations; think of the result in airplane cockpits or operating rooms. Ponder long and hard upon this point. The mere decision to be a surgeon will not magically confer upon you the dexterity, compassion, and calmness to do it.

Even on your first day in the operating room, you must look ahead to your last. An old surgeon who has lost his touch is like an old lion whose claws have become blunted, but not the desire to use them. Knowing when to quit and retire from the consuming passion of your life is instinctive. It takes courage to do it. But do it you must. No consideration of money, power, fame, or fear of boredom may give you the slightest pause in laying down your scalpel when the first flagging of energy, bravery, or confidence appears. To withdraw gracefully is to withdraw in a state of grace. To persist is to fumble your way to injury and ignominy.

Do not be dismayed by the letting of blood, for it is blood that animates this work, distinguishes it from its father, Anatomy. Red is the color in which the interior of the body is painted. If an operation be thought of as a painting in progress, and blood red the color on the brush, it must be suitably restrained and attract no undue attention; yet any insufficiency of it will increase the perishability of the canvas. Surgeons are of differing stripes. There are those who are slow and methodical, obsessive beyond all reason. These tortoises operate in a field as bloodless as a cadaver. Every speck of tissue in its proper place, every nerve traced out and brushed clean so that a Japanese artist could render it down to the dendrites. Should the contents of a single capillary be inadvertently shed, the whole procedure comes to a halt while Mr. Clean irrigates and suctions and mops and clamps and ties until once again the operative field looks like Holland at tulip time. Such a surgeon tells time not by the clock but by the calendar. For this, he is ideally equipped with an iron urinary bladder which he has disciplined to contract no more than once a day. To the drop-in observer, the work of such a surgeon is faultless. He gasps in admiration at the still life on the table. Should the same observer leave and return three hours later, nothing will have changed. Only a few more millimeters of perfection.

Then there are the swashbucklers who crash through the underbrush waving a machete, letting tube and ovary fall where they may. This surgeon is equipped with gills so that he can breathe under blood. You do not set foot in his room without a slicker and boots. Seasoned nurses quake at the sight of those arms, elbow-deep and *working*. It is said that one such surgeon entertained the other guests at a department Christmas party by splenectomizing a cat in thirty seconds from skin to skin.

Then there are the rest of us who are neither too timid nor too brash. We are just right. And now I shall tell you a secret. To be a good surgeon does not require immense technical facility. Compared to a violinist it is nothing. The Japanese artist, for one, is skillful at double brushing, by which technique he lays on color with one brush and shades it off with another, both brushes being held at the same time and in the same hand, albeit with different fingers. Come to think of it, a surgeon, like a Japanese artist, ought to begin his training at the age of three, learning to hold four or five instruments at a time in the hand while suturing with a needle and thread held in the teeth. By the age of five he would be able to dismantle and reconstruct an entire human body from calvarium to calcaneus unassisted and in the time it would take one of us to recite the Hippocratic Oath. A more obvious advantage of this baby surgeon would be his size. In times of difficulty he could be lowered whole into the abdomen. There, he could swim about, repair the works, then give three tugs on a rope and . . . Presto! Another gallbladder bites the dust.

In the absence of any such prodigies, each of you who is full-grown must learn to exist in two states—Littleness and Bigness. In your Littleness you descend for hours each day through a cleft in the body into a tiny space that is both your workshop and your temple. Your attention in Lilliput is total and undistracted. Every artery is a river to be forded or dammed, each organ a mountain to be skirted or moved. At last, the work having been done, you ascend. You blink and look about at the vast space peopled by giants and massive furniture. Take a deep breath . . . and you are Big. Such instantaneous hypertrophy is the process by which a surgeon reenters the outside world. Any breakdown in this resonance between the sizes causes the surgeon to live in a Renaissance painting where the depth perception is so bad.

Nor ought it to offend you that, a tumor having been successfully removed, and the danger to the patient having been circumvented, the very team of surgeons that only moments before was a model of discipline and deportment comes loose at the seams and begins to wobble. Jokes are told, there is laughter, a hectic gaiety prevails. This is in no way to be taken as a sign of irreverence or callousness. When the men of the Kalahari return from the hunt with a haunch of zebra, the first thing everybody does is break out in a dance. It is a rite of thanksgiving. There will be food. They have made it safely home.

Man is the only animal capable of tying a square knot. During the course of an operation you may be asked by the surgeon to tie a knot. As drawing and coloring are the language of art, incising, suturing, and knot tying are the grammar of surgery. A facility in knot tying is gained only by tying ten thousand of them. When the operation is completed, take home with you a package of leftover sutures. Light a fire in the fireplace and sit with your lover on a rug in front of the fire. Invite her to hold up her index finger, gently crooked in a gesture of beckoning. Using her finger as a strut, tie one of the threads about it in a square knot. Do this one hundred times. Now make a hundred grannies. Only then may you permit yourself to make love to her. This method of learning will not only enable you to master the art of knot tying, both granny and square, it will bind you, however insecurely, to the one you love.

To do surgery without a sense of awe is to be a dandy—all style and no purpose. No part of the operation is too lowly, too menial. Even when suturing the skin at the end of a major abdominal procedure, you must operate with piety, as though you were embellishing a holy reliquary. The suturing of the skin usually falls to the lot of the beginning surgeon, the sights of the Assistant Residents and Residents having been firmly set upon more biliary, more gastric glories. In surgery, the love of inconsiderable things must govern your life—ingrown toenails, thrombosed hemorrhoids, warts. Never disdain the common ordinary ailment in favor of the exotic or rare. To the patient every one of his ailments is unique. One is not to be amused or captivated by disease. Only to a woodpecker is a wormy tree more fascinating than one uninhabited. There is only absorption in your patient's plight. To this purpose, willingly accept the smells and extrusions of the sick. To be spattered with the phlegm, vomitus, and blood of suffering is to be badged with the highest office.

The sutured skin is all of his operation that the patient will see. It is your signature left upon his body for the rest of his life. For the patient, it is the emblem of his suffering, a reminder of his mortality. Years later, he will idly run his fingers along the length of the scar, and he will hush and remember. The good surgeon knows this. And so he does not overlap the edges of the skin, makes no dog-ears at the corners. He does not tie the sutures too tightly lest there be a row of permanent crosshatches. (It is not your purpose to construct a ladder upon which a touring louse could climb from pubis to navel and back.) The good surgeon does not pinch the skin with forceps. He leaves the proper distance between the sutures. He removes the sutures at the earliest possible date, and he uses sutures of the finest thread. All these things he does and does not do out of reverence for his craft and love for his patient. The surgeon who does otherwise ought to keep his hands in his pockets. At the end of the operation, cholecystectomy, say, the surgeon may ask you to slit open the gallbladder so that everyone in the room might examine the stones. Perform even this cutting with reverence, as though the organ were still within the patient's body. You cut, and notice how the amber bile runs out, leaving a residue of stones. Faceted, shiny, they glisten. Almost at once, these wrested dewy stones surrender their warmth and moisture; they grow drab and dull. The descent from jewel to pebble takes place before your eyes.

Deep down, I keep the vanity that Surgery is the red flower that blooms among the leaves and thorns that are the rest of Medicine. It is Surgery that, long after it has passed into obsolescence, will be remembered as the glory of Medicine. Then men shall gather in mead halls and sing of that ancient time when surgeons, like gods, walked among the human race. Go ahead. Revel in your Specialty; it is your divinity.

It is quest and dream as well:

The incision has been made. One expects mauve doves and colored moths to cloud out of the belly in celebration of the longed-for coming. Soon the surgeon is greeted by the eager blood kneeling and offering its services. Tongues of it lap at his feet; flames and plumes hold themselves aloft to light his way. And he follows this guide that flows just ahead of him through rifts, along the edges of cliffs, picking and winding, leaping across chasms, at last finding itself and pooling to wait for him. But the blood cannot wait a moment too long lest it become a blob of coagulum, something annulled by its own puddling. The surgeon rides the patient, as though he were riding a burro down into a canyon. This body is beautiful to him, and he to it—he whom the patient encloses in the fist of his flesh. For months, ever since the first wild mitosis, the organs have huddled like shipwrecks. When will he come? Will he never come? And suddenly, into the sick cellar—fingers of light! The body lies stupefied at the moment of encounter. The cool air stirs the buried flesh. Even the torpid intestine shifts its slow coils to make way.

Now the surgeon must take care. The fatal glissade, once begun, is not to be stopped. Does this world, too, he wonders, roll within the precincts of mercy? The questing dreamer leans into the patient to catch the subtlest sounds. He hears the harmonies of their two bloods, his and the patient's. They sing of death and the beauty of the rose. He hears the playing together of their two breaths. If Pythagoras is right, there is no silence in the universe. Even the stars make music as they move.

Only do not succumb to self-love. I know a surgeon who, having left the room, is certain, beyond peradventure of doubt, that his disembodied radiance lingers on. And there are surgeons of such aristocratic posture that one refrains only with difficulty from slipping them into the nobility. As though they had risen from Mister to Doctor to Professor, then on to Baron, Count, Archduke, then further, to Apostle, Saint. I could go further.

Such arrogance can carry over to the work itself. There was a surgeon in New Haven, Dr. Truffle, who had a penchant for long midline incisions—from sternum to pubis—no matter the need for exposure. Somewhere along the way, this surgeon had become annoyed by the presence of the navel, which, he decided, interrupted the pure line of his slice. Day in, day out, it must be gone around, either to the right or to the left. Soon, what was at first an annoyance became a hated impediment that must be got rid of. Mere circumvention was not enough. And so, one day, having arrived at the midpoint of his downstroke, this surgeon paused to cut out the navel with a neat ellipse of skin before continuing on down to the pubis. Such an elliptical incision when sutured at the close of the operation forms the continuous straight line without which this surgeon could not live. Once having cut out a navel (the first incidental umbilectomy, I suppose, was the hardest) and seen the simple undeviate line of his closure, he vowed never again to leave a navel behind. Since he was otherwise a good surgeon, and very successful, it was not long before there were thousands of New Haveners walking around minus their belly buttons. Not that this interfered with any but the most uncommon of activities, but to those of us who examined them postoperatively, these abdomens had a blind, bland look. Years later I would happen upon one of these bellies and know at once the author of the incision upon it. Ah, I would say, Dr. Truffle has been here.

It is so difficult for a surgeon to remain "unconscious," retaining the clarity of vision of childhood, to know and be secure in his ability, yet be unaware of his talents. It is almost impossible. There are all too many people around him paying obeisance, pandering, catering, beaming, lusting. Yet he must try.

It is not enough to love your work. Love of work is a kind of self-indulgence. You must go beyond that. Better to perform endlessly, repetitiously, faithfully, the simplest acts, like trimming the toenails of an old man. By so doing, you will not say *Here I Am,* but *Here It Is.* You will not announce your love but will store it up in the bodies of your patients to carry with them wherever they go.

Many times over, you will hear otherwise sensible people say,

"You have golden hands," or "Thanks to you and God, I have recovered." (Notice the order in which the credit is given.) Such ill-directed praise has no significance. It is the patient's disguised expression of relief at having come through, avoided death. It is a private utterance, having nothing to do with you. Still, such words are enough to turn a surgeon's head, if any more turning were needed.

Avoid these blandishments at all cost. You are in service to your patients, and a servant should know his place. The world is topsy-turvy in which a master worships his servant. You are a kindly, firm, experienced servant, but a servant still. If any patient of mine were to attempt to bathe my feet, I'd kick over his basin, suspecting that he possessed not so much a genuine sentiment as a conventional one. It is beneath your dignity to serve as an object of veneration or as the foil in an act of contrition. To any such effusion a simple "Thank you" will do. The rest is pride, and everyone knoweth before *what* that goeth.

Alexander the Great had a slave whose sole responsibility was to whisper "Remember, you are mortal" when he grew too arrogant. Perhaps every surgeon should be assigned such a deflator. The surgeon is the mere instrument which the patient takes in his hand to heal himself. An operation, then, is a time of revelation, both physical and spiritual, when, for a little while, the secrets of the body are set forth to be seen, to be touched, and the surgeon himself is laid open to Grace.

An operation is a reenactment of the story of Jonah and the Whale. In surgery, the patient is the whale who swallows up the surgeon. Unlike Jonah, however, the surgeon does not cry out *non serviam,* but willingly descends into the sick body in order to cut out of it the part that threatens to kill it. In an operation where the patient is restored to health, the surgeon is spewed out of the whale's body, and both he and his patient are healed. In an operation where the patient dies on the table, the surgeon, although he is rescued from the whale and the sea of blood, is not fully healed, but will bear the scars of his sojourn in the belly of the patient for the rest of his life.

Letter to a
Young Surgeon IV

—⫘—

Let us go. It is seven-thirty in the morning. The men's locker room is a scene of great activity. Surgeons, Residents, Interns, and Students are dressing for the morning's work. There is a nervousness in the stalls, a nickering and stamping. These surgeons are neat; they hang their clothing in the lockers with precision; everything is folded along its creases. Paper boots are fitted over shoes with care, caps tied behind the head just so, the strings of the masks knotted and adjusted. Metal doors clang. The bodies of these men are like the furniture of your house; you have seen them every day for years. They seem beautiful and young, even the old ones. Their hands are pink and warm to the touch from so many scrubbings. Each fingernail is trimmed in a gentle curve. Their talk is all of football and baseball and gold. Surgeons love the notion of teams pitted one against the other, or of single combat. It is fitting that this be so. In the corridors the patients wait. They lie narcotized, silent, yet afraid, on stretchers, each one parked outside the room into which he will be taken. As each surgeon approaches his patient, he, too, grows quiet. Who knows what dreams these surgeons have had?

The women surgeons dress with the nurses. Never mind. The inheritance of surgery is less a patrimony than a matrimony. "Male" is inspired tinkering, a knack for repairing the works. "Female" is softness of touch, an intuition for planes and membranes. Like the poet, the surgeon must incorporate both. If pressed I should confess to the suspicion that women make better surgeons than men. Women know how to fold themselves about life. Women know blood, and they know pain.

The light in the operating room is no less important than the light in an artist's studio. It must be direct, cast no shadows, yet be free of glare. None of these has ever, to my knowledge, been achieved to perfection. It is to be expected then that a surgeon will complain of the poor light forced upon him by malicious electrical influences. But inferior light must not become the excuse behind which a nervous surgeon conceals his fumbling. Operating rooms must be of a certain size. Too small, and there is more likelihood of contamination by the collision of occupants and equipment. Too large, and the mind is distracted. Great empty spaces take away from the proceedings that lovely feeling of a close-knit team on an expedition. Of the two, I prefer small rooms which act to concentrate the thought and discipline the mind. Too much space smothers me. Being slight, I am able to insinuate myself amongst the matériel. Bulkier members of the species are less insertable. Let them have wider ranges.

You wheel the stretcher alongside the operating table and help the patient to slide himself from one to the other. Now you must keep in contact with your patient until he is asleep. Hold his hand if one is free of the anesthetist's use, or place your hand upon his chest, his shoulder. This will suggest to him that a protective spirit hovers over him. Speak quietly, as though privately, to your patient. Dwell upon his awakening. Say the word "recovery." It is a winged word. The sight and sound of you at this time is balm in Gilead to him. No matter how kindly the others are, he does not know them. You are his doctor, the only one who has received his trust. These others are strangers. Tangency in the operating room is both given and received. Often the patient will reach out to touch you, taking comfort from the feel of your body, just as you draw strength from his. The patient is not a plant of the genus *noli me tangere,* whose seed vessels would burst at the slightest touch. He is frightened, feels himself to be alone in a green and clanking place where there are no windows and he cannot see the sky. Let him look into your eyes for whatever distance and space he can find there.

One day you, too, will be a surgeon and stand over a table upon which a patient lies. In a few minutes you will take up a scalpel and lay open his body. Your patient may be, like the man I operated on today, old, wasted, his bowel obstructed by a tumor. All at once, before the induction of anesthesia, this man reached up his two hands. They trembled in the air like weightless dragonflies. The long papery fingers encircled my neck. His grip had a strength that surprised me. Not to strangle but to draw in through his hands all the blood and breath that coursed there. To this, you, too, will gladly submit, knowing that it is a greater offering than any mere surgery. It is only human love that keeps this from being the act of two madmen.

Take care not to get in the way of the anesthetist. During the induction of anesthesia, you have the chance to do small tasks that might assist him—tearing strips of adhesive tape for him to use in securing a needle in a vein, or pressing, if he should request it, the larynx of the patient to ease the passage of his tube into the trachea. It is a privilege to attend to the needs of an anesthetist.

If the anesthetic is to be spinal, help the patient to turn to one side and to curl his body. Now cradle and steady him until it is done. Never fear to be thought unmanly because of such service. Now your patient is ready to go to sleep. To wish each other luck is neither inappropriate nor insensitive. It is honest. The injection of Pentothal is given. You continue to soothe him with your touch and voice. Is there no hidden cabin of the brain, I have wondered, some dark sulcus where he will hold these words you say to him: "Relax. Go to sleep. Pick out a nice dream"?

"That's right, give in. Don't fight it," you say. And he submits. Perhaps one day he will summon these words forth to the blazing courtyard of consciousness. Then he will hear them again and think of you, and smile. Never doubt that he has heard you. Sounds are intensified during the induction of anesthesia. Now he is asleep and hears nothing. Anesthesia is an imitation of death, uninhabited even by dreams.

Like all ceremonies, washing the hands has a wisdom beyond mere practical worth. Like the donning of clean, loose-fitting clothing, it is an act of supplication. It goes without saying that the fingernails are kept short and straight and clean. There must be no sharp points to snag flesh. Nothing sets a patient's pulse to hammering like the sight of a cache of dirt beneath his surgeon's fingernails, for it implies carelessness with the flesh of others. (Between you and me, I can think of one or two surgeons whose natural corruption is such that an impaction of good clean New England dirt under the nails would be absolutely purifying. When I told this to my nurse, Anne Palkowski, she said to give her a minute and she could think of several more. Give her an *hour,* and the whole thing would become a national scandal.)

Take a pointed stick and wipe beneath each nail. Throw away the stick and take up the heavy-bristled brush. Drench it with soap and water. Proceed to scrub a finger at a time, then the thumb—front and back. Advance to the dorsum of the hand, firmly, and with ever-increasing circles. On to the palm. Flex the fingertips, back and forth, back and forth. Now in long, luxurious strokes, up and down the arm, to an inch above the elbow. Rinse, and do it again.

The body of the patient is now uncovered. In the matter of such exposure the surgeon must set the tone for the others to follow. Remember that you and the sleeping patient are one and the same. To expose his nakedness is also to expose your own. Therefore draw upon yourself the mantle of modesty. There are occasions that require the genitalia of your patient to be shown, either for examination or surgery or for teaching. Accept such exposure with a dignified and natural mien. Should the patient be awake during this time, help him to bear whatever discomfort or embarrassment this engenders.

If nakedness is not essential to the proceedings, draw the sheets about the patient so as to cover what otherwise might go uncovered. To cover the nakedness of another is an act of charity. To gape needlessly is to be like the lewd elders who spied upon Susannah sleeping in her garden. This is also the way you must instruct the novice medical student. Embarrassed and threatened by being witness to such things, the student will cast about like a floundering swimmer for the reactions of the others present. He will gratefully anchor himself to your calm, undismayed face, and he will set his own in the same mold. The young woman being readied for appendectomy is not Aphrodite making an earthly appearance. Nor is the surgeon Praxiteles sculpting Venus. She is a work of art, but not by you created.

Doctors who indulge their lust among the patients get nothing but a bad reputation and a guilty conscience. They shall feed upon the dry cobs of repentance. In an act of passionate love the two participants are nude. In the love between patient and doctor they are naked. Both are vulnerable, laid open to chance and design. The true healer retains the nakedness of a child; he remains open to the emotion of love for his patient.

But let us be honest. To gaze upon the beautiful unclothed body is a spur to the lustful imagination. Soon, in your mind, you are fondling this body, kissing it. To deny the existence of these urges is to deny your humanity. To fail to suppress these urges is to accept a condition of bestiality. Suppress, therefore, and do not feel guilty for your lustful thoughts. Even the gods hankered. Only distinguish between nakedness and nudity. It will enable you one day to be touched to the heart by the vanished bosom of an old woman.

The surgeon takes incorrigible delight in the immersion of his own body in that of another. It is a kind of love. But it is never to be confused with eroticism. Dwelling as he does within his patient's body, when a surgeon makes an incision, it is a self-inflicted wound.

Poised above the patient the surgeon is like a priest guarding and preserving fire. He takes strength from this closeness. For the body of the patient is the sun, the whorl of light and heat that radiates life into this room. It is the patient's heat that foments this work, his light that makes it visible and possible. Without the patient this world is dead. He is the nucleus, all the rest, the cytoplasm. He, the seed; the rest, the fruit about him.

When the incision is made, the surgeon gazes through the aperture, and even as he does, something marvelous happens. He himself shrinks to accommodate to the dimensions of this unexplored place. Once, while studying a group of tiny bonsai trees in a tray, I knelt to peer upward into their branches from below. Suddenly it was I who was small and the trees that were large. I was a pygmy in a towering forest. Such is the magic of bonsai, and such is the magic of Surgery.

The abdomen at the same time expands to incorporate him. He descends, reliving his childhood fears. He is once again in a mad, dark cellar with, high above, the fading light of earth.

Once inside, every artery is a red river to be forded or dammed up; every organ, a mountain to be skirted or climbed. The surgeon is a trekker in a land of mystery and beauty. Beneath his feet he feels the throbbing of a great engine. About his head a warm wind breathes. No less than the one he has just left, this new world holds all there is of good and evil. An intimate warmth encloses him. It has the humidity of his mother's unremembered womb. Nor does he once look back at what recedes outside. From the moment of his entry he is totally engaged. He is in a state of *topophilia*, wherein his vision changes. He sees vast dripping caverns, escarpments, lofty ranges. Pink and salmon and maroon creatures drowse in their beds. These creatures are friendly; the surgeon approaches them with affection. But there are fumes, too, a sluggish trickle. Far in the distance a stony gray crater presents itself. One, and then another, and another for as far as the eye can see. There are the very plains of Hell.

For years the surgeon has dreamt of this place, conjured it in his mind, imagined all of its marvels. And now he is there. Unlike the poet's travels, which are figments and phantasms, this is real.

At first it seems that sound, too, has shrunk. There are only vast silences. Soon these silences are violated by the whoosh of blood coursing through hidden passageways and the throbbing of an engine far below. The surgeon experiences systole and diastole, not his own, but a rhythm absorbed from the landscape. A distant wind blows to and fro, folding and unfolding the fine linen that hangs between the flanks. But wait awhile and there are other sounds—whispers, giggling, murmurs, ticktocks retrieved from beyond the auditory threshold.

Once having shucked the outside world, the surgeon's mind has been set free. He is once again a child gazing with the liberated eyes of childhood. But a wise child, for he brings here all the reason and logic and knowledge of that other life. Like a mountaineer who must bring along his own food and oxygen, the surgeon feeds upon his past experience. It sustains him throughout his journey. But he must be certain to bring enough. Otherwise he will surely die in this unterrestrial place. Who would visit this awful place must be like a deer, gifted with presentiment. He must stand as the deer stands—motionless, breathless, quivering, to feel the distant sounds come nearer, the sounds that no one else can hear. He lays his ear to a kidney to hear its soft watery machinery. He listens to the filtration and extraction of the liver, the muddy slide of the gut, the ceaseless chewing of a tumor. He hears the whole cavern of the belly reddening, as though he were under the influence of hashish.

For the surgeon, the distance between the lips of his incision and the prize he seeks, and for which he has been dispatched by his patron, is no more than twelve inches. Still there are gorges to be crossed on narrow swaying filaments, precipices to be scaled, Fate to be placated. All the while on his trek, the surgeon's mind urges toward that tumor. His eye is fixed upon its gray stony parapets. From the moment of incision he is already laying siege to it, tying off its supply routes, burning off the foliage that protects and conceals it, tightening his grip on it, even dwelling within it like a spy, gathering information, taking measurements, looking for signs of weakness. The surgeon hates and loves this tumor that both resists and offers itself to him. It is the object of his dreams. At last, he retrieves the tumor from this dream and holds it up to the light. Hunter and prey have met in one. A man among men in one world, he is a man alone and lonely in this other. Here within, he shares none of his terror or exhilaration. There is only the solitude of terrible works.

Now the expedition is completed. In jubilation or despair, the abdomen is closed. A line of sutures like the lashes of a closed eye marks the passageway. Already the scar begins to form across the entrance—blood, serum, a jelly of fibroblasts and tissue juice gather, all the cellular throng that will barricade with boulders and walls of flesh.

Safe outside, the surgeon turns to gaze at the abdomen, imagining still the maroon and humid walls, the bare gray crags, the moment of victory or defeat. And the pulse beats faster at his wrist. Now the wound is dressed. How quickly an incision becomes a wound! The unbandaged eyes of the surgeon see beyond the sealed gate to the garden within where once, like Adam, he walked in high discovery. This sealed and silent abdomen, this, too, will never be the same as it was. For the surgeon has left his mark hewn into a remote trunk. All about the tumor he has built an altar of metal clips arranged under auspices.

His fingerprint is on the wall. And he has left his dreams behind to glide among the viscera, mute witnesses to what has transpired. The abdomen is closed; the surgeon's dreams remain within. Nor are the organs of this abdomen ever wholly forgotten. They have become part of the surgeon's past. And these organs have imparted to him a certain knowledge, whispered to him secrets that he will pass on to others. Much as a jewel box contains the dreams of a vain woman, or a casket of bones the dreams of a widow, inside this closed belly flit the fitful dreams of the surgeon.

How to Build a
Slaughterhouse

—៣—

It is May and, for whatever reason, I have been invited to serve on
a jury that is to pass judgment on the final projects of a group of
candidates for the degree of Master of Architecture at Yale University.
But I am not an architect. I am a surgeon. Nor do I know the least
thing about buildings, only that, like humans, they are testy, com-
pliant, congenial, impertinent. That sort of thing. When I am faced
with blueprints and drawings to scale, which are the lingua franca
of architecture, something awful happens to the left half of my brain.
It shrinks, or desiccates, collapses, and I fall into a state of torpor no
less profound than that of the Andean hummingbird when it is confronted with mortal danger. Sadly, my acceptance of such an invitation by the Yale School of Architecture is just another example of
the kind of imposturage of which otherwise honest men and women
are capable.

The charge that has been given the students is to design and
build an abattoir. It is understood that prior to this undertaking they
have, as a class, made a field trip to a slaughterhouse in the New
Haven area. For months afterward they have been working toward
this date. It is two days before we are all to meet for the examination
in the seventh-floor "pit" at the School of Architecture. But if I cannot
know what they know of buildings, at least I can have seen what
they have seen, and so I telephone the owner of the slaughterhouse
on the outskirts of New Haven, the one that the students visited

months before. "Yes," he says, "by all means." His voice is genial, welcoming.

It will be no great shock, I think. A surgeon has grown accustomed to primordial dramas, organic events involving flesh, blood, and violence. But before it is done this field trip to a slaughterhouse will have become for me a descent into Hades, a vision of life that perhaps it would have been better never to know.

In a way, it is the last place on earth that seems appropriate to the mass slaying of creatures. Just another grinding truck stop off Route 1 in North Haven, Connecticut, with easy access for large vehicles and, nearby, an old cemetery tossing in the slow upheaval of resurrection. It is 7 A.M. Outside, another truck rumbles into the corral.

THERMOKING is the word painted on both sides of the huge open-sided car filled with cattle. Each cow has a numbered tag punched through an ear. Outside, the enclosure is already ridiculous with lambs. What a sinister probability this truck gives out. Inside it, the cows are, for the most part, silent until one lifts its head and moos wildly. Now another joins in, and another, until the whole compound resounds with the terrible vocabulary of premonition.

The building itself is low and squat—a single story only, made of cement blocks and corrugated metal and prestressed concrete. Behind it is a huge corral. Such a building does not command but neither does it skulk. It carries out its business in secret and decides what you will see, hides from you what it chooses. If only I can come upon it—the undiscovered heart of this place that I know, must believe, is here. Does this building breathe? Has it a pulse? It must.

Now the gate at the rear of the truck is opened. The cattle mill about like bewildered children until, prodded from behind, they move sightless and will-less down the ramp and into a gated pen as if in sleep through an incurable dream. Here they come, slowly, their hooves weighted down with reluctance. The wooden floor of the entryway is scarred, packed, and beaten. The hooves, staggering, thump the timbers. There is a quick lateral skid on manure. It is the sound of those skidding hooves that, months later, you will hear while waiting in line at the bank or getting a haircut.

The cowherd urges them on. They seem afraid of displeasing him. With gentle callings and whistles he inveigles them into the pen. I keep my gaze on a pair of mourning doves waddling among the droppings until, threatened by a hoof, one takes to the air with a muted small whistling of its wings. The other follows in a moment. Against a nearby fence a row of fiery tulips spurts. Into the narrow passageway the cattle go single-file, crowding at the mouth of it, bumping into each other, clopping sidewise so as not to lose their place. It's as if, once having passed through that gate, they would be safe. As if what lay ahead were not extinction but respite, and there were not, just ahead, death bobbing like clover in a pasture, but life. Only the first two or three begin to suspect. One after the other these lift their heads at the sound of the stunning gun. But there is the sweet assuaging voice of the cowherd and the laughter of the men inside to draw them on.

The one at the van shies as she encounters some hard evidence. She balks, stops, the others press against her until, with a toss of her horns, she throws her new knowledge down before the herd, like an impediment. Without warning (do I imagine it?) the leaves on the trees at the periphery of the corral begin to siffle, the grass to stir. Tails rise as if in a wind. Ears and flanks shiver in a cold blast. As abruptly, all is still. But I see it has not been the wind, only death that has swept across the corral and whooshed away.

Inside, the men are waiting. All are dressed in identical uniforms—overalls, ankle-length rubber aprons, high rubber boots, and orange plastic hard hats. The hooks, tracks, scales, tables, and trays have an air of brutal metallic strength; there are no windows nor anything made of wood. The room echoes like a gymnasium. From somewhere too far off to be heard clearly, a silken radio voice announces the morning news. Something about a famine in Ethiopia. . . . There is the smell of cowhide and tobacco. One of the men clicks over the multitude in the pen. ". . . Six, eight, ten, fourteen . . ." he counts. "Plus one hundred sixty. Jesus! a day's work."

The Process begins. There is a muffled whump from the stunning pen, like the firing of a mortar shell. A body arches, the tail blown forward between quivering legs. She goes down, folding on all fours at once, something from which the air has been let out. They drag her a foot or two to the hoist. A chain is placed about one hind leg and the winch activated. A moment later she is aloft above the Killing Oval—a kind of theater with a centrally slanting stone floor and a drain at the lowest point. As she hangs upside down, her coat seems a bit loose, shabby, with all the points and angles of her skeleton showing. The throat slitter is ready. It is clear that he is the star. Enisled in his oval space, alone there with his cattle who, one at a time, stretch out their necks to him, he shines beneath his hard hat. He is blond; his eyes, blue knife blades; hefty, a side of beef himself, though not at all fat. No part of him shakes with the thrust. Still, if physiognomy is any hint of character, he has found his rightful place. The eyes boil from her head; saliva drips from her limp tongue. Up on his toes for the sticking, and oh those chicory-blue eyes. For just so long as the blade needs to burrow into the neck—one second, two—the pudgy hand of the man grasps the ear of the cow, then lets go. He is quick with the knife, like a robin beaking a worm from the ground. The slit is made just beneath the mandible, the knife moved forward and back and withdrawn. In this manner the jugular vein and carotid artery are severed. The larynx, too, is cut through. He has a kind of genius. His movements are streamlined, with no doubt about them. How different from my own surgery, where no single move but is plucked at by hesitation.

In the abattoir there is gradation of rank, at the bottom of which hierarchy is the hoser, often the newest member of the group. Only after a long education to the hose will he be formally instructed in the art of stunning and hoisting. Then on to bunging, decapitation, amputation of the hooves, gutting, skinning, and, if his dream is to be realized, killing, which is at the pinnacle. In this, it is not unlike the surgical residency training program at Yale. Never mind.

The stunner turns their brains off like spigots; the slitter turns on the faucet of their blood, which squirts in a forceful splash toward the stone floor. For a moment the cows are still, megaliths, then a mooing, flailing, kicking as the effect of the stunning wears off. Now and then the slitter must step out of the way of a frantic hoof. It takes so long until all movement stops! As the bleeding slackens the hose is used and the business dilutes into wateriness. The hose flogs across unblinking eyes; it is a storm of weeping. I am tempted to reach out, I am that close, and lift a velvet lip, finger a horn, but I do not. There is rebuke implicit in such acts.

"Two hundred and fifty gallons of water per second," the hoser tells me. It does not occur to me to doubt him. I peer through the scrim of blood and water to the stunning pen, where the next cow has just been felled. It is in the stunning pen that the animals seem most exposed, with no tiny shield of leaves, no small tangle of brambles, such as any captured thing is entitled to hide behind. And all the while the flat mooing of the already-slit, a hollow blare pulled up and out from their cavernous insides that stops abruptly and has no echo. And the howl of the stunned. Now there is a throatful of hot vowel if ever you hear it.

Each cow is impaled at the groin on a ceiling hook and detached from the hoist to make room for the next. These ceiling hooks are on tracks and can be pushed along from station to station. A second hook is used in the other groin. A light touch sends the splayed animal sliding on the rack like a coat in a factory. Already there is a second cow bleeding from the hoist, and the third has been stunned. The efficiency of the men is a glittering, wicked thing. They are synchronous as dancers and for the most part as silent. It is their knives that converse, gossip, press each other along. The smallest faltering of one would be felt at once by each of the others. There would be that slackening which the rest would have to take up. But now and then they laugh, always at each other, something one of them has said. One of them is always the butt. It does you good to hear this chaffing. I see that without laughter the thing could not be done. They are full of merriment, like boys. Or like gods, creating pain and mirth at the same time. A dozen times a day, the hoser, who is younger than the rest and a little simple, I am told, turns his hose on one of the other men, who roars with outrage. Everyone else dies of laughter, then rises again, redder in the face. What are their minds like? Bright and light and shadowless, I think. Disinfected.

There is a sequence to it: stun, hoist, slit, hose, bung, behead, amputate, and gut. Each step in the process is carried out by one man at his station. The cattle are slid from one to the other on the racks. What a heat! What an uproar! Already the sink and scales, all the ghastly furniture of this place, retreat into far corners and I see nothing but the cattle. At one end of the room the heads are lined up on a folding rack, such as might otherwise be used to dry clothes. Tranquillity has been molded into their mouths. The once swiveling lips are still, the brown eyes opaque. Here they are axed open and the brains examined by the inspector.

"What are you looking for?" I ask him. With scissors and forceps he cuts into the base of one brain.

"Pus, spots, lumps," he says. I peer over his shoulder and see instead at the back of the cow's eyes all the black and white of her tribe puddled there. At the base of her brain a slopping pasture, green with, here and there, a savory buttercup to which all of her life she lowered her muzzle. And in her throat, pockets of retained lowing which I think to hear escaping even as he prods the tissue with his forceps.

The beheader is not yet twenty. When he turns to see who is spying there, his smile is hesitant and shy. Around his waist a chain belt holds a bone-handled sharpener and a spare knife. He flashes his wrist, and there is the quick hiss of the blade against the rasp. Later he will show me his knife, let me heft it, turn, flip, feint.

"Nice?" he asks me.

"Nice," I say. "Nice." Abruptly, he kneels to his work. He might be giving first aid to the victim of an accident. Not Judith at the nape of Holofernes nor Salome working her way through the gorge of John the Baptist was more avid than this youth who crouches over his meat like a lion, his blade drinking up blood.

The first slitter has been replaced by another. This one is Italian. His hair is thick and black with just a spot of russet like the flash of a fox's tail. His shoulder is jaunty, his cheek shadowed by eyelashes as he sinks the knife. It is less a stab than a gesture, delicate and powerful, the thrust of a toreador. Against the tang of his knife, the loaded artery pops, and the whole of the cow's blood chases the blade from the premises. I see the slow wavelike pulse of the slitter's jugular vein. Once he laughs out loud. The sound is sudden and unexpected. I turn to watch the mirth emerging from so much beauty of lips and teeth and throat. At eye level a posthumous hoof flexes, extends, flexes again.

All at once, a calf, thinking, I suppose, to escape, wallops through the half-open gate of the stunning pen and directly into the Killing Oval. She is struck on the flank by a bloodfall from the hoist. Her eyes are shining pits of fear. The men view this with utmost seriousness. Immediately two of them leave their tasks and go to capture the miscreant, one by the tail, the other by an always handy ear, and they wrestle the calf back into the pen to wait her turn. Now here is no Cretan bull dance with naked youths propelled by the power of horns, but an awkward graceless show, as the calf robs them of their dignity. They slide on the floor, lose their balance. At last calm is restored. Half an hour later, writhen and giving up the ghost, the calf has her turn. So, there is a predetermined schedule, an immutable order. Why?

". . . nine, ten, eleven, twelve. One dozen." Someone is counting a cluster of impaled and hanging calves. They are like black-and-white curtains ungirt, serious. The men part them with the backs of their hands in order to pass through. They are not just dead; they are more than dead, as though never alive. Beyond, trays of steaming guts; another rack of heads, all clot and teeth. Each head is tagged with the number of its carcass, just so each plastic bag of viscera. Should a beast be found diseased in any part, the inspector discards the whole of it. The men do not wear gloves but plunge boldly into the swim. Are they in a kind of stupor of blood? Oddly spellbound by the repetition of their acts? Perhaps it is the efficiency of the Process which blinds them. I think of the wardens of Auschwitz. At the final station, barrels of pelts. For leather, for rugs.

"A guy in New Jersey buys them," the skinner tells me.

I see that one of the slit and hoisted continues to writhe, and all at once she gives a moo less through her clotted muzzle than from the gash in her neck. It is a soft call straight to my heart. And followed by little thirsty whispers.

"It's still mooing," I say.

"Oh, that," says the slitter.

"How can that be?" I ask. "The larynx has been severed. Hear that?" He cocks his head. There is a soft sucking sigh from the veal cluster farther on, as though someone were turning over in his sleep.

"They do that sometimes," he explains, "even that long after they've been cut." There is an absolute absence of any madness in him which might explain, mollify, soften. He is entirely cool, reserved, intent.

But today they have not been able to kill them all. Some will have to wait overnight in the corral. Thirty minutes after the command has been given to stop, everything in the slaughterhouse is neat and tidy, as much as rinsing and scrubbing can make it so. The tools have been scraped clean, the planks scoured and freshly swept. When it is all done, the beheader snatches a hose from the youngest, the one who is simple, and sprays him in the crotch. Another joins in the play. How young even the older ones look now. They are eager to go home, where I should think them the gentlest of men. This slaughterhouse is a place one leaves wanting only to make love. In the courtyard my nose is feathered by the smell of fresh air. Overhead a gull blows by, beaking at the sky. From my car I see a cow swing her muzzle at a fly, lash with her tail, and fall still. On the roof, along the eaves, doves mourn.

In the morning I arrive just before the men. I wait for them to come. Soon they do. One of them has brought a little dog, a terrier, who scampers along, bouncing sideways and snapping high-pitched chunks out of the silent air. The sight of the dog tickles the men, each of whom stops to pet or scratch. "You, Fritzie," they say, and growl, "little pecker." Now the building awakens, accepting clatter and water gushing into its basins. It begins again.

For two days my new colleagues and I watch and listen as the twelve students present their models, their blueprints. Never, never have there been abattoirs more clever, more ingenious than the abattoirs of Yale. For ease of access the "Plants" are unequaled. Railroad sidings, refrigerated trucks contiguous at one end, attached meat markets. It is all there. And inside, disposable plastic troughs for collecting the blood, fluorescent lighting, air purification, marvelously efficient stunning rooms. "Here," they say, pointing, "is where they are stunned." And, "I have placed the killing alcove here." The faces of the students do not change; they do not tremble at the reenactment of Purgatory. Rather, a cool, calm correctness is what they own. Like the slaughterers, the students have grown used to the awful facts; what concerns them is the efficiency of the process. When they speak of the butchers, they commend their technique. And so do I. So do I. And if ever I should wish to own an abattoir, I would be wise to choose any one of these student architects to make it for me. But there is another abattoir that concerns me now. It is the real abattoir that lies just beneath the abattoir these architects and I have seen.

In the design and building of an abattoir one must remember that once it was that the animals were the gods. Slaughtering was then no mere step in the business of meat preparation but an act charged with religious import and carried out in a temple. The altar was sprinkled with blood. The flame of animal life partook of the sacred and could be extinguished only by the sanction of religion. But, you say, what can architecture do in the face of slaughter? Beauty and spirit stop at the first splash of blood. Better to settle for efficiency. But efficiency gives way before the power of the mythic imagination. And so we shall try:

First, the location. No grinding truck stop on the highway, but a cool glade at the foot of a ridge with, beyond, another ridge and another. Some place beautifully remote, I think, on a small elevation from which the sky and the sun might be consulted. Yet not so high as to be seen silhouetted against heaven from the sea. That is for temples and lighthouses. Nor ought it to be easily seen from any road but must be out of sight, like certain sanatoria, oracular pools, surgical operating rooms. A place without vista, turned in upon itself. And hidden by trees. The gods always play where there are trees that invite mist to their branches. I should build it in a grove, then, to benefit from the resident auspicious deities. And yes, trees, not so much to lend mystery and darkness as for companionship, to bear witness. Let a vivid spring leap nearby with water that is cold and delicious. To listen to its quick current is tantamount to bathing in its waters. Just so simply are ablutions performed. Hand-scooped from the stream, such water will, if drunk at certain susceptible times of the day—twilight and dawn—summon visitations, induce dreams. Pulled up into the throats of the doomed beasts, it will offer them peace, make them ready.

At this place let there be equal parts of sun and shade and at night the cold exaltation, the lambent flood of moonlight. And no nearby houses, for the shadow of this place must not fall across the dwellings of human beings. Killing of any kind has its contagious aspects. Place it thus and the abattoir becomes a god—distant, dignified, lofty, silent. Gaunt and stark until the beasts are ushered in. Only then does its blood begin to flow. Only then is the building warmed and colored, completed. Made human. Such a building is a presence. I would want anyone looking at my abattoir for the first time to fall under its spell, to believe it particularly his as well—there would be that certain tilt of a roof, the phantom shadow of leaves cruising over tile. One glance at such a site and you will say as Oedipus said at Colonus: "As for this place, it is clearly a holy one."

David, it is reported in the Bible, purchased a threshing floor from Araunah the Jebusite upon which to build the altar of his temple. Alas, the Jebusites are no more, and neither are their threshing floors to be found in the land. Even so, I would use stone for the floor, roughhewn granite quarried nearby, granite that will wash black in the rain, turn gold in the setting sun. Granite with beveled edges cut to fit neatly, the gaps between to be filled with mortar. Brick too is permissible, since the elements of earth and fire are combined to form it. Brick is earth which has gone through fire. It is sacrificial. None of this will be understood by those who see but a stone in a stone, a brick in a brick. It is in the precise placement and the relationship of these materials that their sacramental quality lies. The roofs of the inner passageway will be of slate raftered with the bisected trunks of oak trees upon which strips of bark have been left. These trees should be felled in October, for in the spring all of the power of the tree is devoted to the making of leaves. In the fall the wood is more compressed and solidified. Oak is preferred above all others, as much for its strength and resistance to water as for the news whispered by its leaves that nothing is annihilated; there is only change and the return of matter to a former state. Stone, brick, and wood, then. The earth has been burnt; the stone has been cut from its place; the tree has been felled; and all three rise in the form of the abattoir. Yet their texture must survive. The memory of the original tree, clay, earth, stone, is made permanent by the form in which each is made. The builder with his hand and his eyes must do justice to the talent and potential of the material. Nor are these materials passive but offer their own obstacles and tendencies.

Centrally, there is to be a vast open atrium flanked by columns whose capitals are carved as the horned heads of beasts. Everything must reflect the cattle. They are the beating heart of the place. So let there be columns and an unroofed atrium. As nobody can live without the ample to-and-fro of air, so will the building be dead that does not permit the internal play of abundant air. Between the columns of the atrium place lustral stone basins in which water from the stream may be collected for the washing of hands. Columns too, for avenues of light that in the company of the breeze and the high fountain will rinse the air of reek.

The building faces east to receive the morning sun, in which it is best for the men to work. There are to be no steps in any part of the abattoir, only timbered ramps curved like those of a ziggurat along which the animals are led up to the porch or vestibule. This antechamber measures in cubits twenty by twenty. (The cubit being the length of the forearm from elbow to fingertips.) It is the function of this room to separate the profane world from the sacred area which is the atrium. In order to enter the atrium the cattle must pass in single file beneath an arch. It is well known that to pass through an archway is to be changed forever in some way. Who is to say that such passage does not purify these beasts, make them ready to die? The atrium itself is vast, measuring in cubits sixty long, forty wide, and thirty high. As I have said, it is roofless in order to receive the direct rays of the sun. Nor has it any walls on either side but open colonnades. To the rear of the atrium is a third and smaller room where the men take their rest. Inside, the corridors, vestibule, and resting room must be brilliant with light from wall lamps and skylights. Shadows are dangerous in an abattoir. They make you think. There is to be no rebirth here, as we know it. It is a place for endings, where residue is hosed away and no decay permitted.

Let us dwell upon the interior of the building. If a stable has the odor of manure, why, that is fitting to the stable. The smell increases the stableness of the building, confirms it in its role as the dwelling place for beasts. Just so is the odor of fresh-spilled blood apt for an abattoir. You would not expect perfume. Still, I would be grateful for the sacred smell of sawdust or straw—for the sake of the cattle, to conceal it from them. Blood has no smell, you say? And it is true that there is no odor of it in the operating room. But I think that to catch the whiff of blood is a talent beyond human olfaction. Tigers smell blood and hunt it down precisely. And sharks, having shed a single drop of their own blood, will devour themselves. Are you certain that domestication blunts the noses of these animals? No, compassion dictates that we separate the about-to-be-slain from those crossing over. Listen! The stones ring with hooves. And in a corner of the atrium, the sawdust is roiled where one of them has floundered, the cloven hoofprints brimming with red shavings. And no reek in the air.

When, as happens, they cannot all be slain in one day, the cattle are led at dusk from the clearing in front of the abattoir down to a narrow tortuous path lined by thick shrubbery. It is the same path by which they left the world at dawn. Here and there the path forks, suggesting a labyrinth. Such a serpiginous route emphasizes the immense apartness of the abattoir. They are ushered into a pasture at some remove where they spend the night in a world cast in frost and moonlight. Stay with them through these hallucinated hours white as foam and filled with heightened meaning. Be there just before dawn, waiting. Long before you see them you will hear the sound of their lips pulling at the grass of the pasture. Ah, there! Look! The first one—all white, breasting the mist, then coming clear of it, like a nymph stepping out of the woods.

Now they are led back to the slaughterhouse. I hear the soothing murmur of the herder making his sweet deceit. "Come along now, ladies. Be polite. No need to crowd. It's all the same in the end." A moo interrupts.

"Hush, now." Again the labyrinthine path must be navigated. In the early morning the climate of the place is that of a cellar—cool and cavernous. There are the pillars caught in the very act of rising. There is the sibilance of insects and a throbbing of frogs. The mist rises and soon there are drifting veils of water and sunlight, something piney in the air. Pious the feet that pace the stone floor of the atrium. The heads of the men are covered with small caplets. Prayers are recited. One of them holds the knife up to the sunlight, then turns to examine its larger shadow upon the floor. Any nick or imperfection that might cause suffering to the animal is thereby magnified and corrected before the beast is led to it. At the last moment the blade is smeared with honey for sweetness and lubrication. All the energy of the place emanates from the edge of that knifeblade. It is a holy object, a radiant thing. In the dazzling sunlight it is like a silver thorn to be laid upon the willing neck of the beast.

But a cow is not much, you argue. A cow is not beautiful as a trout, say, is beautiful. A trout—made of river water, and speckled stone, and tinted by the setting sun. Nor are cows rare, as peacocks are rare, or certain blue butterflies. These cattle bring with them no paraphernalia of the past. They have none. I tell myself that. For a cow, the sun that rises each day is a brand-new sun, not the one that set the day before and rose the day before that. Humans are the only ones afflicted with a past. But then I think of the many-cattled pastures of my childhood in the milk-drenched upper counties of New York State. I close my eyes and see again a herd upon a green slope. There! One lifts her dripping muzzle to stare at a trusted human being. Nonsense, you say, to deplore this slaughter when with each footstep we erase whole histories. Besides, they do it humanely. What! Would you rescue them? Burst upon the scene with a machine gun and order the animals to be loaded on the truck and driven away? To the country, to the middle of the meadow, and set them free?

I know, I know. But to one who watches from the periphery, there seems no place for this event in human experience.

Hypocrite, you say, why don't you give up meat instead of professing all this outrage?

Give up meat! Oh, no, I couldn't do that, I have eaten meat all of my life. Besides, vegetarianism seems to me a kind of national atonement, an act of asceticism like the fasting that is done during Lent or on Yom Kippur.

So. We are all meat eaters here. The desire for meat is too deeply seated in us. As deeply seated as the desire for romance. The difference between those butchers and you is that they do not come to the abattoir each day with their hearts gone fluid with emotion. They have no patience with the duplicity of sentiment.

It is the next day, and already the event is too far away for grief or pity. How quickly the horror recedes. I pass the butcher shop, whose window is neatly arranged with parts of meat labeled shank, loin, T-bone. For a long time I stand gazing at the display. For one fleeting instant it occurs to me that this window full of meat is less than dead, that, at a given signal, the cut-up flesh could cast off its labels and cellophane wrappers and reassemble, seek out its head and hooves, fill with blood and *be* again. But the thought passes as quickly as it came.

"Is the veal fresh?" I ask the butcher.

"Slaughtered yesterday," the man says. "Can't be much fresher than that."

"Let me have a pound and a half of the scallopini," I tell him. "Nice and thin, and give it a good pounding."

Diary of an Infidel:
Notes from a Monastery

—ɯ—

Wanderers know it—beggars, runaways, exiles, fugitives, the homeless, all of the dispossessed—that if you knock at the door of a monastery seeking shelter you will be taken in. A bed will be provided, and food and the opportunity but not the obligation to pray. Those inside will know it too, the monks, and they will act accordingly. After all, the most unlikely visitor has the possibility of having Christ within him. So the monks are taught and so they believe.

It is evening. I am standing on the pier of San Marco in Venice. If I have been fleeing, it is from no physical hardship, but only from the dilemma of life. In my haste, I have made no hotel reservation. For some hours I have traipsed from one *pensione* to another. No luck.

"What is that place out there in the bay?" I ask a stranger. I point to a small island, every inch of which is occupied by a great church and attached buildings.

"That is the Abbey of San Giorgio Maggiore," he tells me. All at once I know that it is the place I have been seeking.

Let it be said at the outset that I am no frequenter of churches. The very buildings have become invisible to me. So that were I to pass a house of worship in the street I would be unlikely to see it. Long ago I accepted the notion that faith is something given to selected men and women, like perfect pitch. It cannot be sought after. No amount of yearning can produce it. Whatever adherence I had to the concept of a hereafter vanished at puberty. Nor did its departure cause me discomfort. I felt, rather, disencumbered. Unlike heaven or hell, oblivion could be approached with equanimity. (As for sin, I have committed my share and failed to regret it enough.) Truth to tell, I love sin. And magic, and the possibility of a grand mess, the whole place caving in. Which posture has caused me to stumble from one humiliation to another with some frequency. Call it impulse then or impertinence or just perhaps *nostalgie de la croyance* that finds me aboard the vaporetto, leaving the orange fire of Venice and making for the island of San Giorgio in the bay. "Just a happen," Emily Dickinson would have said of the trip. Later, the monks will say that I have come in accordance with a will other than my own. But that is the way they talk. We shall see what happens.

The approach to San Giorgio is from the west. Physically San Giorgio seems a dead place, without periodicity. It has a solid heavy look, a sinker. Or anchor. Yet held afloat by something. All about the boat, the lagoon is flashing with gulls and gondolas. At last, with a thump and a scuffle we are at the wooden pier.

"San Giorgio!" calls the boatman. *"Permesso, permesso, signore, prego!"* And he pulls back the bar. I cross the great stone terrace and rap on the door. It is answered by a monk in a loose floor-length black habit that flows about his legs.

"I am a wayfarer seeking shelter," I say. "I would like to stay in your guesthouse, *il foresteria*," I tell him.

"I am Dom Pietro, the guestmaster," he says in English without the least surprise. He does not ask my name or whether I am expected. "I will show you to your room." He pivots momentously and leads the way into the abbey. He does not offer to carry one of my bags. Perhaps the idea does not occur to him. Perhaps it is his unworldliness. Perhaps he is rude. The staircase is narrow and winding. Ahead, he is all grace and figure, while, clumsy with baggage, I bump and scrape to keep up with him. At the door to what I see is to be my room, he pauses.

"Enter, Christ," he says.

"Well, not exactly," I say.

"Four hundred years ago the abbot himself would have come to bathe your feet."

"How long have you been here?" I ask.

"We have been here one thousand years."

The room is not a cell but good-sized with a high beamed ceiling. A large casement window opens out to reveal the Byzantine domes of San Marco directly across the water. The furniture is heavy, Renaissance. The floor, marble; there is no rug. I count three crucifixes, a woodblock print of Pope John XXIII, and an etching entitled "S. Franciscus de Paola in a State of Ecstasy." The Virgin Mary occupies a niche by the door.

"You have arrived very late in the day," says Pietro. "It is just now time for Vespers. Come." I deposit the suitcase and typewriter and follow him down a long corridor, descend a curved flight of stairs, cross a foyer, and step into what proves to be the side door of a great church. Inside it is black. Never, never has there been darkness like this. It is the first darkness, undiluted from the beginning. I can see nothing. Ahead of me the monk's black habit has become part of the immense blackness of the church.

"Come," he whispers. "We shall be late." I take one blind cautious step and pause again. A hand slips into mine and exerts firm pressure. We walk for what seems a great distance, then stop. The hand is disengaged and with a sweep of pale palm I am invited to sit. In a moment he is gone. Slowly my eyes accommodate and I understand that I am entirely alone in a huge vaulted building. Far away, two small candles, like stars. And like stars, they shine but give no light. I sit for a long time in the absolute silence. Slowly the church forms itself about me. I establish the site of the nave, the great altar. High above, an angel hovers in full finial display.

All at once, there is a barely perceptible noise, a soft rumble as of thunder. The sound dies without discovery of its nature or source. It returns, seeming to come from all directions at once, like ventriloquy. One moment it is subterranean; the next, it gathers from on high. Is it the wind? Tricking among the roofs and towers? A construction of the water? A vagrant noise from the Piazza San Marco? At last it emerges from its mystery, grows into a tremulous hum and solidifies into chanting. The music has no tempo. There is no breathing audible in it. No one voice stands out; it is the fusion of all that produces the effect. Long-held notes which at last modulate again and again in the calm rhythm of the heart. Systole, diastole. Something, I think, that must be performed in tranquillity, a kind of respiratory yoga. I am suspended in the sound. And charged. My fatigue lifts and is replaced by a drowsiness. The headache which has plagued me for three days is a distant muted pulse at my temple.

The chanting dies away as gently as it began. Once again there is the unanimous voice of silence. In a moment Dom Pietro is back. I have no idea how long the service has lasted. Time, it seems, as well as space is immeasurable here.

"It is time for the evening meal," the guestmaster says as we leave the church. "When you enter the refectory the monks will be standing, each behind his place. You will be seated at the head of the U-shaped table next to the abbot. Stand in front of the table and wait. Soon Padre Abate will arrive. He will come up to you at once and hold out his hand. You must take his hand in yours, bow, and kiss his ring. He will then conduct you to your seat. The meal is taken in silence."

"Kiss his ring?"

The abbot is bulky but he is not obese. Rather, his body is conscious and suave. It has the gracefulness of power. His smile is warm, papal. Behind those hooded eyes burns a superb intelligence. When he holds out his ring I bob to it. Against my lips it has the unyielding smoothness of a ram's horn. I sit next to the abbot on his right at what amounts to a high table. The others are seated at the two long tables of which we are the connecting link. Scanning the tables I see that all but one of the monks are big, fleshy men; that one is candle-thin. The monk serving the meal places a large tureen of soup on the table from which the abbot serves first me, then himself. The tureen is borne away and placed in front of the monk nearest me. This man takes from it and passes it to his neighbor. Now the abbot tinkles a small silver bell. One tink. And a young monk seats himself at a lectern. He begins to read aloud, in Latin first, then Italian. His voice, though monotonous, is devoid of weariness or boredom. I do not get much of it. The lives of the saints, I think. Or the Rule of Saint Benedict.

A cruet of red wine is at each place along with a small loaf of bread, fat in the middle and tapering at the end, thus repeating the bodily configuration of its devourer. The abbot takes my glass and, holding the cruet of wine high above it, pours so that the red stream appears to have a solid permanence. Not a drop is spilled or runs from the lip of the vessel. The meal, other than the soup of rice and noodles, consists of hard gray meat encased in a jelly. I think of toads and half expect one to poke its nose up for air. I can eat nothing but the bread, wine, and apple. The eating of such food could never be thought sinful. I think of the thousand marvelous restaurants in Venice.

The monks, even the thin one, pile their plates high. Looking neither to the right nor to the left, they eat. As they do, their faces take on the lesser intelligence of dumb submissive beasts. At least three are out-and-out gorgers, slurping, mopping, belching. I spend the time worrying my food into insignificance on the plate. Another tink! and the silenced reader takes his place at the table. It is the time for talk.

"You are most welcome to our abbey and our table." The abbot's voice is smooth and practiced, furry. "But you have eaten nothing." A smile shows concern.

"Please pay it no mind. I am famous for it."

"It is the rule here that you must finish everything on your plate."

"Then permit me to serve myself."

"It is my pleasure to serve my guests."

"But you all eat so much. One is not accustomed."

"Saint Benedict has said that he who works shall eat."

"Then I must have some work to do here. You must give me a

job. I am not comfortable when I am idle and all about me are fully engaged."

"There is no work for you here."

"Then I am to be an ornament? Please, I am a doctor; I can give the monks each a physical examination. Or, if you prefer, I would be happy to help in the kitchen or laundry. The garden. Whatever."

"No." He smiles. "You are not to work here."

"But I have always worked. Upon my tombstone shall be carved 'He kept busy.' "

"No."

"Then why am I here?"

"The reason has not yet been revealed to me." The small white hands part briefly, then rejoin, and I understand that the subject is closed. Well, then. I shall develop my unrealized genius for elaborate repose. If I can do no work here, so much the better. Like the poet, I'll loaf and invite my soul.

"Tell me," says the abbot, "perhaps you can help me. Is there an English word—*tempiternal*? I read it the other day. How does it differ from *sempiternal*?"

"I think it was a misprint," I tell him. He laughs. Just that, and we are to be friends. He fingers the bell, and we rise. One of the monks with his cowl at full mast and his arms hidden in his surplice recites a prayer of thanks. The others listen very carefully. No one in the refectory but bows his head and folds his hands into a long pale flower bud. Spying, I see the thanker exchange the briefest, tiniest smile with one of the novices grouped at the farthest end of the table. A private joke. Why does this make me so happy? The departure from the refectory is made in silence and then there is a procession that is very far from the kind of academic slouch which I am used to at Yale commencements. They go *en file*. Moments later they are cowled silhouettes merging with the night.

At the door of the refectory I am retrieved by the guestmaster. So far as I can tell, none of the other monks has so much as glanced in my direction. Once again in my room, Dom Pietro becomes the perfect chamberlain.

"The bathroom is just outside your door. No one else is permitted to use it during your stay. The armoire is fifteenth-century Florentine. The bed, too. Only the desk is Venetian. All of the icons are of the same period save for the amethyst crucifix on the desk, which is thirteenth-century. The bed is firm and comfortable. The pope slept in it on his last visit."

"I am to sleep in the pope's bed?"

"It was before his election."

"Oh well, then."

Pietro lifts one eyebrow.

"By the way, Dom Pietro, what are the rules? I must tell you that I am incompletely housebroken and do not want to disgrace myself. Tell me what I must not do."

"The only rule here is that of Saint Benedict, and that, of course, does not apply to you. But there are three things: Turn out the lights when you leave the room. If you smoke, collect the ashes and butts and give them to me to discard. Do not put them in the wastebasket."

"Where, then?" He points to an inkwell made of horn on the desk.

"That will do fine. Above all, close the window when you leave the room."

"That's all?"

"And oh, yes, one other. You must eat everything on your plate."

"It was hardly Belshazzar's feast."

"Nevertheless, you must. It is the rule here."

"*Per la penitenza,*" I murmur. Pietro is not amused.

The temperature is frigid in this place. I am shivering and my nose has begun to run. In the morning I shall have to chip myself out of bed with a little pickax. I fit the stopper in the huge claw-footed tub and turn on the faucets. From one, there is nothing at all; from the other, a pathetic twine of cold water. While waiting for the tub to fill I go to the windows and push them open. Venice snaps open like a fan. Directly across is the Piazza San Marco and the Palace of the Doges. Below, the ghostly night traffic of the lagoon. My room is on the second story at the front of the abbey adjacent to the facade of the church. I shall be able to pick out this window from the vaporetto. I lean on the ledge until a huge black shape erases Venice. Silent as a monk the freighter noses toward Yugoslavia beyond the sea. The wind of its passage blows the smell of cuttlefish into the room. The spell is broken and I go to my bath. After half an hour, the vast bathtub holds three inches of cold water. For my sins. I strip and tiptoe in. There I crouch, not daring to sit, and with the help of a soapy rag, rearrange the dirt on my body. No towel but a regulation-sized washcloth. I air-dry. It seems that my suffering soul is forcing my body to keep it company. No sooner have I re-dressed then there is a knock at the door. Pietro. Am I to have constant attendance?

"Ah, I see that you have bathed."

"In a way. Might you have a bath towel?" He goes to inspect the bathroom.

"But you have washed the tub. I am to do that for you."

"The monk does not live who washes my tub. My rule." He disappears briefly and returns with an ancient frayed towel that I could conceal entirely in one of my ears.

"Also fifteenth-century?" I ask.

"Will you be smoking tonight?"

"Yes. Do you mind?" I light up. "I don't suppose you . . ." Pietro smiles and reaches out to accept. I light it for him. He drags pro-foundly and exhales slowly. I see that he has not had a cigarette in recent memory.

"Will you have a brandy?"

"You have brought brandy here?"

"One does not set out to explore a savage country without bring-ing something to appease the natives," I tell him. And pour two large hookers. He sips with pleasure.

"Padre Abate and I are the only ones who speak English. The others are not permitted to speak with you unless necessary."

"Do you have many visitors such as I?"

"Guests are rare here. The occasional priest on his way to Rome, a visiting abbot come to concelebrate mass with Padre Abate, and of course, once, the pope."

We smoke three cigarettes each and drink another brandy.

"It is strange," I tell him, "the austerity amidst these gorgeous surroundings, all this vast treasure."

"Not austere enough," he says. "We are too fat." And he taps his belly with two fingers. "I myself should have preferred a thornier path. But it was not given me."

"Whatever for?"

"The conquest of self is the more complete in a severe convent."

I am extremely tired. Pietro does not notice and makes no effort to leave. All at once, I am set rattling by the sound of a loud bell. It is exactly like the bell used to mark the end of a period in Public School No. 5 in Troy, New York, and, five minutes later, the beginning of another. It is a harsh, prisonlike jangle, meant, I think, to startle rather than remind. In a country full of beautiful bells it is the cruelest noise that calls these monks to prayer. At the sound Pietro stands.

"Compline," he says. "Come and you will hear me sing."

"Another time," I say. "I am through for the day."

"I shall not be coming to meals regularly," I tell him, "other than breakfast."

He urges me to relent and come to the noonday meal.

"It is the best one," he says. "Very good pasta, fish."

"No, I cannot eat so much."

"It is you who are the monk, a Carthusian. On a single loaf of bread a week."

He laughs at his joke.

At last I am established in my room, the noise of the tiny far-off world on one side of the window, and on the other side, the limitless silence of the monastery.

Once I am alone the feeling comes over me that I have lived in this monastery room before, as though this were not my first coming but a return to a beloved room after a long absence, an awakening after a wintry hibernation. The bed, the table, the casement, the floor, even the crucifixes seem to have taken on the kind of familiarity that belongs to the objects of one's childhood, everything unchanged, as it was.

On the pillow of the bed someone has placed a hand-printed card of the day's activities:

ORARIO MONASTICO

ORE:	5:00	sveglia
	5:30	mattutino
	6:45	laudi/messa
		conventuale (cantata, concelebrata)
	7:30	colazione (fino alle 8:30)
	12:50	sesta
	13:00	pranzo
	14:00	riposo
	15:30	sveglia
	15:45	nona
	19:35	vespri (cantati)
	20:00	cena/ricreazione
	21:00	lettura/compieta (cantata)
	21:30	riposo/silenzio

It seems no different from my own hectic hours in surgery where bits and pieces of day and night are pinched off, each full of its own obligation and necessity, though unannounced by bells.

Morning, after the very soundest sleep. The bed, though narrow, is deep. It molds itself to fit the body so that one is not so much in it as of it. All night long there were the lapping of waves and the dark shapes of freighters gliding past. I have begun writing an essay on surgery. My plan is to work on it a few hours each day. I have just taken a seat at the desk when Pietro arrives.

"Padre Abate wishes to give you a tour of the monastery."

I follow him to the foyer just inside the front door, where the abbot and four other monks are waiting. With the abbot presiding, I am led from one spectacle to the next: the refectory with its great ornamental lavabos, the twelfth-century cloister of the cypresses, a monumental staircase, a long pristine white dormitory with, on either side, the black doors of the cells, each with its little wicket. For spying, I suppose.

The church, designed by Palladio, is in the form of a cross with a cupola above and an adjacent campanile affording, I am told, the best view of Venice. The facade, facing San Marco square, is of the finest Istrian marble.

From the outside, the dome of the basilica is one big tonsured scalp. Inside, it is wallpapered with scenes from the Bible. The Annunciation. There is the archangel impregnating Mary with words. Mary, herself, looking up from her book with that "Who, me?" expression on her face. There, the Last Supper. The Israelites collecting manna. At the head of the nave is the choir where the monks worship. It is four steps higher than the presbytery, where the great altar is situated and which, in turn, is three steps higher than the main portion of the church. The whole is a great prismatic box where light and stone interact to produce something greater by far than either one—a conspiracy.

There is no stained glass, for which I am grateful. I have always resented stained glass, its way of getting between me and the sky, always demanding attention. Whenever I see it I imagine the wickedest sins being committed behind it. The building is made entirely of stone and has the coldness of stone. What little there is of wood is in the furnishings, the ornately carved choir, the crucifixes. The altar is decorated with a large round copper ball placed over four figures of the Evangelists. It is this that serves as the tabernacle for the Holy Sacrament. All this is explained to me by Padre Abate. To me this church is a vaulting paradise where voices ascend, multiply, and are gathered beneath the dome, where pillars and arches stretch away and away in every direction into far distant darkness. Here is a building that is never still, but alters its angles and curves to fit each new position of the body, pressing against one until it occupies the heart. I am struck by the great number of angels placed strategically upon every ledge and mantel, a whole host *tenentes silentium*.

It is too beautiful, too perfect, the columns too straight and soaring. Humility alone dictates that one wall be defaced, one pillar be pulled askew by ropes.

Several hours later we pass through a pair of immense carved doors into a great hall or throne room. It is a huge square space about the periphery of which have been set three semicircles of thrones in tiers, twenty-four in each, as in an amphitheater. Below and in the center is an altar bearing twin candelabra. In one corner of the room, a small black potbellied stove with a chimney. On the wall in back of the altar, a large painting depicting Saint George having just impaled the dragon on his lance.

"Carpaccio," says Pietro.

"This is the Conclave Room," says the abbot. "In the history of the church only one pope was elected outside of Rome. It was here that the election took place. The year was 1700. The College of Cardinals gathered to this place. These are their thrones, preserved just as they were. The name of each priest is carved at the back. There," he points, "the little stove where the ballots were burned while across the lagoon all Venice watched for the puffs of smoke. We are very proud of this room." Dom Pietro touches the abbot's arm and they speak together in Italian. The abbot turns to me.

"Dom Pietro has reminded me that you are still tired from your journey. We shall rest here. Please," he motions, "be seated."

Gratefully, I climb the first step to the middle row of thrones, walk in one, two, three, and sit in the fourth. All at once the four monks turn to each other and begin to jabber, using their hands wildly. I know at once that I have committed a gaffe. Something Pietro neglected to warn me against. I spring to my feet.

"What is it?" I ask. "I have done something wrong."

Padre Abate explains. "You have chosen to sit in the place of the man who was elected pope in this room. You must forgive our agitation."

My relief is as vast as their excitement.

"A coincidence," I say. The abbot shakes his head firmly.

"Providence," he says. And that's that.

O twice elected! I sleep in one pope's bed; I sit in the throne of another. From that moment I have free rein to go anywhere in the monastery. Only the dormitory of cells is forbidden me. About them I am immensely curious. To think that tucked within such grandeur there are those little pockets of modesty.

It is only with Pietro that I can speak freely, converse. His visits to my room, made in the role of guestmaster, are frequent and pro-longed. While, in the beginning, the unpredictability and duration of his presence were annoying, I find myself less and less exasper-ated. I tell myself that it is because he speaks English, but I suspect I have grown fond. Honesty forces me to admit that I look forward to that soft rapping at the door, the inch of opening through which looms that great mound of black.

What a great powerful woman of a man he is. A diva bursting with temperament. Well over six feet tall, and hefty, with skimpy blond hair combed straight forward to conceal frontal baldness. Much the tallest of the monks, he holds himself ramrod-straight, which accentuates his height above them. His voice is baritone with just the hint of brogue. He is, after all, Irish from Dublin. The eyes are Anglo-Saxon blue, the nose fleshy with mobile nostrils. When he turns to speak, it is with his whole body rather than his head only, as though he were on a stage and playing to an audience. It is a flattering gesture in that it lends the impression that his en-tire attention is given to you alone. Turning, he lightly fingers the material of the habit which he does not so much wear as model. Whereas the others seem unaware of their costume, Pietro makes every use of it to express himself. By carriage and mien he is apart from the community. In file across the cloister the heads of the others are downcast and forward. Pietro's head is down too, yes, but with the chin turned slightly to the side as though he were listening. The others are merely monks. Dom Pietro is pure figure. He seems to have come to understand this abbey with his body the way an old sailor does his boat—the shadows made by the archway, the exact step in the marble staircase where his voice echoes most thrillingly from the domed ceiling. And in these places he lingers to submit,

encouraging the building to express itself through his body. In his
company, I feel all the more an old clothes-bag.

"Everything we do is in the interest of unity and uniformity," he
says. "Our identical habits, the way we walk in line, heads bent,
hands hidden in the surplice. Such an unchanging rhythm sets the
stage for the appearance of God."

It is the chain reaction of monastic life. They have but to look
at each other moving toward glory with submarine grace and their
zeal is fired.

"But your walk is different," I tell him. "I would know you at
once in a crowd."

He does not hide his pleasure at this.

Pietro has been appointed to look after my needs. Whatever
I am to see and hear will be filtered through him. To see more I
shall have to stand tiptoe and peer over that massive shoulder. Each
time he leaves my room I turn the crucifix on my desk thirty degrees so that, sitting there, I am out of the line of fire. Each time
he comes his first act is to turn it back until once again I am a
bull's-eye.

"When are you going to stop being so childish?" he asks.

"Never," I tell him.

"Padre Abate has given me permission to take you for *un pas-
seggio,* a walk outside. I'll be back for you at half past three. . . ."

"Good," I say. "Until then I can do my writing." Whereupon he
sits down, lights one of my cigarettes, and begins.

"You eat nothing," Pietro accuses me. "You are all wrist and rib
like one of the desert fathers. It would be different if you were fasting
out of penitence."

"I was the runt of the litter," I explain. "It makes you finicky."

"You do not like our food."

"That is putting it mildly."

"What is wrong with it? It is tasty and nourishing."

"No, it is all some ghastly mistake you are making in the
kitchen."

He flashes me a look of mingled exasperation and affection.

"Show me," I persist, "where in the Rule of Saint Benedict it says that the food must be part of the penance."

He laughs with almost physical violence. At this moment he seems less a monk than I do. All at once he makes a quick pass at his temples, raises his eyes, and becomes holy again.

Three-thirty and Pietro is at the door. We take the vaporetto to the next stop and walk the length of the Giudecca, making a number of side trips into the small secondary streets. I am struck by the cleanliness and tidiness of the neighborhood. And the silence. Although it is late afternoon there are few people in the streets. The glow of Venice lights up our hands and faces. I see his glance turn sidelong at a window full of food. We stop in a bakery and I buy two heavy moist sweet cakes. We stand there as he wolfs his down in a state of enormous happiness. I give him half of mine and he does away with that too, snuffing up the crumbs. The woman in the bakeshop smiles at the naked pleasure of the monk. He could eat ten more, he tells her. As a reward he takes me to the convent of the Franciscan Poor Clares of the Most Holy Trinity. Or a name something like it. It is a severely enclosed nunnery where some fifty women live in abject poverty and total isolation from the world. The windows of the cells are slanted so that the nuns cannot look down into the street, only up at the sky. The convent is presided over by a quite beautiful abbess of about forty. She, like the others, goes barefoot. From behind a wooden lattice she visits with us. Pietro jokes with her in a familiar manner. She has a full-cheeked heart-shaped face with a dimpled smile and clear gray eyes. She passes a bottle of wine and two glasses out to us on a turnstile. Pietro fills our glasses and I toast her. She takes no wine.

"How long have you been here?" I ask her.

"Twenty years."

"Only Lot's wife has had a longer sentence," I tell Pietro in English. He relates this to her in Italian, whereupon she claps her hand to her mouth and laughs.

"What do you do all day?"

"We pray. At night too. We are busy all the time, and very

happy." It is apparent that she has foretold my doubt. Pietro and the abbess engage in a long informal chat in Italian during which they both bubble over with what can only be construed as unalloyed pleasure. It is the shared experience of prayer that binds them together. Once again I am a goy among the Jews.

Here at the Abbey of San Giorgio each room and corridor is aware of every other room and corridor. Perfect in itself, yet in Perfect resonance. It is forbidding. And the whole of the island enveloped in solitude, cut off. What could have possessed the early founders to plant their abbey here? Were they fishermen, sailors by nature that must never be parted from the water? This glowing house, these walls and columns and cloisters that divide up the way of life of the Benedictines—no road winds toward it from afar. It reigns over no fields, only sparkles like a chip of bright stone in the lagoon. And all this doting upon permanence, antiquity, which to gaze upon is just as disheartening as it is to peer into the future. Permanence gives a feeling of oppressiveness to a building. Here is a fifteenth-century table. There hangs an icon from the twelfth, and beneath this little glass bell you can see a few strands of Saint Lucy's hair. So instructs Pietro, dropping centuries the way others drop names.

And what a sobersided business it all is. This routine: Vigils, Primes, Tierces, Sexts, Nones, Vespers, Compline, and those meals which are only variants of the holy offices rendered in gastrointestinal terms. Then at dusk two dozen doors close; two dozen bolts are shot. And we are enclosed.

The objects and furniture of my own room, although doubtless arranged without a decorative intention, have achieved a certain harmony. I cannot imagine them in any other placement, as though the only way possible were with the bed against the inside wall and the armoire on the outside wall next to the window, the desk in the center of the room with the horn inkwell at the far right hand of the blotter, the amethyst crucifix at the far left, the woodblock print of John XXIII above the bed, with the Madonna guarding the door. Each object keeping its exact distance and relationship, each respecting the singularity of the other, yet at the same time complementing the others, offering planes, patterns, buttresses and corners against which each can measure its position in the world. It is the deadest room of my life.

In the inner courtyard there is a collection of flowerpots each holding a plant of some kind. Mostly roses and camellias, but I see lilies and geraniums as well. They are grouped about a white stone Virgin whose hand is raised in blessing. This garden is presided over by Dom Lorenzo, the oldest in the community. He is also the barber and the infirmarian. So far as I know, he is unable to speak a single word in any language, at least he has never done so in my presence. Nor even cleared his throat. Still he is filled with the deep breathing that I recognize as contentment. It is good to be near him. After the noon meal I go to the courtyard to watch him work. Now he examines a camellia, stroking the leaves one after the other, lifting the stems on his thick burry fingers. Now he palms a brick-colored pot. And like all lovers he hums an impromptu tune. I am envious of his work.

Part of the courtyard is fenced off as a cage for a large orange cat.

"What is his name?" I ask Lorenzo.

"He has no name." These are the first words I have heard him utter.

Now that is real poverty. To own nothing, not even a name. Dom Cat, then. And what a dispirited thing he is. The cats I have known watch every leaf on its way down, hear the last click of a mouse's teeth upon a grain of rice. But this orange monk watches and hears nothing. He has renounced the world. I see that he is very thin. Don't they feed him enough? I open the gate of the wire fence and step inside. The cat raises his head. In the depths of each slotted eye, a blazing yellow cross. I go for him; he arches, snarls, and backs away. Again I try, this time from the rear. I long to hold even that ugly irritable creature in my lap, would risk every scratch and bite to feel for a few moments its hum upon my thighs, its rough tongue on my skin. Now I offer a hand. He reels, spits, and rakes it with relish, offering three red stripes in return. The beginning, they say, is always painful. Never mind, I shall try again. I cannot let him live and die without knowing once the happiness of a human lap.

When I leave the cage, I see that Lorenzo has departed. Against the wall, a pitchfork! Here, where there is neither hay nor manure. Perhaps it is there for me to murder the cat. More likely it is used by the monks to drive out their lust. Just at that moment an errant pigeon lights within the wire enclosure and steps to within inches of the cat, which intrusion the cat makes no sign of having noticed. It is blind? The pain in my hand tells me it is not. One peck at the sanctified stone convinces the bird of its miscalculation. Off it heads for the riper pavement of San Marco. One marvels at the ways of bird and beast.

Among the flowering plants in the courtyard I notice a small graceful twine of ivy. Its leaves are glazed with dust, the clay pot that holds it is whitened by mildew and caked with dried mud. I glance about to see. No one. Only Dom Cat behind his wire fence. I pick up the pot of ivy and hurry back to my room. Who can blame a man for taking what he really needs? Kneeling at the tub, I wipe each leaf with a damp cloth, then scrub the pot. Now, where to put it? I place it on the small night table to join *The Rule of Saint Benedict,* but it doesn't do. I move it to the desk. No. The floor? At last it sits upon the narrow window ledge. But there too the ivy is all wrong. It looks awkward, straggly, as though having intruded upon this museum, it has paid with its gracefulness. This room which hates, yet retains, me has rejected the plant. I am oppressed by its presence; a balance has been upset. Pietro knocks and enters. He sees it at once.

"Ah, you have taken a plant."

"It needed a haircut and a bath."

"Dom Lorenzo is both barber and gardener here."

"It looks terrible where it is," I say. "I'll take it back to the courtyard."

"Yes," he says.

Pietro arrives to collect me for the noonday meal. Foolishly, I relent and go with him to the refectory. Boiled beef floating in fatty water. I cannot eat it and that's final. Also a limp variant of cold cabbage with a cheese sauce. Altogether awful, but I am determined, and down a bit of it goes. The implacable sweet wine and bread. A pear for dessert. This last I devour ostentatiously down to the gist, hoping to draw attention from my wastefulness. Still the monk who clears the table holds up my ruined meal with a look of mingled sorrow and reproach. I dare not look him in the eye.

Padre Abate and I are chatting during the brief period after the meal when discourse is allowed. All at once, he is distracted by two of the older monks, one on either side of the table, who are enjoying a rather noisy joke. There is loud laughter. It is Balm in Gilead. But the abbot is annoyed. He waits for me to finish speaking; I see that he is no longer listening. The moment I am silent, he turns toward the vociferous pair.

"*Piano! Piano!*" he commands. Instantly the men are silent, abashed, deflated. It is a ruthless slice. I suffer for their humiliation.

"Do you love each other?" I ask the abbot.

"Oh, yes. We do. They are brothers. I am their father. Of course I love them. But they must be ruled, like all children." He laughs genteelly. I see that he does love them, but not the way my father loved me nor the way I love my children. He loves them the way a shepherd loves his flock, or a mariner his crew, without passion and without recklessness but with an undercurrent of mistrust. The abbot sees my embarrassment for the monks.

"One must not love the excess of laughter," he explains.

"There can never be too much laughter," I say. "The world is so sad."

"Our world is not sad. It is only silent."

"Any silence would be pleased to be broken by the noise of such laughter."

The abbot reaches for his bell. Tink! And the time for talking is over.

Monochromatic, narrow, undeviating are the monks, yet how they stir my imagination. I want to know everything about them. Had I brought my dissecting kit, I'd have scraped them down to the hair follicles, just to see. But then, I suspect the direct, frontal gaze is less informative than a peep through the shrubbery or from behind the pedestal of the Mother of God.

To Venice for more brandy and cigarettes. Also bread and cheese. Venice is seen best by the myopic and the astigmatic, which is why I move my glasses to the top of my head. The elongation of the eyeball enhaloes the city, lends it a radiance, like the glory of Saint Benedict on his way to paradise. In such a light the least act is bathed in goldish colors. The café where I shop is full of men barking at each other like walruses but with an implied courtesy. Two women enter. One is wearing a bright yellow skirt. One of the men calls out to her. He says something which makes the other men laugh. A moment later the women have joined them. I cannot take my eyes from it, the implication of it. How they animate each other, all the while, it seems to me, considering each other's needs.

One day into its night, and again a day with all the hours jumbled. I watch the monks cruise from the refectory after the evening meal like widows on some melancholy errand, and I continue my patrol of the premises. Prowling through corridors and staircases, I come upon a pair of great doors most emphatically shut. I open one and find myself in the Conclave Room, the scene of my earlier triumph. It is windowless and therefore dark save for the light given by four candles burning upon the altar. I sink into one of the thrones in the first tier, close my eyes, and drift toward sleep. Something keeps me from it. It is whole minutes before I know that I am not alone here. A monk is kneeling on the stones directly before the altar. Why has he come here? It is not the time of a holy office. It is the time for rest and recreation. I am curious but wish not to be indiscreet. I lean forward thinking myself to have been unobserved. We are not more than a dozen feet apart. And a world.

Although I cannot be sure, I think it is Vittorio, the novice master. "A very holy man," Pietro said. In the candlelight the face of the monk is made of wire and glass and wax. He retains only the smallest suggestion of human nature. From his mouth comes a continuous whisper, now and then punctuated by a sigh. It is as though I am watching through a keyhole the upward flight of a soul. I can make no sense of the words. They are whispered conspiratorially, the syllables like pebbles worn smooth by rubbing. He seems in a painful state, a delirium. I am moved by a desire to relieve him of it, to jostle him out of his nightmare. But even were I to shake him, shout in his ear, he would not budge.

His passion rises. *Aves* come foaming from his agile mouth. Next to his lips my own lips are cripples. There is something epileptiform about it—the trembling, the shaking. Has he eaten some marvelous drug? Hashish? Mushrooms? When at last he raises his head, I know the difference between a face and a countenance.

There is no speck of egotism in his love, while the love I have known has been full of nothing else. This kind of love would vanish at the first attempt to analyze it. Its existence depends upon participation in the mystery. I watch him exploring all the limits of his longings and feel in myself for the first time the painful absence of God. For him these visions are privileged moments. He has learned how to summon them forth. My own dreams come of their own volition, without the fanfare of prayer. What is it that he sees each time, all in ocher, burnt sienna, carmine, and flesh? Does he hear the shouts of Roman soldiers, the footsteps of women on the *via dolorosa*, the hammering of spikes? What must it be like to feel trailing at one's feet the whole of the gorgeous Christian epic—immaculate, murderous, risen? It is a triumph of the imagination. My own fails me at this point. I have no visions. Only, now and then, strange noises in my blood. There are tears on his cheeks! In each drop, a tiny candle flame reflected.

At last, he crosses himself one last time, rises, and, still murmuring, comes to sit beside me. He is totally relaxed, unselfconscious. He smiles, his face still moist. His teeth are white as peeled almonds.

"But you were crying," I say. Vittorio raises his eyebrows as though I have just given him news.

"It was not grief," he says.

"What, then?"

"It was the hard labor of prayer."

Laboring, then, toward that moment when abbey will stop being abbey and become heaven.

Sunday. I go to Mass. A German priest has come to concelebrate with Padre Abate. There is an air of importance about the event. The community scurries to prepare. The presbytery has been chained off and seats set up in the center of the nave so that the rite takes place at a great distance. The monks file in. It is so drafty that a wind stirs hair and lifts the hems of habits. A little chain tinkles against a silver box. As if on command, puffs of incense rise from behind the altar, filling each rift and corner. Beginning in small fire, they bellow into patterns of ostentation. Each dense head of smoke punches into the diluter curtain made by its predecessor. Upon the ledges, the wings of angels ruffle. The mass is a self-absorbed omophagy, a meal partaken of only by its celebrants and their acolytes. The rest sit or kneel, watching and waiting for the moment to line up and receive the consecrated Host in their mouths. From the distance the face of the German priest is golden and waxed, a thing of closed contentment. His lips boil over with Hail Marys, incense ashake in his breath. The chant reverberates, becoming distant and hollow, as though great earthenware jars had collected and reissued it. To dwell on Christ a dozen times a day and never tire of Him! It is like gazing at the photograph of a beloved. One never wearies of the face that each time evokes the same powerful onrush of love. The monk seems to me like a child whose father has long ago died, before his eyes had had their fill of him, but whose image the child keeps forever in his heart and draws forth at will. I leave the church in the middle of the service, go to stand on the terrace in front. I must leave this place, and soon. Something is closing in on me. I feel myself to be quarry, something backed away, to be taken.

The high water that has covered the terrace for days has receded. Here and there in the declivities in the stone, puddles of water have been trapped. They seem mysterious openings onto something rather than reflective surfaces that might give the world back to itself. I am drawn to these windows in the stone. They are like apertures into the past and the future, broken-off pieces of sky. In one, a gull wheels, its breast whiter by far, its eyes more glittery than if seen in the air. He opens his beak and carries the whole sky in it. It is the first time I have seen my reflection in weeks. I look for signs of wickedness. If bloodshot eyes and crow's-feet are clues, then the evidence is stacked against me. Otherwise, it is just a face bearing here and there the mark of an old humiliation, a half-remembered pleasure.

Away, away from this trance of an island and all that has and has not happened.

It is shortly after Vespers. The monks have left for the evening meal. Nearby in the gathering darkness I hear the sound of scuffling, breaths drawn in haste. I approach and find Lorenzo, the old infirmarian, on his hands and knees feeling about the floor of the stall.

"What is it?" I ask him. "What are you looking for?"

"Miei occhiali sono perduti. Non posso vedere."

"Your eyeglasses? Which is your seat?" He points; I find them at the back of the choir stall in which he was sitting. He puts them on, all the while thanking me for the gift of sight restored, and hurries away. We both enter the refectory late to find that the meal is already in progress. I take my seat next to the abbot and murmur an apology. Lorenzo walks to the center of the room, turns toward the abbot, and kneels, on his face an expression of abject remorse. He is like a dog who has misbehaved and now is begging forgiveness. For several minutes the abbot continues to eat as though the man were not there. At last he gives a tiny nod which sends Lorenzo scurrying to his place. Still, clearly, it is a rebuff rather than a release. Dessert is a handful of unshelled peanuts. The abbot cracks cruelly.

"Lorenzo lost his glasses in the choir," I explain later when talking is permitted. "I stayed to help him find them."

"Punctuality at meals is part of the Rule of Saint Benedict," he says. They are not merciful to each other, I think. Mercy is a rough-edged shaggy thing. The Rule of Saint Benedict is too sealed and gleaming. Any lapse, however human or innocent, will be warily forgiven at best. What is sought here is not illumination, then, but submission. When it comes to God, I prefer a certain discretion, a courtesy rather than this all-out, overheated embrace. Besides, sin, as is well known, is the shortest cut to Heaven. I must spend more time away from here. Tomorrow I shall go to Venice.

Only three weeks in the monastery and already everything is both extraordinary and familiar. The effect is to make me a bit giddy. I feel like laughing. The smallest thing tickles me. My room has taken on a certain liveliness. Even the furniture seems capable of expressing itself; the crucifixes have achieved a state of movement. The green brocade bedspread threatens to overflow the bed and spill itself upon the floor. I am invigorated by it. I see that the life here is meant to facilitate visions. Here is a building that has been built and decorated by man to lure God. Perhaps that is all that one can do. Provide an altar with candles and incense, then kneel and wait.

Just below my window spreads the great terrace at the front of the church. It is made of fitted square flagstones of marble. Here, in the evening, singly or in twos and threes, the monks come to stroll and gaze across the lagoon at Venice. Who knows what thoughts they have? Now and then their faces take on a wistfulness. A longing betrays itself.

Although talking is allowed on the terrace, more often than not, out of long custom, the monks are silent. What is there to say? Only, they walk, pausing to gaze across the water, eating the golden mist of Venice.

From this terrace, steps descend into the water so that the whole island seems to belong as much to the water as to the land. Sometimes, at the highest tides, when the *acqua alta* covers the stones,

raised wooden platforms are placed between the abbey and the landing pier.

Directly behind and beneath my room is the cloister, punctuated
at the center by two ancient cypresses, and at one end by a white
stone lavabo. It is the stillest spot that ever was. A cloister, unlike a
park or an orchard, is not the place to sit and have a long chat. First
of all, there are no benches and one can hardly think of sprawling on
ancient sacred grass. Nor, somehow, are the carved hedges and colonnades hospitable to the chasing to and fro of conversation, unless,
I suppose, it be muttered in Latin. One walks in a cloister. Up and
down and all around, slowly, steadily, letting the thoughts turn inward until the mind becomes the very cloister in which one walks.
All this silence is just as well, for I am quite unfit for chat. I don't
know what's happened to my mind. It's become like a crocodile half
in the ooze and drowsing. Every now and then it yawns and snaps
shut around a wisp of thought. Then hours of cold-blooded lethargy.

Though sparsely populated, the abbey is crowded with presences,
full of its own story, self-involved, and presenting a profound indifference to the world across the lagoon. Except for the two cypresses
in the cloister it is so treeless a place—just bare buildings exposed
to the eye of Heaven. Oh, for a bit of dim leafage to sin behind. And
someone considerate to do it with. The inhabitants of this place have
amputated the past, torn themselves free of their childhood. What
fills that place in the mind where memory rules? They are unstirred
by the nostalgia and sentiment with which the rest of us alternately
console and torment ourselves.

There is the time of work and the time of prayer; the time of
rest and the time of eating. It is an immutable order which prevails,
a childlike rhythm. They are children but without the child's lovely
ignorance of loss and decay. If they yearn for the farmhouses and
boulevards of long ago, one can detect no sign of it. Nor do they
miss the faces that were once dear and utterly familiar—parents,
brothers and sisters. For them there is only the long, long present
lived out in the company of each other.

Every day the coast of Venice seems farther away, receding. It is a perception that now elates, now terrifies me. The abbey is more and more a labyrinth into which I have stumbled and from which I either shall or shall not emerge. What was at first a troubled silence has become a sheltering hush. Having no habit, I wear what amounts to a coat of many colors—red polo shirt, blue jeans, green sweater, and horn-rimmed glasses. In my present state of dishevelment, I should be unrecognizable to the mother who bore me. Yet I am spared the sight, for there are no mirrors. Except in the rare puddle, I have not seen my reflection, nor have I heard my name. I have asked Pietro and later the abbot to call me by name, but they do not. I am always addressed directly but never by name. Soon I shall have forgotten it and be forced, like each of the novices, to adopt a new one. It is as though I were disappearing, receding into insubstantiality. Now and then I light a cigarette and let the smoke curl slowly from my pursed lips, studying the jet for evidence that I still exist.

Again and again I read *The Rule of Saint Benedict*. It makes no mention of the likes of me in the abbey. Hospitality alone explains my presence, setting aside the possibility of my being Christ. Or perhaps my coming is an opportunity to test their faith against worldly contamination?

The trick to being celibate is to forget that you are a man. Easier said than done, as Saint Jerome discovered in a desert. Saint Benedict too had his problems. On the back of each choir stall is carved a scene from the life of the saint. In one he is shown building a monastery; in another, he converts the heathen soldiers; still another has him being assumed to glory. My favorite shows the horny old saint fighting off a serious attack of lust by throwing himself into a clump of thorn bushes. Best not to talk. In a week or so I shall be sporting a full rack of antlers. All you have to do is drive out your nature with a pitchfork, make a desert of your heart, and call it peace. Yet I am struck by the evidence of happiness on the faces of the novices. I cannot fathom it. It is a gladness that can come from no human source. I mention this to the abbot.

"It is the gladness of Heaven," he says.

Along with human love, what is missing here is reproduction. Nothing, no one, is born here. There are no new eyes, new breaths. There are no natives; everyone has come from somewhere else. All the fecundity is in the long ago. It stopped at the womb of Mary. Sixteen men, then, full of unspent sperm, dry as chalk. By what magic do their faces remain unscored, their hair full and black, their hands youthful and soft? With what is their flesh nourished that each one looks twenty years younger than he is? As though he were being returned to the condition of Adam before the Fall. While, I, pouched and sacculate, am at the height of my beshrivelment. It is the refrigerated condition of their lives, I think, that holds back decay. Thousand-year-old insects trapped in amber share the same incorruptibility. I watch their shadows fall across each other in the cloister, one monk darkening another who in turn darkens the next. It is their only manner of touching. As for myself, I shall, in the matter of chastity, proceed day by day, secure in the folk wisdom that one does not go blind in the absence of sex. But, oh, to gather and spread a woman's hair upon my bare shoulders. Personally, I think it felicitous of man to have sinned his way out of the Garden of Eden, which must have been claustral and dull. O give me Babylon or Nineveh. I am just a few days short of adding Venice to the list.

At San Giorgio instead of irony there is humility; instead of satire, sermon. Irony is the human glance. I am used to it. Eternity is the cool perspective of God. And this God is not ironic; he is earnest and high. This evening I return to the church, trying to feel what it is that is expressed there seven times a day and what lingers in the intervals. Faced by the passionate striving of the last rays of the sun and lingering wisps of scent, I have to remind myself of the inanimateness of stone. At such moments, I would greatly appreciate a reassuring sign from heaven. Whichever way I look I see carved an endless variety of sunlit patches—spaces, angles, arcs. In contrast to the dark half shadows below, the upper galleries deliver an atrium of light that transforms that well of shadows into a luminous cave. I spy on the monks as they chant, drawing as close to the choir as I can without disturbing them. Here, even the faces of the old have the tenderness of youth. They seem to listen as they sing, abandoning themselves, while translating the universe.

Back in my room it is quiet, quiet, only the quick small slide of my hand across the paper as I write. But my atheist pen is marching out of step here. I glance up to capture a thought, and through the forest of crucifixes see the bottle of brandy on the nightstand. The pen discarded, I stand at the window, sipping. Two gulls wheel; I call out to them, just to hear the sound of my voice. First one, then the other answers me. Well, good, then. I shall converse with the birds. Like Saint Francis.

I have been given the run of the monastery. Only the cells of the monks continue to be forbidden me. The complex of buildings is vast and the monks, engaged in their prayers and duties, are largely invisible. A whole day will go by without my meeting one of them. On the occasion that I do, the monumental silhouette floats near, lowers its head, and hurries past with, at most, a whispered. *"Buon giorno."* More is not permitted. For one who believes that a good chat is the highest development of civilization, this interdiction of conversation is hard to bear. I miss that low hum, more audible to the heart than to the ear, by which a lived-in house announces itself. Sometimes, while sitting in the park or while writing at my desk, I have the feeling that I am not alone, that others are present. I know they are not. Still, I turn around to see. And sometimes I think— Good Lord!—perhaps the whole of the community who lived here has fled, and to the millennium of spiritual influence, now I alone stand heir.

A great drowsiness has come over me, as though the air here were webbed and I trapped within it. I relieve myself of a dozen yawns an hour. As many as a monk does prayers. No sooner is one yawn expelled with jaw-dislocating emphasis than the next bubble gathers in my head. By tomorrow I shall be in deep coma. In such a convalescent state, for that is what I have diagnosed it to be, I can explore only by small ambitions, hithering and thithering as far as the Conclave Room for a long solitary sit-down, lethargic as a turtle on a sunny rock; on to the sacristy—another daydream; then up to the top of the campanile, where I feel like a muezzin on a mosque. Once again Padre Abate has refused to let me work. Oh, well, if there is nothing whatever to do here, then I am just the man to do it. Every evening I return from a ramble in the cloister to find that my room has been swept clean, the cigarette ashes taken away, and the bed, which I had made, remade according to some fierce precision of which I am ignorant. Who did it? The angels?

Time and again the great church of San Giorgio Maggiore coaxes me inside her. I have taken to sitting there at odd hours. Truth to tell, I am far more attracted to the bells, incense, and statues of a religion than I am to its dogma or Talmud. It is the child in me craving diversion. And this church is brimful of spectacle, what with John the Baptist shaggy on the wall, Lazarus half in and half out of his shroud, and, of course, Saint George in full metallic fig. In the absence of human beings I have been keeping company with the statuary. Just today in the church at twilight a gray angel soared over my head. I could feel the breeze of its passing. But what is this! In the midst of perfection I have discovered that one of the host of angels, the third to the left of the main altar, has been imperfectly rendered, one wing being rather too centrally rooted at the back, and more than a little lower in its thoracic attachment than the other wing. The corresponding shoulder droops, giving a kyphoscoliosis of the spine. Such an angel would hover askew, list to the affected side. Here, I think, is a cockeyed creature made from a bumpy hunk of marble by hands less skilled than willing. Still, something about her miscreation is endearing, as though her sculptor had not yet learned the dishonesties of art. I say "her" because of all the race of angels on this island, only this one suggests specificity of gender. Aside from Michael, Gabriel, and the one who wrestled with Jacob, about whose masculinity there has never been any doubt, the others are sexually indeterminate. The gender of angels is not readily told. One does not turn them upside down to see. Nor is it of the least importance, as the whole idea, I gather, is that they be neuter. But this crookback to the left of the altar is, beyond peradventure of doubt, womanly—the female of the species. It is something about the elbows, the knees, whatever. Nor does she have the basic seraph's countenance with plump cheeks and serene brow all framed by ringlets. Instead, she is stringy. All wrists and ribs. The face too owns a certain gauntness of features, the suggestion of fatigue. The mouth is a thin slit; the expression is less one of ecstasy than of endurance. This face has witnessed; it has tolerated. Now and then I have the fleeting thought that I have seen this face before. But where? Whose is it?

It is three midnights later. I awake suddenly and lie there in bed rummaging about in what I used to call my mind. All at once, I am bolt upright. In a moment I have pulled on my clothes, grabbed candlestick and matches, and am racing along the hallway, down a flight of stairs. I push open the side door of the church. It is full, still, of the sweet smell of incense. And, oh, that black that does not hold itself back but comes charging at you like a panther. I light the match, touch it to the taper. But why do my hands tremble so? I watch my shadow become involved with the dormant church as the flame is batted in the draft. The great altar looms; now to the left. One. Two. Three. I hold up the candle at arm's length. Flashes of gold from the monstrance. The stillness rages in the very pillars. And I know. I am certain.

Some months before I left New Haven, a nurse who had worked in the recovery room retired. For thirty-five years, each day, Adele Cleary had received into her care dozens of postoperative patients, each of whom shared the single condition of unconsciousness, being either fully anesthetized or in emergence from that state. Upon leaving they would be amnesic for their time spent in this room. While one would flail about in danger of injuring himself, another, driven by some drug-released urge toward violence, would strike out at those who tended him. I remember one of her black eyes. Part of the job, Adele had said afterward. Still another patient would vomit or choke or suffer cardiac arrest and so must be resuscitated by mouth-to-mouth breathing, and receive a beating upon the chest

to coax back a heart in standstill. Nor did a single one of her patients remember Adele. Were she, later, to pass one of them in the
street, he would give no sign of recognition. To all of this Adele
presented an unruffled expression. It was more than tolerance or
endurance; it was acceptance, it was obedience. Adele Cleary was
a hunchback. Despite the fact of her crooked spine, which was ill-
concealed and even accentuated by the thin blue scrub dress she
wore at work, there was no awkwardness in her ministrations. In the
recovery room, if nowhere else, she was graceful. At her retirement
she was presented with a purse containing one hundred dollars collected from the others. The chief of surgery proposed a toast with
ginger ale.

"What are you going to do now, Adele?" he asked. "Are you
going to travel? Or just loaf?"

"Now?" said Adele with a shy smile. "Now I am going to recover
from my life."

I saw her once after that. There is a small park in the center
of New Haven. It is called the Green. In good weather people go
there to eat lunch, play chess, or walk their dogs. One day I was
crossing the Green on some errand or other when I caught sight of
her sitting alone on one of the benches that line the paths. Several
people walked by. All at once she rose and walked quickly to catch
up with a man who had just passed. When she had come within
arm's length she raised one hand to touch his sleeve. I saw the man
turn, look at her for a moment without expression, then wheel and
walk briskly away. After a moment, Adele returned to her seat. I
stopped to talk.

"Who was that?" I asked her. We were that easy with each other.

"Oh," she said. "Someone I thought I knew. But I guess not."

"One of your patients?" I said. Adele smiled and looked at something farther and farther away.

Later that day, sitting in my office at the hospital, I thought of her
again, of how many thousands of people in the city she had steadied
and thumped and rubbed and blown her breath into; of all the vomitus and phlegm and blood with which she had been spattered; of all

the prophecies she had sown: "You are going to be all right." "Pretty soon you'll be back in your own bed"; all her crooning, her coaxing back, her padding against mindless battering; all those magic acts of intercession; that endless braiding of tubes and wires about pale sick faces. And no one could remember having seen her!

Before I left for Italy I saw her name in the obituary column. Isn't that just the way? You work all your life, and the minute you stop and begin to enjoy . . .

For a long while I gaze up at the statue of the angel, the third from the left of the main altar, the hot wax from the taper begloving my hand in tightness and heat which races up my arm and across my chest where my heart beats hard against it. Look! She bends to peer at me, lifts one hand as if to wipe a brow, then slowly relents into marble. So! Adele, I say aloud. I might have known.

Minutes later, back in my room, I snuff the taper. There is the sad smell of candlewick. And the singing of wings.

To search for faith in a monastery is to deny its existence elsewhere. True morality is directed outward toward others. It has nothing to do with self-perfection. Besides, it is less what goes into man than what comes out of him that matters.

Take Dom Pietro. Eighteen years in a monastery and he has remained a personage. I can see him carried across the Piazza San Marco on a *sedia gestatoria* shedding benedictions on the crowd. Listen:

It is only months ago. I am visiting another surgeon's operating room. The woman on the table has lost the circulation in her right arm. Weeks before, a new artery was grafted between her aorta and the blocked blood vessel. For a while, the pulse returned to her wrist, but then came fever. The pain in her hand returned and the pulse vanished. An infection has developed in the graft, and now not only her arm but her life is at stake. Wayne Flye is a young surgeon newly arrived at our hospital from Texas. This is to be his first operation in New Haven. I am present out of a spirit of comradeship. I want to keep him company. I observe now as he reopens the old incision

in her chest, splitting her breastbone in two. He raises the sternum
as you would raise the two halves of a hatchway. But as he does
there is a great bang of blood. In a moment the chest is full of it,
with more lapping at the gunwales. Adhesions 'from the previous
surgery and from the infection have been torn. But you could not
tell from watching this surgeon. His voice is Texas-slow, quiet; he
murmurs to his assistants, the nurse. His manner is controlled,
oaken, as though the hemorrhage has somehow strengthened his resolve. His fingers enter the chest, submerge. It is a gentle burrowing
as they sniff out the site of the bleeding.

"Here," he says, at last. He has found what he was looking for.
"Suction." And the lake of blood is drained. Now the chest cavity is
dry. One finger has discovered the source and stanched the flow.
With his free hand he begins. From the periphery in toward his
finger, he dissects in a circular pattern. Each snip of his scissors clears
away more of the infected scar. Now and then a hidden sac of pus
is exposed and wiped away. The superior vena cava appears. More
camouflage is mowed. He closes in. All barriers to the truth are
broken down until at last there is only his index finger emerging
from a rent in the great vein whose wall, weakened by infection, had
given way. Only the plug of his finger inside the vein prevents ex-
sanguination. "Curved arterial clamp," he says. His voice is flat, calm.
He fits the jaws of the clamp about his index finger, sits it down
upon the wall of the vein about the gash; he withdraws his finger;
there is a spurt of new blood, then the sound of the teeth of the
clamp clicking into place, once, twice, three times, and the bleeding
has stopped. All that remains is to stitch up the tear and release the
clamp. Done, he swiftly removes the infected graft and replaces it
with another. Looking over the shoulder of this surgeon, I see a
faithfulness to vocation, a testimony to the exorbitant demands of
two hearts—the patient's, heaving there within view, and his own.

Later, in the locker room, we are drinking coffee.

"How do you do it?" I ask him.

"I just follow things as they are," he says. "There are always
spaces between, where you can go."

There is no speck of irony in him. In this alone is he like a monk.

But I think there was something besides vision and touch and memory at work here. Call it intuition, or a quality of the spirit. The senses have nothing to do with it. Had the lights gone out, he would have finished in the dark. He could be blind and deaf, I think, and have done it as well. There is a place where knowledge and technique stop and the spirit moves where it wants. The surgeon had better follow.

As with the monk his rosary, so with the surgeon his instruments; the handling of designated objects induces a feeling of tranquillity. But Wayne Flye does not attach a mystical significance to his work. For him it is the tangible that counts.

"You're good," I tell him. "That was close."

"Think so?" He smiles. "Nowadays the tools do it for you."

Days, nights, days, nights. So many hundreds of dark and light hours.

For some time I have been utterly depressed. Already the chant is becoming tiresome to me; all so patterned, divorced from humanity. It sounds about as vivacious as the strewing of ashes on a sidewalk. There is something of insanity in it. My room, which I had grown to love, seems bewitched, a bare tidy cell from which something essential has been banished. Its very tidiness disturbs. How can I be expected to find anything in a place so uncluttered, empty, really, as though all of the furnishings have been removed to prepare for a visit by the exterminator. I can find things only if they are left lying about in the open. It is the same with all these antique masterpieces. Saint George in love with the dragon; in love with his killing of the dragon, his flat face pale with spent lust rather than religious ecstasy. And the paintings of Tintoretto with which this house is smeared. A whole pantheon of gross, sexless indecencies in the name of Christ. All those pretty bodies devoid of honesty. They have no more to do with Christianity than I do. I do not see faith in them; everything depicted is so inert, remote. Two dozen beautiful youths draped upon crosses, with their clean bloodless wounds, their pale dry brows, their impeccably trimmed beards, their penislessness. I much prefer the German version with gouges running blood and runnels of sweat and skinny twisted legs. Perhaps it is the surgeon in me.

Even had I been among the faithful I should have eschewed icons. They are unnecessary, a hindrance, something between God and me that draws the eye to themselves.

I suppose the abbot's treatment of Lorenzo in the refectory has something to do with my frame of mind. And then there is Pietro. This morning at breakfast, the novice who was pouring coffee asked me shyly and in newly found English whether I would like milk and sugar. Delighted to be addressed by someone if only on this level, I accepted both despite the fact that I take my coffee straight. Another small door had opened. In the evening, this from Pietro:

"These monks are all so unspiritual. I would much prefer a stricter abbey. How sweet the life in the old monasteries must have been. This place is positively unedifying. If you don't watch them every minute, the novices do wicked things."

"Like what?"

"Speaking directly to guests, for one."

"Come now, Pietro, you're jealous over that novice asking me how I took my coffee. That's it, isn't it?"

"He knows the rules as well as I do. They are dumb Italians," he says. I am shocked.

"That is stupid," I tell him. "And furthermore, you are bored and boring." Hurt to the bone, he whisks himself from the room with a single stroke. An hour later he is back with a little bar of lavender soap that he has hidden away. But it won't do. More and more I see him as a rabid and afflicted soul, a born Inquisitor who sees sin in the least twitch of an eyelid. Therefore constant watchfulness is necessary, as though he alone were called to great tasks. Such a man places high value on the outer proofs of virtue—the downcast glance, the purity of the singing voice, all of that. He is the sort of priest who would convert with the sword, if need be. I see that, in an odd way, the abbot relies on his severity and worldliness. Why? But it is not just Pietro and the abbot. It is all this praying for the sake of praying. Do they really believe in the efficacy of their acts of prayer? Or are these simply rites that must be performed? Like chores in a garden? I imagine them praying the way a sheep grazes, on and on, without a pause, without a thought. More and more I see them as a tepid black coagulum flowing listlessly this way and that. But I am a guest here! Discretion, do not abandon me. Even to think such thoughts, much less write them down, is to act the asp in a basket of fig leaves.

"I'm going to Venice today," I tell Pietro.

"Will you be back for the evening meal?" asks Pietro.

"Absolutely not."

"Have a good time," he says. But I do not. From San Marco, the abbey is a hulk that has been blown in from the sea and all of whose sailors have been dead for years. Venice, which only yesterday was a magic dream of beauty and so full of possibility, seems a giant cloaca, carved and frescoed over every millimeter, into which filth of all kinds is collected. What a sour, rankled old man I have become, a stateless person. By evening I am once again aboard the vaporetto laden with Grand Armagnac and a large box of chocolate creams. From the boat the facade of the monastery has caught the last pink. It seems to me at this moment to have captured its whole past, retained it somehow, and now to be reflecting it in a continuous even glow, the way ruins reveal to us their previous complete existence. To my mingled surprise and indignation, I find myself impatient to get there. I hurry to the refectory, where the monks are standing each behind his place. They have just come from the choir, and their habits are still singing the last notes of the chant. Later, I give Pietro a strudel I have bought for him. He carries on about it with unfeigned joy. Lickity-split! And it is gone, with the creature sighing and mopping his chops. It is moving to see how much of the world he loves and denies himself. Thrown into ecstasy by candy yesterday and strudel today. What purpose is served by the denial of strudel?

Up at dawn. In the cloister strolling off the night's lust. Then to the refectory for sweet strong coffee and the stale crusts they call toast. Then again to my room to begin a morning of writing. My life is as rhythmical and obscure as if it were being passed at the bottom of the lagoon. The weather has turned unaccountably sultry. I open the casements wide and let in the honeyed air of Venice. Directly ahead, in the lagoon, men in gondolas are poling in unison. They are not slim, but hefty, beefy, and they wear identical striped shirts and stocking caps. I assume that they are members of a team of athletes. There is a great delicacy in the way they handle the poles. It is more than mere strength. It is grace and precision as well.

I am drawn from my desk to the open window by a frantic buzzing. The noise is made by two large dragonflies in the act of mating on the very ledge. How did they come there, so far from the least vegetation and fresh water? Never mind, their presence is no more strange than my own. They are tail to tail and glued, but now, it seems, full of second thoughts. All four wings row hard to break a terrible suction. The single crosshatched tube that is the fusion of their bodies bends as if to snap. Joined, they are a single lunatic insect in the throes and striving for separation. If this be sex, I'll have no more of it. At last, the wretched four-wings gives up its struggle, and taking off sideways, awkwardly settles for being airborne. It is like Achilles dragging off the body of Hector. One must beware of love. Like certain Bedouins, you can die of it.

To the park, then, since there is again to be no writing. I follow one of the gravel paths to a point where it intersects with two others. Lining the paths, ancient white capitals hung with marble grapes. Standing guard at the juncture, a large stone angel with wings half raised. Gabriel, at the very least, or Michael. On the pedestal a paste of droppings and feathers. So! Angels too molt; they defecate.

No sooner have I taken a seat on the bench than I hear the pebbles of the walk crunching beneath light footsteps. A quick scattering that identifies the maker long before he comes into view. "Dom Sebastiano," I call out. A moment later he is standing before me in the usual posture of humility—head bent forward, eyes lowered, as though feeling the weight of his sins. Of them all he is the only thin one, lean as Cassius. Of them all he alone conforms to my notion of the physiognomy of Christ—gaunt, sallow, his face harried, preoccupied. I can imagine this one reigning from the tree, surrounded by a golden nimbus. His movements have none of the heaviness of the other monks. He is quick and jerky. His fingers flicker, his head too. Even his habit is caught up in the commotion and trembles at the hem. When he raises his eyelids I see that his eyeballs bulge, showing altogether too much white. This gives him the expression of a horse skittering above a rattlesnake. His face is drained of color save for a swatch of bruise beneath each eye. Standing still, he seems to be containing himself by an effort of will lest his entire body break apart. In his company my own body speeds up, feeling the need to keep pace. What, I wonder, did he do before he entered the monastery? Often it is possible to guess. One of the monks has retained the slow clumsiness of a peasant farmer. Another, the impetuosity of a soldier. Still another, the grace and balance of a mariner. But here is someone who gives not the least sign of how or where he lived before becoming a monk. Although he looks to be thirty years old, I know that it is quite possible that he is much older.

"Will you sit with me for a while?" I ask him. He blushes and picks at something that might have happened to his habit. Still, he does sit on the very edge of the bench, as though to spring to his feet at any moment.

The sun had come out; my first view of it in a week. Within minutes the days of damp and cold have evaporated. In his heavy woolen habit, Sebastiano perspires frantically. His skin radiates heat.

"What do you wear in the summer?" I ask.

"This," he says, "the same thing."

"But it must be hot. You are wet all the time."

He smiles.

"The wool absorbs the sweat," he says. "I do not mind too much. Still, I prefer the cold."

I see that he does mind, a great deal, and that the summer months are hell for him.

"Where are you from, Sebastiano?"

"Tuscany. An old village. Monte San Savino. My family are farmers in the hills there."

"Have you always wanted to be a monk? Even as a child?"

"No, not always. I was a student at the university. But I studied too hard. Something happened to my mind. I could not pass the examinations. For a long time I could not think. Then God spoke to me and brought me here."

"Are you happy here?"

"Oh, very happy. I am a good monk. I place myself in God's hands. He will see that I am rescued."

"Rescued? From what?"

But he had already sprung from the bench and hurried away.

I awake feeling somewhat ill. My sides ache and I am coughing. I should hate to become sick here. Since it is only death that they trust, I should be afraid that they would not take my flesh seriously, leave several stones unturned. Would their physical diffidence keep them from resuscitating me mouth-to-mouth or massaging my heart? I rather think they might gather round the bed and rejoice, as long ago the nuns did in the hospital in Troy, New York, where I followed my father on his hospital rounds. I remember them grouped like lamps in a darkened room, the face of the patient graying away, their own aglow with an imperturbable golden light. Not for me the festive air of the deathbed. No, thanks. I can wait for the wonders of eternity. Wrap me not in tranquil joy. A shot of penicillin will do just fine.

It is the morning of the next day. I am once again in the little park. The sound of gravel crunching leads me to where Sebastiano is pacing to and fro. I block his path with my body. He looks for all the world like a blackbird—raising one wing or unclasping a twig to some indeterminate purpose.

"What is it?" I ask him. "Something is wrong."

"It is nothing. Nothing. I am tired. Please let me pass." His face has the fatalism of a slave.

As we talk, he holds one hand at his chest to brace against some shortness of breath. Or to pry loose a stone.

"Tell me," I say.

"I cannot sleep. All night I toss and turn. In the morning I am tired. I come to the park to rest."

"Your appetite," I say. "I have watched you in the refectory. You eat as much as the others."

"You are not the one to criticize." He tries to smile. "You are already famous here for eating nothing."

"Never mind about me," I tell him. "You are thinner even than when I arrived." The man appears to be in a state of dread and exhaustion. I see him mounting his cot each night and riding it furiously toward dawn.

"Hold out your hands," I tell him, "and spread your fingers."

He does and I examine his palms, half expecting to find stigmata other than those of thyrotoxicosis. What a rage for the terrific I am developing here.

I tear a sheet from my notebook and lay it across his outstretched fingers. The paper vibrates, then falls to the ground.

"Look up," I say. Again he obeys. "Now down." The veined marble lids drop over the proptosed globes, leaving a rim of white sclera showing above the iris. I see that no matter in which direction he gazes his pupils are surrounded by white. The whites of his eyes are bloodshot. In the bright sunshine, he blinks and tears.

"Look here," I say, and with one quick movement reach up and pull down the front of his habit to expose his neck. Sebastiano is shocked.

"Please," he whispers. "I must go."

"I want to feel your neck," I say. What I am seeking is there. A soft diffuse swelling that occupies the front of his neck. With one hand securing his shoulder, I bend to place my ear against that swelling. He jumps at the contact.

"Don't breathe," I say. "Hold your breath." He does and I hear the loud bruit of blood eddying there. Against my ear there comes the confirmatory thrill. For a long moment I hold him in the diagnostic embrace, listening to the malicious huff-puff of that hyperthyroid gland.

"It's called Graves' disease. Your thyroid gland is making too much hormone. It makes your body run too fast. That is the cause of your nervousness, your sleeplessness. There is a medicine. First you need to have a blood test to make sure."

"No, no," he says. "Dom Pietro is right. I am possessed. The abbot has seen these things before. He knows what to do."

Possessed! It is my turn to recoil under the force of a word.

"You are no such thing," I say. "You are sick and you need medicine. In a few days you will feel better. You will be able to sleep."

"No," he says. "When Padre Abate returns from Rome, we will have an exorcism."

"That is crazy," I say. "Where do you find an exorcist around here?"

"Dom Paolo is an exorcist. He will do it."

Paolo! The portly old choirmaster, with his music teacher's gold-rimmed glasses. I try to imagine him, masseters clenched about a hiss of incantation, habit hitched, cincture tightened. Now he takes up the silver crucifix and advances upon the devil. . . .

"But you must take the medicine. If I am wrong, it will not hurt you to take it for a few days. If I am right, you will be much better. What do you say?"

"No. I must go. Let me pass."

"This afternoon I go to Venice. I return with the medicine."

"No." And he breaks free from my grasp and is gone. A gull flies overhead, its testy scream long outlasting the shadow of its flight upon the footpath.

I am in my room waiting for the inevitability of Pietro. He comes.

"What's the big idea of telling Sebastiano that he is possessed? He is suffering from hyperthyroidism. He bears all the stigmata of it." I list them. "The rapid pulse, the bulging eyes, the voracious appetite accompanied by weight loss, the fine tremor, the intolerance to heat, the unrelenting anxiety."

"You examined him?"

"I certainly did."

"That was an infraction. Padre Abate will be angry." Pietro himself is furious.

"Say what you will, I'm off to Venice for the medicine."

"You have no understanding of our lives. Perhaps if you would kneel and pray . . ."

"I am less a kneeler than a bower down who keeps the stones of this earth close in his vision. Besides, there are my pagan arthritic knees."

But he is not to be disarmed. He spins and sweeps toward the door, sending his habit from his ankles with cold grace.

"I'll take the matter to the abbot," I say.

"Padre Abate is in Rome for three days. He has other duties, you see."

"I'm not waiting."

"The exorcism has been planned for some time. Sebastiano desires it. The abbot has delayed only because he has felt that Sebastiano is not strong enough for the ordeal. It is to be performed upon Padre's return from Rome."

"Sebastiano needs propylthiouracil," I call after him.

For the hundredth time I try to decide why I have come here. I might as well have spent a month among cannibals. I am determined to treat Sebastiano, although it will mean that I must leave San Giorgio. What it will mean for Sebastiano beyond regaining his health, I have no idea. I suppose I should care more about that. He will have broken his vows of obedience. Perhaps they will cast him out. The thought chills me. He belongs here most emphatically.

I have it. Enough for two weeks and the promise of a continued supply of the medicine. It took less than I anticipated. A few phone calls, the word *Yale,* the other word *professor.* Such syllables in Italy have a magical incantatory power of their own. I find Sebastiano in the laundry, to which he has been presently assigned.

"Here." I press the bottle of pills into his hand. "Take one four times every day at regular intervals. And don't skip."

"No," he says. "I cannot."

"You fool! Take it or go to Hell!" I am shocked by my outburst. It matters much more than I thought. I must have this . . . this evidence.

He is hesitant, reluctant. But the bottle is in his hand.

"It is not permitted," he says, but now without conviction. I have him.

"Listen, Sebastiano. Listen to me. I shall explain it all to Padre Abate upon his return. He is a kind and reasonable man. He loves you. How happy he will be to find you better. For two weeks only. If you are not improved, then go ahead with the exorcism. I'm dying to see one anyway. In the meantime, if I were you, I would not try to pray. It is too exhausting for you."

"Not pray?" The wild eyeballs threaten to pop their sockets. A day without prayer is a day lost. How does one talk to these aliens? Their citizenship is elsewhere. But I have him. I can tell by the glance he gives to the pills. It is the glance of a man looking at a food strange to him and wondering what it will taste like. If this works, I shall know why it was that I came here.

Back in time for Vespers. The church already dark. Why is it that night falls faster in a church than anywhere else? And is more absolute? More than night is falling here. I push open the side door, but for a moment the darkness will not let me in. I press against it, but it has no give where I am concerned. There is no floor in it. It is bottomless. I advance one foot, toeing for a hold. Within, I stand quite near the choir, yet hidden from them in a small alcove. In a moment the monks file across my path, close enough so that I can see them in the candlelight. They open their mouths as one, and now come those phrases and strains that, even as I listen, leave the realm of music and direct themselves toward what I presume to call the soul. It is not so much voice as echo.

Right smack in the middle of Vespers, from out in the courtyard, Dom Cat breaks his vow of silence and begins to yowl. Forced, desperate cries of sexual desolation that begin low in the throat, then rise quickly to the soprano range. It is like the whine of a chain saw moving through a plank of oak. For a moment the chant falters, then gathers itself. Do I imagine a streak of repressed desire among the silver monotony? On and on the creature howls for all the rest of us, the reservoir of lust of seventeen men, overflowing. Nor does he stop with the end of the chant but continues to spray the night with his rage until eventual sleep deafens us.

"What in the world . . . ?" I ask Dom Pietro in the morning.

"The devil." He smiles.

"Oh, good," I say. "We may yet have an exorcism."

Once again Pietro warns me not to interfere.

"It is none of your affair," he says again. "You do not understand us. . . ."

Now I must leave the Abbey of San Giorgio. It is not mere work that I am forbidden; it is my work—that respectful interference in the lives of others that constitutes the diagnosis and treatment of disease. I simply cannot remain here to watch a man with thyrotoxicosis exorcised for demons. Here, among the kidnapped, the never-set-free. Strange black flowers they are that cannot live in the sunlight. Plucked and laid upon an altar. I suppose what bothers me most about them is that they lack scope. These decades of stagnation have made them unfit for the company of man. How they wrong themselves by refusing to be part of their own age, neglecting what exists now. Assuming the existence of God, the monk is possessed of Him in exact proportion as he is dispossessed of everything else. Dom Pietro is right. I do not understand it. Not at all.

It was a mistake to come here. Were I ever to express my belief in God it would be a courteous salute into the distance, and smartly delivered rather than this groveling in a reliquary where men do not tend their aging parents, or carry the burdens of others, or accept the honest concern of infidels. In one hour, I leave for Venice for more propylthiouracil. If I have to cram it down his throat.

On the way back from San Marco I struggle against the possessive motion of the vaporetto, the monotonous shuddering of the boat demanding from me an admission of contentment. And I *am* happy to be returning to the abbey. Going home, I think, and the idea takes me by surprise. To be receptive; to wait, that is all. But then comes evening. And with it, the lamps of doubt. What is it that in this hushed house, in these hushed hours, draws near? Then recedes? There! It comes again. Circling and circling, pausing, darting away.

—∞—

Padre Abate has returned from Rome. Within an hour I am sum-moned to his presence. The change in his manner from benevolent warmth to icy shuddering rage stuns me. He himself looks sick with displeasure, his face gray, sweating. Is this difficult for him too? I begin, knowing that it is hopeless.

"I hope that you have had a pleasant trip. By now you know of my treatment of Sebastiano. You will be pleased to learn that he is already much improved. He is calmer; he is sleeping well."

"It is the infirmarian's duty to look after our health." His voice is terrible, frigid.

"Then I am happy to have been able to assist him in this."

"I did not give you permission to work here, nor Sebastiano permission to accept your ministrations. It was wrong of you to do this, wrong of him to accept. You have violated our rule." All at once I am like a child who is being scolded for having misbehaved. To my astonishment, tears of humiliation spring to my eyes. Why should I care what he thinks of me? I am not one of his monks. But I do care.

"You are overtired, Padre Abate. You yourself look unwell. The rigors of your journey, and now this . . ."

He glances up.

"Your diagnoses are presumptuous. Perhaps it would be best for you to leave the Abbey of San Giorgio."

"And Sebastiano?" I ask.

"That is none of your affair."

My temper flares. "It was not his fault. I forced him to comply. You simply cannot bear that such a benefice be delivered by an infidel. That's it, isn't it?"

With a small nod, I am dismissed.

I have packed my bags and stacked them near the door of my room. Now I stand at the window inhaling for the last time the honeyed mist of Venice. I cannot wait to get out of here. *Precipita-tamente. Hic et nunc.* First vaporetto in the morning. Of all the things I could have done in Italy, I had to come to this dismal monastery and get thrown out to boot. Take care, God. If the gift of prophecy has not deserted me, you dwell in the last of your houses. Your days are numbered. These sixteen relics are your only worshipers left. Soon you will exist solely in paintings and statues, nothing but the work of art you were always meant to be.

It is nine o'clock in the evening. Time for *Riposo e Silenzio*. Two dozen doors are shut, twenty bolts shot. Grate, clang, thump, click . . . and the monks are through for the day.

Toward midnight I am startled by a knock at the door. Pietro, I think. He is the last person I want to see.

"Go away," I call out.

A pause and then another knock. That would not be Pietro. He would have barged in. I open the door to see old Lorenzo. He is plainly distraught.

"What is it, Lorenzo?"

"It is Padre Abate. He is very sick. Will you come?"

"I am not permitted. In any case, I am leaving here in the morning."

The old monk takes me by the hand and tries to draw me toward the door.

"What is the matter with him?"

"You will come?" I follow Lorenzo down the long dark corridors and through doors leading into the living quarters from which until now I have been forbidden. The infirmarian opens the door and steps aside. The room is tiny and painfully neat, devoid of depth and looking like something flat that has been stretched on a frame. It is without wrinkles, webs, or laps. To step into it is to lose a dimension. The small armoire, open, is bare save for a few black socks, a short pile of white linen, and one black habit. On a writing table, several books, pen, and paper; on the walls, a wooden crucifix, and, set in black velvet and framed, a bit of yellow bone. Under it, the legend RELIC OF SAINT BENEDICT (VERIFIED). But who shall say where sentiment may not exist?

The abbot is neither sitting in his chair nor standing to receive me, but is lying facedown upon his cot. Nor does he turn his head to glance in my direction. The infirmarian lowers a blanket to the abbot's waist. There, bristling between his shoulder blades, I see a huge abscess. It has been present for weeks, I am certain. The area of inflammation is fully ten centimeters in diameter with bubbles of pus issuing from multiple sites of drainage in the already gangrenous skin. The mass crepitates beneath my palpating fingers. A gas-producing clostridium? The man's skin is hot, his breathing comes in short little gasps. He seems in a profound lethargy, yet is fully awake, I know it. Solemnity issues forth from his already perished flesh.

So, I think, His Augustitude hath contracted a boil!

"It is a carbuncle," I say. "It needs to be lanced. Now." Neither man makes any reply.

"Show me what you have," I say to Lorenzo. We go to the infirmary. I look over the meager equipment on his shelf. There is only unsterile cotton, a small bottle of what looks and smells like Mercurochrome, and an antique scalpel with MADE IN GERMANY carved into the handle.

"Do you have such a thing as a local anesthetic? Novocain?" Lorenzo is mystified.

"Bake the cotton in the oven for twenty minutes. First wrap it in paper," I tell the old man. I take up the bistoury and test it for sharpness. It is hopelessly dull. I shall have to whet it. I find a pumice stone used by the infirmarian to abrade calluses and a cruet of olive oil. Half an hour of circular honing, and the knife is usable. Barely. We boil it in water for ten minutes and return to the abbot's cell. He has not moved in our absence. His body has a deflated look, as though the voluminous flesh has slipped from his bones and he has already begun to sink in. A light, greenish phosphorescence, the emanation of decay, shines from his cavernous skull. For a moment I think he is dead. But then he breathes.

"There is no anesthetic," I say. "I will apply ice to reduce the pain of the incision, but it will hurt. I must make two cuts, a cruciate incision so that it will stay open." Silence. I hold the ice to the surface of the boil, then pour the contents of the bottle over the lesion.

"Now," I say. And think to myself, don't scream. I am praying silently for him not to. I want him to succeed. I cut. And the man on the cot howls—a cascade of vowels that bounce back from the high ceiling. I steel myself against the sound and draw the knife along the fiery mound for its full length. Because it is dull, I must press firmly. Again, in the same track, a third time. Midway through the third stroke a wave of foul-smelling greenish pus lifts from the cut and runs across the back of the man. My hands are warm and wet with it. All the while the abbot cries out; his body is racked with sobs. Now for the second incision. I reach around with my left hand and clamp it over his mouth.

"Shhhh. The others will hear and be frightened," I whisper. And I cut. The force of his cry bursts through the slats of my fingers. But what comes out is only the snorting of a horse. Gentle pressure expresses a great amount of putrefaction. Lorenzo gasps and crosses himself as the stream continues for minutes. When, at last, the flow has dwindled, I insert a twisted wick of the cotton into the wound to hold it open. I cover the place with a small towel.

"*Ti calma,*" I say. "It is done. *Respira forte.*" It seems right to use Italian. "Soon you will feel better. Already, the pain is not so severe?" For the first time he raises his head and nods slightly.

"Stay with him. I will be back in one hour."

In my room I find three of my shirts washed and neatly folded on the precisely turned-down bed. That Pietro! I scrub the dried corruption from my hands and pour a glass of brandy. The hot ribbon of liquor winds down through me. I pour a second, and carry it with me downstairs to the side door of the church. To my surprise it is morning. The sunlight streaming through the high dome picks out each facet and edge, defining, washing, coloring the stone. I sit, listening to the whole island beating like a heart, and I sip the brandy.

Did he think he could vanquish pain merely by being one of the serene elect? Arrogance. Or was it a trial he had set for himself out of pride and obstinacy? And oh that bellowing, that terrible yowling, as though something, a passion which had been contained for a lifetime, had broken free. The whole biography of the man had been written in that single episode when, for the first time, derobed of his habit, he wore the genuine lineaments of suffering mankind. Had he not sent for me, had he chosen instead to die, he would have done so in the full understanding of why he had lived. But he was afraid. Now it is too late.

It is time to visit the abbot. He is sitting on the edge of the cot. I hardly know him. His face is white as a gardenia. In spite of his bulkiness, he is strangely diaphanous. All of his features have relaxed, "given" in a way, even his shoulders and spinal column— crumpled. He seems shorter, rounder. Nor is this pitiable to behold, but rather a change toward the human, the harmonious. This man, I think, will henceforward be incapable of silencing the laughter of monks with a pair of chilly *pianos*.

I accept the seat offered by his gesture and wait for him to speak.

"Do you know that I am from peasant stock?" he says at last. "My family are farmers from the hills around Como. I am one of nine children. We were very poor." I feel obliged to respond.

"To be born ignobly is a lesser misfortune than to live so."

The abbot smiles.

"In any case," I say, "let me change your dressing. Then you must rest. Lorenzo will bring you food."

I go to stand behind him, help him to lift the habit from his back, and gently push him forward. The towel is stuck to his back by the dried effusion. I pick out the cotton. It is chased by a slide of new purulence. But the swelling and redness have begun to subside. The lips of the incision remain widely open, allowing for drainage.

"Warm compresses, now," I tell Lorenzo. "And Sebastiano?" The abbot nods.

Outside the door, a wave of elation. I can stay! I can stay!

The others of course had heard. That passionate bellowing, those howled vowels that had been contained all his life and only now had gathered from somewhere deep within and flung themselves into the farthest reaches of his abbey, to the cells of his monks where they lay in their beds and trembled.

"Did you really cut into him?" Pietro asks. Before I can answer he covers his eyes and shudders. "No, don't tell me."

"There are few things I can count on in this world," I say. "The squeamishness of the religious is one of them."

"Speaking for the community, we are grateful for what you have done for our beloved Padre." He says this with precision. Elocuting, really.

With the lancing of the boil comes an unexpected benefice. Pietro spells it out for me.

"Padre Abate wishes me to tell you that in the time immediately following *Compieta* and prior to *Riposo e Silenzio,* the older monks, two or three at a time, may visit with you for dialogue. This is to continue for as long as you wish it during the remainder of your stay with us, which the abbot hopes will be lengthy. It is the expectation of the abbot that the community, excepting the novices, of course, will make your further acquaintance through these conversations. In the interest of uniformity he suggests that these visits take place here in the guest room." It is apparent from his tone that Pietro is resentful. The message is delivered with ill-concealed distaste. I do not try to hide my own elation.

"Personally," says Pietro, "I doubt any good will come of it. Some of them are really rather dumb Italians." I am shocked at this second slip of bigotry.

"Listen, Pietro . . ."

"It goes without saying that you are to keep in mind at all times the holiness of this house."

"Did the abbot tell you to say that?" By his silence I know that he did not. Pietro is jealous.

"Come tonight, then, and bring Lorenzo and Antonio."

"Lorenzo! Holy Mother of the Word Incarnate!" He leaves. My plan is to loosen their tongues with brandy, ravish them with chocolate creams. And ply them with questions.

The first to arrive is Lorenzo, scarcely five feet tall, a cap of cropped white hair over an unmarked face. He has been in the monastery for sixty years. I pour him a glass of brandy.

"*Un biccierino?*"

"*Mille grazie.*" The others arrive. Antonio, with whom I have never exchanged a word, and instead of Pietro, Vittorio, the holy novice master. The sounds we must make to converse cause us to smile. They are a mixture of Italian, French, German, and English. Even Latin is made use of *in extremis*. It is the Tower of Babel all over again. Yet somehow there is comprehension. It is an understanding beyond grammar and accent. Soon it is all wickedness, *chez moi*. Glass is clinked, a cigarette is lit, a chocolate cream is popped, and with it ecstasy oozes across a long uncandied face. The temperature of the room rises. Now and then there is wafted to me the smell of ripe monk. Come to think of it, I have seen no other bathtubs save my own Gethsemanic appliance.

"Where do you bathe?" I ask.

They laugh happily but do not reply. About this, I see, I am to remain ignorant.

"What brought you here?" I ask Antonio.

"I love God," he says. A moment later I hear him say with the exact same intensity, "I love chocolate creams." The flesh of none of them, I suspect, is entirely dead. They all have much work to do. An hour later, they leave. The last to go is Lorenzo, plump as a pincushion and with many more colors in his face than when he arrived. Antonio, too, might be expected at this moment to be as besotted with wine as he is with Christ. It has been a lovely evening.

Now, each night, there is company. With what eagerness I wait for the sound of their soft knocking at my door. I have taken to leaving it ajar so that I can spy on them as they approach. Clotheslines have been strung the length of the corridor leading to my room. Sheets, pillowcases, underwear, handkerchiefs, and socks are hung there. The monks must part the laundry with the backs of their hands as though it were beaded curtains. Dom Paolo, the choirmaster-cum-exorcist, comes each night. He, it seems, is to be my sparring partner; he will guard the others against contamination from my worldliness. This is the way we speak:

"Where are you buried?" I ask him.

"In the crypt beneath the floor. You see how convenient it is? We simply disappear into the premises. There is nothing for the world to dispose of. Just so do we become our beloved abbey."

"How old were you when you entered this monastery?"

"I was ten, but long before that, I knew that I was to be given to God, that I must learn not to trifle. But we do not any longer take in children. It is thought wiser to let them have a taste of the world first."

I disagree. I tell him, "I think it more natural and wiser to enter as a child before having been seized by life. At least it would forgo the need for painful renunciation. Or later, perhaps, much later in life, after a series of failures. Then it would seem a blessed haven."

"You quite misunderstand the monastic urge," he says. "And the concept of the *formation* of a monk."

"What if one of you gets appendicitis?"

"We are very healthy."

"But appendicitis, after all."

"Ah well, you see that we have not." Then, as an afterthought: "We place ourselves in the hands of Christ."

"You are more severe than your predecessors who lived here seven centuries ago. They, at least, were open to medicine. Even that delivered to them by infidels from the East."

"You live among us like an angel," says Vittorio.

"More like a ghost," I say. "Or a bumblebee visiting a secret garden. I should much prefer to do some work. But Padre Abate will not permit it."

"The abbot knows best."

"Well, then, if I am to be an angel, I shall put my head under my wing and think of nothing."

"Ah, there you are, Dom Lorenzo," I say. "Today I caught you sleeping at your orisons." He blushes; the others laugh gently. *"Dolci?"* I pour him a large brandy. He has brought me a postcard upon which is a photograph of San Giorgio from the other side of the lagoon. He points to a dot which is the window of this very room. I *am* thrilled. I listen as he tells the others once again that I saved the abbot's life.

"Once," says Paolo, "not so very long ago, when one of us died, Dom Tommaso, a very holy man—" he looks at the others; they nod in agreement—"when we went to prepare his body for the crypt, we saw that he still wore the cincture about his waist. So tightly had he drawn it that it had bitten into him. The flesh had grown over it."

I make no reply to this.

"But we no longer tighten the cincture." He sighs at the passing of a happier time.

"How do you support yourselves?"

"We are not a mendicant order. Only if someone wishes to give us a gift."

"I see." And make a mental note.

"Who decides which duties each of you is to perform? The refectory, for instance?"

"Each of us must serve a turn at kitchen and table."

"Pietro says he hates it," I betray shamelessly. Then hurry on.

Within days, the debate peters out and like true companions we fall to telling stories. Vittorio tells a story about Saint Euphemia, whose church is the oldest in Venice. The others know the story and give encouraging nods.

"Not long ago," he begins, with the air of someone who has invented a new sauce, "it was discovered that the church was in danger of collapsing. Workmen were called in to shore up and reinforce the structure. During the digging, the shovel of one of the workmen struck a hard object buried beneath the foundation of the church. The object was uncovered and found to be the coffin of none other than Saint Euphemia herself. The shovel had broken the ancient wood of the box and had stuck the still undisintegrated head in the nose. From the wound thus caused, fresh blood flowed." Vittorio's eyes blaze at the thought of the miracle. Yet he speaks of it as though it were an ordinary event, something expected.

"It was in all of the newspapers," he says.

"Really?" I say. There is no irony here. Only my presence among them is ironic.

"Padre Abate," I begin, "told me today that Ezra Pound used to visit him often here. Do you know that Pound was a Fascist, a bigot, and a traitor to his country?"

"But you did not know," Paolo exonerates, "that Ezra Pound was hung up in a cage by the American soldiers in Pisa? When he died, the body was placed in a gondola and poled away. How sad it was. He was not a bad, bad man. His funeral, how desolate, the lone gondola disappearing from the island, bearing only the body, *solo, abbandonato.*"

All through these evenings, Pietro remains silent. I think he is sulking. Only now and then, like a diva who cannot bear to leave the stage, he makes his bit of noise in the wings.

"Why is it that you do not pray?" This from Vittorio, the holy.

"These buildings say my prayers for me; I don't have to. Besides, I have bony spurs on my knees. Exostoses, they are called. It hurts to kneel. See?" I pull up my pants to show him.

"Then you must kneel and offer it up," says Paolo, barely glancing.

"Easy for you to say, Dom Paolo. Raised out of this world, you feel no pain in knee or back."

"We do feel it," he replies. "It is an opportunity for virtue."

"What possible virtue can there be in pain? Remember, I am a doctor."

"To do penance is virtuous. The path to God is hard and rugged."

"Yes," I say. "I see that it is."

"I saw that you did not finish your plate again tonight."

"Oh, that."

—ɯ—

Outside the room the mist gathers. Soon there will be rain. Although they do not know, tonight is to be the last of it. I have told Padre Abate of my departure. I wish only to make them smile one last time. I point to the crucifix crusted with amethyst.

"Do you know why the stone is purple?" I ask and go on. "One day Bacchus, the god of wine, angry over some imagined slight or a falling-off of worshipers, swore that the very next human being he saw would be devoured by the tigers that ran always at his side. Just then a beautiful innocent young girl happened by. The tigers leaped. At that instant, the girl cried out to the goddess Athena for help. Athena took pity on the girl and instantly turned her into a pillar of pure white stone. Now when Bacchus saw what he had caused, he was filled with remorse, and in atonement he poured over it the juice of his sacred grapes. And that, my dear, dear friends, is how the amethyst came to be purple." They are enchanted, the way children are enchanted by a story. We all have another brandy; there are more *buona seras* than in the last act of *The Barber of Seville*.

When they have gone, I open the windows and the rain rushes in. Here and there the lagoon leaps up to grab the fresh drops, zealous to convert them to salinity.

Tomorrow evening I shall leave San Giorgio. It is no less painful to leave than it would be to stay. Exile simply cannot be the proper condition of man. Heaven is for the heavenly, and I am not one of those, each of whom is like a river that leaves behind its name and shape, the whole course of its path, to vanish into the vast sea of God. I cannot do that. I love my name, which was my father's name, and the name of my children. I am proud of my few accomplishments, ashamed of my many failures; there are human beings I would die for. And so I depart this antechamber of the hereafter where faith is like a fierce orange cat who might claw the one who reaches out or settle to its belly and purr. You never know. Winning faith is like trying to tame a wild animal. One can try too hard. A little coyness is better.

Pietro feeds ravenously off me.

"Stay," he pleads. "Stay if you want to. For as long as you want. Where will you go?"

"To Florence, and then home."

"Florence! Such a long train ride; it will be crowded, noisy. What is there in Florence that we do not have here? You must go to Torcello, the other islands here in the bay of Venice. You have not met the Armenian fathers at San Lorenzo. Byron studied there, you know."

O my batch of monks! Shall we ever meet again? Not here, I think. Perhaps in the plains of air. For I shall not return. Already it seems to me that the Isola di San Giorgio does not exist except as the island within myself, that isolated interior place upon which for a brief time I was marooned, and whose every corner I searched for the illumination of faith, and failed. I have not learned to pray. The closest I have come to praying is to ask this island to reveal the secrets it knows. But no building has the power to change a man's soul or produce a Sabbath of the heart. Still, still, I have become simpler. I shall no longer question or ask for proof. The fact remains that I can only find happiness in human love. The love of God won't do.

Perhaps I should not have come. But there was no way to avoid it. I had come, I suppose, seeking someone who possessed the key to something which all my life had been a mystery to me. Someone human, yet who had risen above his humanity. I did not find him here. Now I go back to my life. I shall practice no rites, say no prayers. Instead I shall permit myself superstition. It is simpler than religion and has not the burden of morality. I shall continue to make sacrifices to urban and forest deities, believing as I do that symbolic gestures enhance the sense of oneness with all of nature. I shall go on doctoring lest I be tempted to lie down and cherish my sorrows. I shall watch the birds. I shall content myself with a few nuggets of laughter and memory. And I shall try to find human beings to hold in my arms. I am skeptical of great notions such as Mankind or God. It is nature that I love and man.

—m—

Padre Abate and I sit together in my room on the eve of my departure. It is the first time he has come. I offer him a glass of brandy.

"Grand Armagnac," I tell him.

"I know." He smiles. "I have been told. I have wanted to taste it for a long time." We sip for a minute in silence.

"Speaking metaphorically . . ." he begins and hesitates.

"That is always the best way, Padre Abate."

". . . I should say that what you let out of my body was the putrefaction of pride. I am all the more grateful."

"I long ago learned not to minimize the ailments of my patients. To the boiled, his boil is the worst boil in the whole history of boil-age, his lancing the most painful and dangerous. Still, Padre Abate, it was just a boil. I have seen many like it. It is hardly worth the myth of martyrdom." I am talking too much, too cleverly.

"Your mockery, too, is incisive. But I shall hold to my metaphor, if you don't mind. It serves me well."

I do not answer, for it occurs to me that while I have played, often recklessly, with everything in life, this man does not play with his faith. He cannot afford to. I pour more brandy.

"I told you once," he says, "that the reason for your coming had not yet been revealed to me."

"And?"

He rises and walks to the window, and with one hand opens first one, then the other casement.

"Air and light pass through a window in both directions," he says and turns to leave. I rise to face him. He holds out his hand. I take it and bend to kiss his ring. But before my lips can touch the stone, he turns his hand, grasping mine in a candid American hand-shake. The convent does not exist in the world into which human love cannot force an entrance.

It is sunset. The community gathers on the terrace. Only the abbot is missing. No one speaks, as though we had vowed. Paolo holds my suitcase, which he does not set down; Sebastiano, the typewriter;

Lorenzo, the briefcase. The vaporetto, famous for its punctuality, is late. Why doesn't it come? I implore it to come. The waiting is too hard, too hard. At last, it thumps against the pier. "San Giorgio!" calls out the boatman. The suitcase is handed aboard, then the rest. "*Arrivederci*. Goodbye, goodbye. *Ciao. Ci vediamo.*" Fifteen hands are clasped.

I do not look back until the boat is well into the lagoon. At last, I must. I turn to see them on the terrace gazing after me, swaying on the stems of their bodies as though their souls were stirring. They are grouped together, all except for Pietro, who stands a little apart, erect, his habit billowing, stealing the last scene. Of them all it is he for whom my departure is hardest. Even so, I have to smile. If Isola di San Giorgio were to sink into the lagoon and the order came to evacuate, it would be Pietro and Pietro alone who would remain to die with his beloved abbey, black and erect upon the steps of the church, an exclamation point dissolving into the flood.

All at once, the sun sinks behind Venice, and as it does, for one precise moment the final rays strike the facade of the monastery, turning it red. Every window is filled with flames. The whole of the abbey is a crucible. Every window burning. Except one. Mine! And that one is black as night. It is the window which the abbot flung open in his dramatic act of ventilation and which I have forgotten to close. *I have broken a rule.*

Months later I shall wonder, and try to remember, what it was I felt then. Relief that I had made my escape through that black hole, or regret that I had gone from that holy house, every detail of which lies buried forever at the back of my eyes.

Rounds

—⚉—

I hereby call for a moratorium on the hideous custom of naming a hospital *Memorial* something. Or something *Memorial*. As in Veterans' Memorial Hospital or Massachusetts Memorial Hospital or just plain Memorial Hospital. The word has too mortuary an odor. In such a crepuscular place the doctor himself is a shade who has only his familiarity with pain to offer. Here, there can be no hope—only the fulfillment of death. O give me happier hospitals: Veterans' Recovery Hospital or the Massachusetts Palace of Healing, or the Strong Comeback Clinic where, should a patient fail to get well, it would be an injustice rather than a foregone conclusion.

Sometimes, in the Memorial Hospital where I work, I feel like a survivor wandering dazed through burning streets. I pause to study a corpse splayed upon the tines of a great gate. Was he, I wonder, looter or defender? And then I hear the ghostly moan of one not yet dead of his wounds, but still calling out in the language of the living. At the end of just such a night I went to the Maternity floor (I had no business there) and stood in the corridor outside the Delivery Room. Through the closed doors I listened and heard the first cry of a fellow human being. When I heard the newcomer . . . miracle! I was healed.

I understand your reluctance to leave your ward and move on to the next Service. I, too, suffered such dislocations. There is a certain melancholy one feels in passing through a ward full of new patients about whom one knows nothing but for whom one is to be responsible. It is the same sadness a forest ranger must feel in the contemplation of bonsai whose fate it is to be bound, twisted, and amputated into facsimiles of healthy trees. But dwell among these patients for a day or two, become familiar with their wounds and their pain, and all at once you feel a surge of happiness. It is the gift of the patients to you—your knighthood conferred upon you by them. Now you are in a position for healing.

Within days, this new ward is like a village of friends into which you have stumbled and to which you are attached by chains of trust. These patients would risk everything, their lives even, to save you. You can see this from the little smiles they let play upon you when you pass. And you will love them to the point of pain and beyond. But loving them is not enough. To be of real help you must wish to prolong by one second some comfortable moment of their lives. To do this, a doctor must be able to do what even he cannot imagine doing.

Let us go then, you and I, to make Rounds together in this Memorial Hospital. It is a companionable thing for doctors to do.

ROOM ONE

A man carries a small bouquet of violets into a room where a woman lies sleeping. His feet both hurry and drag at the same time. As though his right foot were in desperate haste, and his left were reluctant. This man is not used to holding flowers. He is a plumber; his hands are stained with grease, and scarred. The violets seem even more fragile in his great burry fist. Now the man leans toward the bed, watching the face of the woman. His own face wilts under the onslaught of her labored breath. He stuffs the violets into a glass of water and sets the glass on the window ledge. He sits by the bed. Before long, he dozes. In the chair, he seems a pair of overalls with nobody inside.

Before, when she was still at home, when he was able to care for her there, she was awakened each night and many times each night by a housewifely summons heard through her dreams—a screen door to be closed or a cake to be taken out of the oven. He had always to be on guard then. Once, she had burned her hand with matches. Once, she had wandered out into the street. Then one day he pushed her bed against the wall. Thereafter he slept on the floor next to her bed. It was her bare feet stepping on his body that would awaken him.

"Come along now," he would murmur. "You don't want to be getting up. It's still dark." And he would nudge the woman back upon the bed.

"But the cake," she would protest. "It needs to come out of the oven."

"I'll take the cake out. You rest," he'd say, and lie back down on the floor, holding himself where her soft cool feet had pressed his belly.

Now, in the hospital, when he awakens, it is to the sound of water and gas churning in a pipe. It is an old sound to him, a sound equipped with fingers that reach for the deepest, cleanest place within him. It is a minute before he realizes that it is the sound of her breathing. In the mirror over the sink he catches sight of himself. The color of his eyes has faded; once, they were blue. His head droops. He cannot hold it up. On the window ledge, the violets blaze on.

ROOM TWO

Melanoma. An eggplant and three plums plucked from the belly of a man. Split open upon a tray, the black meat bulged. Nor could the sprung flesh be restuffed in its casing; it was already too large. It is a wild pigment that races like bad news from the founding mole into the farthest reaches of the body. Listen! The sound of chewing. He is like an oak tree infested with gypsy moths.

Out in the solarium his wife and two young sons wait. The woman wears garnets in her earlobes and at her neck. Her eyebrows are darkly penciled, her lashes elongated, caked with dye. She is dressed in black. As though the man's tumor has metastasized conjugally. I tell her the news.

"It's a great loss," she says. "My husband was a brilliant man."

"He is not dead yet," I protest.

"Does he know?" I nod. "How did he take it?"

"He showed no reaction. He asked no questions. That will come later." The woman shakes her head.

"His mother used to punish him for getting sick," she says. All at once, her eyes lake and the mascara slides in runnels toward her mouth. One of the sons, the younger, lowers his eyes to cover the nakedness of his father that she has uncovered with her words. A silence. Then:

"Is it growing fast?"

"Very fast." I think of the gypsy moths.

With a sudden movement the woman places her hand on my arm, and a faint smile blackens her lips as well. I watch her large buttocks grinding down the corridor toward his room. Garnets are wifely stones, I think, for the touch of blood about them.

ROOM THREE

Goiter. A tall blond woman with a long neck. From the front of this neck a mass the size of a lemon rises. She sits up in the bed, and offers the tumor with a simple gesture of her hands. A tiny gold locket in the shape of a heart rests upon the promontory. To either side, a chain burrows beneath the collar of her bed jacket. To each beat of the woman's heart, the little gold heart responds with a shudder of its own. It has a brassy, impacted malice. It is the tumor's heart, I think. Perhaps all I have to do is reach behind her and undo the chain.

"Let me see," I say. And I go for the clasp.

ROOM FOUR

Acromegaly. Her pituitary gland makes too much growth hormone. She is a great tree, but the trunk only, with none of the arboreal graces. See how she fills the bed with the pile and strew of her bones. The bed is too short for her. Overreaching the end, the immense feet of a granite Assyrian queen. Her head is unfinished—unequal halves opposed. One jaw shovels the air about it, the other is dented. Her nose deviates to follow a smell at its left. As though, years ago in the womb, she was set aside for some more insistent errand. A smudged work in progress with His thumbprints still upon it. The slow head swivels to face us, the eyelids half drawn, the mouth hanging. All at once, she sees us, and *something* softens the landscape of that face. The crags and ledges shift, are not where, a moment ago, they were. She smiles, and is completed.

ROOM FIVE

All night the old man bays at what, to him, I suppose, is the moon of dread but to me is the lamp on his bedstand. Each breath is a bone he attempts to dislodge from his throat. Such suffering, I think, must atone for any amount of wickedness. This man will die out of debt. Into the sheet each night he looses his saliva, urine, sweat, and blood, impregnating the linen with his own oils and gums and resins until the sheets grow heavy while he grows ever lighter. Every morning a nurse comes to change the mummy's bed. But the old man does not die. Day after day, and many times each day, he must be turned in his bed, and lifted, and fed and injected. He has lost the control of his bowels and bladder. Pus drains from openings on his abdomen and thigh.

His wife is small and frail. She, too, is old.

"I'm taking him home," the wife tells me.

"But it will be too much for you," I say. "He needs too much tending to. A nursing home would be better . . . for . . . domiciliary care." She smiles at the word.

"His domicile is at 1834 Maple Street. That's our house."

"But what about all the mess?"

"How much mess can one man make?" she answers. And I am silent. For she has told me what I already knew, but had forgotten. Tending the body of another is an act of infinite loneliness, and carried out alone, a solitary commitment for which one is equipped only from the storehouse of his own heart. "How much mess can one man make?" I hear her words and I feel that I have been handed a secret letter which one day I must hand on to another, knowing all the while that this letter contains whatever there is to know about the care of the sick. When all else fails, the old woman teaches, take up reverence and proceed. In the throes of anguish one is far more likely to uncover his nobility than one is to show his cowardice. We are cowardly only in the expectation of distress. Once engaged, we shuck the ballast and, disencumbered, climb to higher ground. Disease magnifies both the sufferer and those who tend him. The patient in full dress of a wasting disease has no more clothing than a beggar. His skin is no more to be coveted than mendicant rags. His jaundice is a mark of autumn. Soon, he knows, it will be winter—cold and pulseless. No doctor worthy of the title will walk past such a dignified sadness unmoved, unstirred to give of himself whatever might be of comfort. As one can love a beggar about whom one knows nothing, so can one love a dying patient who has openly declared the bankruptcy of his flesh. I have known a vain and selfish woman who had done no secular act more arduous then the application of cosmetics to her own face, yet who, when called upon, irrigated the colostomy of her dying husband, and dressed his oozing bedsores. Why deny even to Narcissus that the face in the pool may be that of another?

Homer understood the power of the wound over those who both suffer and tend it. Toward the end of the *Odyssey* we find Ulysses at last deposited upon the shores of his homeland, the kingdom that he had left twenty years before. He is the very picture of the vagabond, dressed in rags and with his hair and beard tangled. Trembling with emotion he makes his way to the gates of his palace and gazes within. What he sees fills him with horror and dismay. The suitors of his wife, Penelope, have assumed control of the palace. They are conducting orgies and revelry; they are squandering his treasure, defiling his house. Penelope and their son, Telemachus, have been helpless to stop them.

Now the crafty Ulysses steps inside. He has decided to keep his own counsel, to let the tatters and dishevelment of twenty years of wandering hide his identity. He is led to Penelope, who engages him in conversation. She likes him, but she does not know him. She requests of him any news of her husband. He offers none. Sighing, Penelope calls for the old nurse, Eurycleia, to bathe the feet of the stranger and to make him welcome.

Now it had happened that forty years before, Ulysses as a boy of ten had gone to visit his grandfather in another country. While there, he had been taken on a boar hunt, during the course of which he had been gored in the thigh by the tusk of a wild boar. The wound was severe and quickly became septic. For a long time it was feared that the boy would die. It was this same nurse, this Eurycleia, who had then been placed in sole charge of the wounded Ulysses. She it was who bathed and treated the wound. I see her applying unguents and herbs, and pressing out the poisons, and cherishing the blood of her little patient as though it were the last of the wine. Until, at last, she saw that the necrotic tissue at the base of the wound had separated and sloughed. New pink buds of granulation tissue appeared. These coalesced to form a healthy bed across which the epithelium raced, and the wound healed.

It is forty years later. The old nurse kneels at the feet of the stranger. Suddenly she feels the scar on the man's thigh.

> *This was the scar the old nurse recognized;*
> *She traced it under her spread hands, then let go,*
> *and into the basin fell the lower leg*
> *making the bronze clang, sloshing the water out.*
> *Then joy and anguish seized her heart; her eyes*
> *filled up with tears; her throat closed, and she whispered*
> *with hands held out to touch his chin:*
> *"Oh yes! You are Ulysses! Ah, dear child!*
> *I could not*
> *See you until now—Not till I knew*
> *My master's very body with my hands!"*

It was not his wife or his son who had recognized Ulysses. It was his nurse. It was the wound that had awakened the buried past, the wound that was the emblem of all the shared pain and despair, the disappointment and the exhilaration that are the measure of the tending relationship.

WARD THREE NORTH

The General Surgical Service, Men's Ward. Rounds with Ora Guilfoyle, the Head Nurse. She is the kind of nurse who, by the mere smoothing of a pillow, can induce sleep in a febrile insomniac. We make Rounds in the manner of people who have come to count on each other over the years. We advance through the ward behind a dressing cart. At each bed we clatter to a halt. The chart is reviewed, the data recited. A wound is exposed, examined, re-dressed. We move on to the next bed. As we come to the end of the row, I am called to the telephone at the nurses' station at the other end of the hall. Ora is annoyed.

"I'll make it fast," I tell her. From the phone, I see her approach the next patient. She takes out her bandage scissors as though to begin removing the dressing from the man's leg. All at once I see her move to the head of the bed. She bends to peer into the face of the man lying there. Suddenly, she flings herself upon his body. One knee on the bed and she is aboard, her skirt hiked. Now she straddles the man and bends to clamp his mouth with her own. As though her tongue were a key that would unlock the secret that lies in his body if only she could find the right way to insert it. She beats his chest with her fists, and huffs, blowing into a grate to keep a meager ember alive. The whole bed rattles and slides.

Such a passion would raise the dead. And so it did. Almost at once the man groans. A breath is taken. Another. Ora straightens, lifts her bruised purple lips away, pressing her mouth with the back of her hand, daring him to abandon her again. A minute later, Ora Guilfoyle has been replaced by the machinery of resuscitation. There is a team of doctors and nurses about the bed. They are all very young. A hectic gaiety prevails, a monitor beeps, a tube emerges from the man's windpipe.

Ora and I resume our Rounds. I am suddenly shy, silent. I think to say something that will acknowledge this event. But I do not. I have seen this woman at her fiercest—wild and desperate. I have seen the rhythmic jounce of dead men's feet. It is best to keep silent. We finish our work and wheel the cart to the nurses' station. A woman is there. It is the man's wife. From the distance, she has watched the coupling of her husband with this nurse. The woman raises one hand as if to speak to Ora. Ora hesitates. But the woman, too, does not speak. There is a glance between them. Then they move apart, the one toward, and the other away from, the bed where it took place.

MATERNITY WARD

The door to one of the Labor rooms is ajar. A young woman half sits up in the bed. She is moaning in pain. Another young woman leans at the bedside. With one hand she presses the back of the one in labor. With the other hand she rubs the huge belly, all the while murmuring. I know them! They are famous in New Haven. A year ago I saw them fighting in the street. It was a summer evening on Congress Avenue where I had gone to make a house call. I emerged from my patient's house to see them come percolating out of a doorway. They had all the arrogant intentions of cooch dancers: a tangle of shrieks and fury, punching, slapping, clawing. One was fat and with a furious fat-man's face. The other was slim and mean-eyed. She had small translucent teeth. Both were blond, the big girl's hair close-cropped, that of the smaller one, ivory, waist-length. It tossed and writhed about its mistress, falling across the face of her opponent so that she could not see, wrapping itself about the big girl's neck, loyally fighting alongside its lifelong benefactor. Or was this hair an agitated wraith trying to make peace? The big girl swore from her throat. Her lips and teeth took no part in the words that barked up from her windpipe in solid lumps. "Fuckin' whore," she yelled. She was powerful and soon had the upper hand, beating the thin girl with relishment. But the desperation of the underdog was great and she found a way. Her translucent teeth indented an assertive, roaring breast.

Oblivious, the women had given birth to a circle of men who enclosed and nourished the struggle as though it were a flame that must be kept alive in a stiff wind. The faces of the men were wet with lust. They warmed themselves in the heat of the women. Their hands were in their pockets. They shifted from one leg to the other, whimpering and squirming like boys who need to urinate. I thought then of the ovaries and uteri of these two, and felt sick. What an elderly refined stomach I have, used only to the cooler colloquy of minds. But all that punching and blood, all that "fuck" in the air. There was a real possibility that I might vomit. I must leave this place, I thought. But I did not. I, too, had to watch. It was like spying on the faces of women in orgasm while they know nothing but their own passion.

"You'd never know they were sisters," a man said.

Sisters! Of course! Only sisters could hate like this. Mere friends would never care so much. At last I could not stay. Blind and deaf I hurried to my car and drove away, only then daring to think of those two, how it was their way to cling and grapple and bite. How eagerly they accepted the tyranny of the flesh that had always, from infancy on, been offered and taken in love and sincere battle. The next day or the day after that, these sisters would slip the straps of their clothing to show the marks left by nails and teeth. Then they would laugh together heartily. One day they would help each other through husbandless childbirth.

THE EMERGENCY ROOM

A man has been stabbed in the neck. I undress the wound. A clot comes loose from his carotid artery and I hear his leaping blood cry out: Tallahassee! Tallahassee! Tallahassee! before I stifle it with pressure. When blood escapes from a rent in a large artery, each jet makes a little noise, not much more than the whisper of gas that escapes from a burning log. It has, I suppose, to do with eddying and the flow of liquid through a narrow place to the outside air. I don't know about that. But when the man died during the night, I wasn't as surprised as you might think to find out where he was born.

"Oh, come on!" you say. "You *must* have known it beforehand."

No matter. I know now that blood is a loyal conductor. It announces a man's native land just in time for him to get off the train at the place he holds nearest to his heart.

MINOR SURGERY

A thin, dark woman lies on the table. She looks to be forty years old. She is dressed in red, slacks and a blouse. Her eyelids are smeared with blue and silver; the lashes are long and caked. Near the outer corner of her left eye there is a small, star-shaped laceration. A bruise surrounds it. A few sutures will be needed to close the wound.

"How did it happen?" I ask her. She makes a small gesture of impatience. I see that it has been caused by something blunt. A fist, perhaps?

"Do a good job," she says. "My eyes are my only good feature."

"That's not true," I say. "You're very pretty." The skin of her face is thick with makeup. It comes off brown and grimy on my alcohol sponges. I must use many in order to cleanse the wound.

"Will I have a scar? My eyes are my only good feature." She says it again. Her hair is anthracite piled artfully. It is sticky to the touch and dry as hay. Not a strand moves when she turns her head to watch me draw the local anesthetic into a syringe. I must lift the hair away from her temple in order to work. When I do, I see the infected cyst just in front of her ear. A drop of pus hangs.

"What's that?" I ask. She makes no move as I inject. It is not pain that concerns her.

"I have an awful habit. I pick at it. There's one on the other side, too. I can't help it. I pick at them. I'm so nervous." I begin to stitch and tie.

"Can't you give me something to keep me from picking at myself? I'm so nervous. Valium helps me." Her mother stands nearby. She is a short, stolid woman also extravagantly made up and coiffed. She has an expressionless face.

"Please help her, Doctor," says the older woman.

"Give me thirty. Five milligrams," says the woman on the table.

"No," I say, "I couldn't do that. I'm a surgeon. I don't prescribe those drugs. Have you seen your family doctor lately?"

"He died," says the mother quickly.

"Give me forty. Just to keep me from picking. I'm such a nervous girl."

"Help her, Doctor. Give her something." They are like gypsies. Their voices sway together, chant.

"Please help her, Doctor. Help my daughter."

"Give me fifty. Fifty Valiums."

"You ought to do something about those infections," I tell her. "I will prescribe an antibiotic ointment. Apply warm compresses. When the drainage stops they should be removed. It is a smallish operation."

"Valium," she sings.

"Valium," they sing together.

"Help her, Doctor."

"Valium."

ROOM SIX

There are two sisters. They are neither young nor old. One, having married well, is rich. The other is poor. The rich sister has far-advanced leukemia. She will die unless she receives a bone marrow transplant. It is her only hope. The doctor of the rich sister has just asked the poor one to submit to an aspiration of her bone marrow in order to match the tissue with that of the patient. Only in that way, he tells her, can he predict the success or failure of the transplant.

"There is a good chance that it will work," he says. "With sisters." They are sitting together in his office.

"How do you do it?" asks the woman.

"A local anesthetic is injected in the skin over the breastbone," he explains. "A tiny incision is made. Then a thick needle with a cutting edge is introduced. A small hole is bored in the crust of the bone and the marrow is sucked out. It is examined under the microscope."

"Does it hurt?"

"There is some pain. I cannot say there is not. Of course, we will try to keep it at a minimum."

"When does it hurt?"

"When the bone is punctured and when the marrow is drawn out."

Suddenly the woman shudders, then hugs herself as though her skeleton were a suitcase she is fearful of having stolen.

"No," she says, "I can't do it. I don't want to. I couldn't stand it."

"It is not really so bad. Perhaps I have made it sound worse than it is. It takes only half an hour."

"But then if I match up with her, you'll take a lot more."

"Yes. That is the hope."

"No. I can't. I won't do it. I'm sorry, don't ask me to. It is too much to ask—to give away my organs . . . my body like that. There's something wrong about it; it's not natural."

"But you have donated blood?"

"That's different. This is deeper. You drill a hole. It's tissue. You said so yourself."

"So is blood. Tissue. And you will make it up in a little while."

"Look, I'm not going to do it. You asked me, and I told you. The answer is no." She rises, takes out a handkerchief, and dabs at her eyes, the corners of her mouth. "I'm a very nervous person." She begins to cry. "The idea of it—being sucked out. Like a boiled beef bone." The doctor is silent, but the woman knows that he is disappointed.

"What will you tell her? Does she know you are asking me?"

"I will tell her that you do not feel that you can do it. I will try to make her understand."

"Look, Doctor, I may as well tell you. We never got along. Even as children. She's never lifted a finger to help me. She's been lucky up till now. I'm the one that's had to struggle." Her voice rises with unexpected ferocity. "Did she give a damn about me? No! I don't owe her a thing. And I'm not going to do it."

"Then it is not because you are frightened?"

The woman starts as though caught off guard.

"Of course it is because I'm scared. The other has nothing to do with it."

"It's all right," says the doctor. He shows her to the door.

Now he is alone in his office. Cowardice, he thinks, is easier to admit to than hatred. It is also more acceptable.

I no sooner step out into the parking lot than I hear from high above plum-colored clouds the honking of geese. The only light in the sky is a moon so thinly carved as to have been a skin graft taken by a plastic surgeon. The geese cannot be seen. Their sound is all. I pause before getting into my car, listening. Do they honk to cheer each other up? Or is it a delirium that is the only state in which the long migration can be made? I am told they ride the air currents that stream back from each other's wings. But I think it is the cloud of honks they ride. On and on they flap, each adding to the sound that is the cushion that carries them, and that they must replenish.

Even so, not all of them make it. Now and then one goose will lose the rhythm of the chant and slip off, his tiny heart all honked out. Down he slews, delivering his small parcel to the ground. Far away and high above, for a little while there will be a gap. Then the others will shift a bit, drawing forward to fill in the line. Ever fainter the fallen goose hears the honking of his tribe until it is only the memory of a sound. Nothing to do with him, and he turns to face his lonely feral exile.

I think I need a vacation. If it weren't such a long trip, I'd go south for a while.

I am called back from home to the Emergency Room. An elderly woman lies on a stretcher. She is stout and gray-haired. Her apron is heavy and wet with blood. An hour ago, she was beaten and robbed in her own kitchen. I bend to examine her smashed purple face. There is a smell about her, a wild smell. It is in her hair, upon her clothing. His smell. As though a wolf had urinated upon her before loping off.

"What did he look like?" the police ask. "Can you describe him?"

"It must have been awful for you, dear," says a nurse.

"He was afraid," says the old woman. "He shook all over as

though to take a fit. I could see way into his eyes. After a while, when he didn't stop hitting me, I just stood there and hoped he'd kill me. I wanted him to. There wasn't another person in the whole world. Just him and me. He was the only one who could help me. But," she sighs, "he didn't.'"

ROOM SEVEN

The man does not yet know that he is dying. His wife sits in the corner. They are conversing.

"How do you feel, Frank?"

"I don't know. I'd have to read my chart to find out."

"What were you thinking about just now?"

"How embarrassing it all is."

"There's nothing embarrassing about it, Frank."

A small woman, she is made even tinier by the equipment that crowds the room—IV poles, cardiac monitor, cooling blanket, respiratory machine, suction.

"He says he has to pee and can't," she announces. I irrigate the indwelling catheter in his bladder. It is plugged. It will have to be changed. I send for the catheterization tray.

"Why don't you step outside for a few minutes, Edna? I'll call you when I'm done."

She stands and picks her way through the machinery to the door. I notice again that she is dainty and very good-looking. I see also that she really does not want to leave, that she is surrendering him to me. When she has left I remove the old catheter, put on sterile gloves, and take up his penis in my left hand. I bathe it with antiseptic solution. Then I insert the new catheter and connect the tubing to a plastic bag. He sighs. I go to the solarium to find her.

"We're in hot water, aren't we?" she says.

I nod.

"I feel so sorry for him," she says. "I understand these things. I've lived through it. Two years ago I had a brain tumor removed. I was supposed to be ninety-five percent blind. But look at me." She smiles. "But Frank is so innocent. He's never been sick in his life.

Such a good, good man. What should I do? Tell me. Should I stay or go home? Should I go down and put another quarter in the parking meter?"

"Go home for a while," I say. "Come back at eight o'clock. I'll tell him in the meantime."

"Oh, God," she says, remembering. "My mother phoned this morning and told me not to worry. It'll be all right, she said, because of the raspberry bushes. She gave him some raspberry bushes to plant. She said he'd be just fine in the spring when they bore fruit. What about radiation?"

"No," I say. It's too late for that.

"How do you do it?" she asks. "I feel sorry for *you*. Never mind about me. I'm tough. But you, how are you?"

"How are you?" I reply.

"It's all that equipment," she says. "The tubes, the suction, and that ghastly bed that moves up and down and sideways and does everything but make itself. I've lost him, haven't I? To the equipment. I sit in that room and feel him recede farther and farther away from me. Already I wonder if I loved him so much as I thought. The man with all those tubes in him—I never knew *him*."

She stands abruptly.

"For God's sake, peel it all off. Pull it all out. I want to give him a kiss."

At eight o'clock I am waiting for her in the room. Frank and all of the equipment have been taken away. The room is vast, barren. Edna and I sit on opposite sides of the empty bed. Our voices echo. We are hollow-voiced survivors.

"I'm sorry," I say.

"You should be," she says. "You gypped me."

An Absence
of Windows

—⁓—

Not long ago operating rooms had windows. It was a boon and a blessing in spite of the occasional fly that managed to strain through the screens and threaten our sterility. For the adventurous insect drawn to such a ravishing spectacle, a quick swat and—Presto!—the door to the next world sprang open. But for us who battled on, there was the benediction of the sky, the applause and reproach of thunder. A Divine consultation crackled in on the lightning! And at night, in emergency, there was the pomp, the longevity, of the stars to deflate a surgeon's ego. It did no patient a disservice to have Heaven looking over his doctor's shoulder. I fear that, having bricked up our windows, we have lost more than the breeze; we have severed a celestial connection.

Part of my surgical training was spent in a rural hospital in eastern Connecticut. The building was situated on the slope of a modest hill. Behind it, cows grazed in a pasture. The operating theater occupied the fourth, the ultimate, floor, wherefrom huge windows looked down upon the scene. To glance up from our work and see the lovely cattle about theirs calmed the frenzy of the most temperamental of prima donnas. Intuition tells me that our patients had fewer wound infections and made speedier recoveries than those operated upon in the airless sealed boxes where now we strive. Certainly the surgeons were of a gentler stripe.

I have spent too much time in these windowless rooms. Some

part of me would avoid them if it could. Still, even here, in these bloody closets, sparks fly up from the dry husks of the human body. Most go unnoticed, burn out in an instant. But now and then they coalesce into a fire that is an inflammation in the mind of him who watches.

Not in large cities, but in towns the size of ours, it is likely to happen that an undertaker will come to preside over the funeral of a close friend; a policeman will capture a burglar only to find that the miscreant is the uncle of his brother's wife. Say that a fire breaks out. The fire truck rushes to the scene; it proves to be the very house where one of the firemen was born, and the luckless man is now called on to complete, with ax and hose, the destruction of his natal place. Hardly a civic landmark, you say, but for him who gulped first air within those walls, it is a hard destiny. So it is with a hospital, which is itself a community. Its citizens: orderlies, maids, nurses, X-ray technicians, doctors, a hundred others.

A man whom I knew has died. He was the hospital mailman. It was I who presided over his death. A week ago I performed an exploratory operation upon him for Acute Surgical Abdomen. That is the name given to an illness that is unknown, and for which there is no time to make a diagnosis with tests of the blood and urine, X rays. I saw him writhing in pain, rolling from side to side, his knees drawn up, his breaths coming in short little drafts. The belly I laid the flat of my hand upon was hot to the touch. The slightest pressure of my fingers caused him to cry out—a great primitive howl of vowel and diphthong. This kind of pain owns no consonants. Only later, when the pain settles in, long and solid, only then does it grow a spine to sharpen the glottals and dentals a man can grip with his teeth and throat. Fiercely then, to hide it from his wife, his children, for the pain shames him.

In the emergency room fluid is given into the mailman's veins. Bags of blood are sent for, and poured in. Oxygen is piped into his nostrils, and a plastic tube is let down into his stomach. This for suction. A dark, tarry yield slides into a jar on the wall. In another moment a second tube has sprouted from his penis, carrying away his urine. Such is the costume of Acute Surgical Abdomen. In an hour I know that nothing has helped him. At his wrist a mouse skitters, stops, then darts away. His slaty lips insist upon still more oxygen. His blood pressure, they say, is falling. I place in my ears the earpieces of my stethoscope, this ever-asking Y. Always I am comforted a bit by this ungainly little hose. It is my oldest, my dearest friend. More, it is my lucky charm. I place the disc upon the tense, mounding, blue-tinted belly, gently, so as not to shock the viscera into commotion (those vowels!), and I listen for a long time. I hear nothing. The bowel sleeps. It plays possum in the presence of the catastrophe that engulfs it. We must go to the operating room. There must be an exploration. I tell this to the mailman. Narcotized, he nods and takes my fingers in his own, pressing. Thus has he given me all of his trust.

A woman speaks to me.

"Do your best for him, Doctor. Please."

My best? An anger rises toward her for the charge she has given. Still, I cover her hand with mine.

"Yes," I say, "my best."

An underground tunnel separates the buildings of our hospital. I accompany the stretcher that carries the mailman through that tunnel, cursing for the thousandth time the demonic architect who placed the emergency room in one building and the operating room in the other.

Each tiny ridge in the cement floor is a rut from which rise and echo still more vowels of pain, new sounds that I have never heard before. Pain invents its own language. With this tongue we others are not conversant. Never mind; we shall know it in our time.

We lift the mailman from the stretcher to the operating table. The anesthetist is ready with still another tube.

"Go to sleep, Pete," I say into his ear, my lips so close it is almost a kiss. "When you wake up, it will all be over, all behind you."

I should not have spoken his name aloud! No good will come

of it. The syllable has peeled from me something, a skin that I need. In a minute, the chest of the mailman is studded with electrodes. From his mouth a snorkel leads to tanks of gas. Each of these tanks is painted a different color. One is bright green. That is for oxygen. They group behind the anesthetist, hissing. I have never come to this place without seeing that dreadful headless choir of gas tanks.

Now the gauze sponges paint red tracks across the bulging flanks of the mailman, marking the area of confrontation. They are harbingers of the blood to come.

"May we go ahead?" I ask the anesthetist.

"Yes," he says. And I pull the scalpel across the framed skin, skirting the navel. There are arteries and veins to be clamped, cut, tied, and cauterized, fat and fascia to divide. The details of work engage a man, hold his terror at bay. Beneath us now, the peritoneum. A slit, and we are in. Hot fluid spouts through the small opening I have made. It is gray, with flecks of black. Pancreatitis! We all speak the word at once. We have seen it many times before. It is an old enemy. I open the peritoneum its full length. My fingers swim into the purse of the belly, against the tide of the issuing fluid. The pancreas is swollen, necrotic—a dead fish that had gotten tossed in, and now lay spoiling across the upper abdomen. I withdraw my hand.

"Feel," I invite the others. They do, and murmur against the disease. But they do not say anything that I have not heard many times. Unlike the mailman, who was rendered eloquent in its presence, we others are reduced to the commonplace at the touch of such stuff.

We suction away the fluid, which is rich in enzymes that have escaped from the sick pancreas. If they remain free in the abdomen, they will digest the tissues there, the other organs. It is the pancreas alone that can contain them safely. This mailman and his pancreas— careful neighbors for fifty-two years until the night the one turned rampant and set fire to the house of the other. The digestion of tissues has already begun. Soap has formed here and there, from the compounding of the liberated calcium and the fat. It would be good to place a tube (still another tube) into the common bile duct, to siphon away the bile that is a stimulant to the pancreas. At least that. We try, but we cannot even see the approach to that duct, so swollen is the pancreas about it. And so we mop and suck and scour the floors and walls of this ruined place. Even as we do, the gutters run with new streams of the fluid. We lay in rubber drains and lead them to the outside. It is all that is left to us to do.

"Zero chromic on a Lukens," I say, and the nurse hands me the suture for closure.

I must not say too much at the operating table. There are new medical students here. I must take care what sparks I let fly toward such inflammable matter.

The mailman awakens in the recovery room. I speak his magic name once more.

"Pete." Again, "Pete," I call.

He sees me, gropes for my hand.

"What happens now?" he asks me.

"In a day or two, the pain will let up," I say. "You will get better."

"Was there any . . . ?"

"No," I say, knowing. "There was no cancer. You are clean as a whistle."

"Thank God," he whispers, and then, "Thank *you*, Doctor."

It took him a week to die in fever and pallor and pain.

It is the morning of the autopsy. It has been scheduled for eleven o'clock. Together, the students and I return from our coffee. I walk slowly. I do not want to arrive until the postmortem examination is well under way. It is twenty minutes past eleven when we enter the morgue. I pick the mailman out at once from the others. Damn! They have not even started. Anger swells in me, at being forced to face the *whole* patient again.

It isn't fair! Dismantled, he would at least be at some remove . . . a tube of flesh. But look! There is an aftertaste of life in him. In his fallen mouth a single canine tooth, perfectly embedded, gleams, a badge of better days.

The pathologist is a young resident who was once a student of mine. A tall lanky fellow with a bushy red beard. He wears the green pajamas of his trade. He pulls on rubber gloves, and turns to greet me.

"I've been waiting for you." He smiles. "Now we can start."

He steps to the table and picks up the large knife with which he will lay open the body from neck to pubis. All at once he pauses, and reaching with his left hand, he closes the lids of the mailman's eyes. When his hand is removed, one lid comes unstuck and slowly rises. Once more he reaches up to press it down. This time it stays. The gesture stuns me. My heart is pounding, my head trembling. I think that the students are watching me. Perhaps my own heart has become visible, beating beneath this white laboratory coat.

The pathologist raises his knife.

"Wait," I say. "Do you always do that? Close the eyes?"

He is embarrassed. He smiles faintly. His face is beautiful, soft.

"No," he says, and shakes his head. "But just then, I remembered that he brought the mail each morning . . . how his blue eyes used to twinkle."

Now he lifts the knife, and, like a vandal looting a gallery, carves open the body.

To work in windowless rooms is to live in a jungle where you cannot see the sky. Because there is no sky to see there is no grand vision of God. Instead, there are the numberless fragmented spirits that lurk behind leaves, beneath streams. The one is no better than the other, no worse. Still, a man is entitled to the temple of his preference. Mine lies out on a prairie, wondering up at Heaven. Or in a many-windowed operating room where, just outside the panes of glass, cows graze, and the stars shine down upon my carpentry.

Copyright Acknowledgments

Essays in this collection have appeared, in slightly different form, in other publications as follows: "The Exact Location of the Soul," "The Surgeon as Priest," "Lessons from the Art," "Bone," "Liver," "Skin," "The Corpse," "Bald!" and "The Knife" in *Mortal Lessons*; "Down from Troy, Part I" in *Down from Troy*; "Fairy Tale" in *The Seneca Review*; "A Question of Mercy" in *The New York Times Magazine*; "Textbook," "Letter to a Young Surgeon I," "Letter to a Young Surgeon II," "Letter to a Young Surgeon IV," and "Rounds" in *Letters to a Young Doctor*; "How to Build a Slaughterhouse" and "Diary of an Infidel" in *Taking the World in for Repairs*; and "Rooms Without Windows" (titled here as "An Absence of Windows") in *Harper's*.

The author is grateful for permission to use an excerpt from *Homer: The Odyssey*, translated by Robert Fitzgerald. Copyright © 1961, 1963 by Robert Fitzgerald. Copyright renewed 1989 by Benedict R. C. Fitzgerald, on behalf of the Fitzgerald children. Reprinted by permission of Farrar, Straus and Giroux, LLC.; from "Lot's Wife," from *Poems* by Anna Akhmatova, translated by Lyn Coffin. Copyright © 1983 by Lyn Coffin. Used by permission of W. W. Norton & Company, Inc.